FAITHFUL PARENTS /// FAITHFUL KIDS

Faithful Parents,

GREG JOHNSON

/////////////////

Faithful Kids

AND MIKE YORKEY

 Tyndale House Publishers, Inc.
WHEATON, ILLINOIS

Library of Congress Cataloging-in-Publication Data

Johnson, Greg, date
    Faithful parents, faithful kids / Greg Johnson & Mike Yorkey.
       p.   cm.
    Includes bibliographical references and index.
    IBSN 0-8423-1248-X (HC) :
    ISBN 0-8423-1369-9 (SC)
    1. Family—Religious life. 2. Christian education—Home training.
I. Yorkey, Mike. II. Title.
BV4526.2.J55 1993   93-13866
248.8'45—dc20

Printed in the United States of America

99 98 97 96 95 94
10 9   8   7   6   5   4   3   2   1

//////////////////////////////

To you, Mom,
a faithful and
loving parent
for so many years.

GREG JOHNSON

To *my* faithful parents,
Pete and Anne.

MIKE YORKEY

CONTENTS

////////////////////////////////////

COMMUNICATION: WHAT TO TALK ABOUT, WHEN, AND HOW TO DO IT

If you think peer pressure begins during the teen years, you're wrong. We must work extra hard to guide them through the struggles they'll face.

SHAPING YOUR CHILD'S VALUES

Adolescence can be exhilarating—and exasperating. During these turbulent times, will your children grasp on to their faith, or will they seek their own paths?

CONTEMPORARY ISSUES FACING TODAY'S FAMILIES

"Leave It to Beaver" families belong to another era. Today's families are facing issues that were unheard of a generation ago.

BUILDING A LEGACY

Like Old Man River, some things about families never change. Keep your priorities in order and your kids will pass down a lasting legacy greater than any six-figure retirement plan.

APPENDIXES

Quotes, notes, and a few more stories from parents we surveyed and interviewed

ACKNOWLEDGMENTS

Writing a book requires a lot of time—and a lot of help.

We want to thank our wives, Elaine Johnson and Nicole Yorkey, for their suggestions and support.

To all the parents and adult children who took the time to fill out our comprehensive surveys, we thank you. Without you, there wouldn't be a book. We know who you are, and we greatly appreciate your cooperation.

To Bob Newman for his humorous help with the Top Ten lists scattered throughout the book.

Also, thanks to Larry Weeden and Nancy Sutton for reading an early manuscript and giving us ideas on how to improve *Faithful Parents, Faithful Kids.*

FOREWORD

////////////////////////////////////

Have you ever been lost in a large city? *Really lost?*

Recently, I happened into the "loop" in downtown Chicago during rush hour. Nearly one million people work in this labyrinth of high-rise buildings and twisting streets. And it seemed like they all decided to head home the minute I showed up.

Between trying to read the map I held in one hand and avoid running into cabs and pedestrians as I steered with the other, I ended up driving in circles for over two hours. I know for a fact that I crossed one river no less than six times.

In total frustration, I made the mistake of rolling down my window and asking for directions. Most people just ignored me, several scoffed, and the few who did answer shared "shortcuts" that multiplied my confusion. In fact, the best advice I got was from a rough-looking policeman who said, "Buddy, why don't you just park that thing and take a cab? *You'll never get out of here!*"

And that's exactly what I did!

After two hours of total exhaustion, I parked my car and caught a cab to my appointment. And then an amazing thing happened. While most big-city cabbies come complete with attitude, I had picked the one cabby whose attitude was pleasant and helpful. As he expertly guided me to my destination, he pointed out where I'd gone wrong so many times, how to get back to my car after my appointment, and even the best way to find the freeway to the airport.

What I learned that day in Chicago was when you're lost, having a map is fine. But having a personal guide is ten times better.

When it comes to finding our way as parents—and especially to developing faithful children—I'm thankful I know two expert, personal "guides" named Mike Yorkey and Greg Johnson. As they write, from their unique position with Focus on the Family along with their careful research and heart-grabbing stories, you'll feel like you're being personally escorted into home after home that produced faithful, God-honoring children.

Many of you who have picked up this book are just like me: More than anything, I want my two children to grow up knowing, loving, and trusting Jesus with a faith that will strengthen them all their lives. But I didn't come from a Christian home, and neither did my wife. We never had godly models in dealing with conflict, communication, and the contemporary issues facing today's family. And at times, just having a map hasn't kept us from wandering down the wrong road.

Mike Yorkey and Greg Johnson have interviewed hundreds of parents and now-grown children to discover the key factors that produce faithful parents and faithful kids. From shaping your children's values, to making them feel unique and special, to building into their lives a legacy of godliness that will never change, you'll read what actually works in homes just like yours and mine.

An aging apostle puts words to the thing that brought him the greatest joy: "I have no greater joy than to hear that my children are walking in the truth" (3 John 4). In speaking with parents across the country, I can testify that there is no deeper hurt than hearing them share about a child who has walked away from the faith.

If you're serious about sending your child off with a heart filled with Jesus' love and presence, and you'd like some practical, biblical advice from two of the best guides in the country, this book is for you.

John Trent, Ph.D.

INTRODUCTION

////////////////////////////////

Have you ever laid awake wondering whether your efforts to pass on your faith to your children are doing any good? That's what this book is all about.

Faithful Parents, Faithful Kids will help you raise children who will one day walk out your front door with Jesus in their hearts. Of course, we can't offer a money-back guarantee; in researching this book, we heard many stories of kids who rejected their parents' faith no matter how much spiritual input was given. In fact, we came across one study that said just 30 percent of churched kids wind up "owning" their faith by the time they graduate from high school.

You can be comforted in knowing that ultimately it's God's responsibility to reveal himself to your children in ways they will accept. But that doesn't release us from making our best effort, does it?

A wise pastor once told me (Greg): "What will it profit a man if he gain the whole world, but lose his own son?" That pretty much lays it on the line. If, at the end of our lives, we've built financial security and purchased nice homes, but our children haven't taken a strong hold of the Lord's hand—what will our lives really have counted for?

That's why Mike Yorkey and I decided to write this book.

We work together at Focus on the Family: Mike is editor of *Focus on the Family* magazine, the ministry's flagship publication; and I am editor of the teen magazine for guys, *Breakaway*. On top of that, we're right in the middle of this child-raising stuff: we both have kids in grade school. I have two boys: Troy, ten, and Drew, eight. Mike has a girl and a boy: Andrea, ten, and Patrick, nine.

Mike and I approached hundreds of parents with grown children in their twenties and thirties, and we asked them to fill out extensive essay-type surveys. Then we sent surveys to hundreds of adult children, asking how their parents raised *them*. Their ideas, quotes, and stories make up a large portion of *Faithful Parents, Faithful Kids*. (For confidentiality's sake, we've used fictitious names and cities throughout the book.)

But we didn't stop with just what we saw in the surveys. We took to the phones and interviewed more than fifty parents and adult children. We transcribed those interviews into reams of stories and anecdotes—100,000 words' worth! Though we were deluged with scores of great ideas—and quite a few parenting secrets we hadn't heard yet—we also discovered that this Christian parenting business isn't as black and white as we had expected.

Looking Ahead
The chapters that follow are filled with loads of how-to advice, interesting lists, fun stories, and a fair amount of humor (we just can't resist a few David Letterman–type top-ten countdowns). There is, however, one overriding principle that we hope you'll spot throughout the book: It's our *relationship* with our kids that matters most to God, not their good behavior or

whether we escorted them through the church doors every time they were open.

If you're the parent of young children, be advised that nearly all of the fathers and mothers and adult children we spoke with told us the adolescent years (ages eleven to nineteen) put a strain on the parent/child relationship more than any other time. However, if the seeds of a quality relationship are planted early in the child-rearing years, you'll enter the turbulent teen years in much better shape.

Along with describing how to form—and keep—a strong relationship with your kids, we'll also answer the questions parents are asking most as they raise their kids in the nineties.

If raising faithful children is something you've been thinking about, stay tuned. We hope this book will provide dozens of helpful ideas on how to pass the baton of faith to your children. This act is *the* most important thing we'll ever do, and we usually get one chance to do it right. Thanks for joining us as we journey down this trail called parenthood.

DEALING WITH CONFLICT AND DISCIPLINE

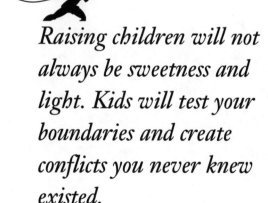

Raising children will not always be sweetness and light. Kids will test your boundaries and create conflicts you never knew existed.

CHAPTER 1

TUNING IN THE BIG PICTURE
Parents and Spiritual Values

Always keep three points in mind about passing the baton of faith to your children:

(1) It's God's job to bring your children to faith, not yours. He offers his free gift of salvation and then waits patiently until they receive it with a whole heart.

(2) All children have free will, and that plays a big part in whether they choose to follow what they've been taught.

(3) The parents' role is to instill spiritual values and point their children toward Christ. While we don't shoulder the entire load, we do have the responsibility to be faithful stewards of those little lives God's given us.

What can you do as a parent to hasten this entire process? Plenty! Where should you start? First, you have to take the long view. Ask yourself: *What type of Christian do I want my children to be when they're twenty-five?*

Hey, we know that's a tough question. But think about it a minute. Then ask yourself this easy follow-up: *Do I want my children to have a faith like mine?*

All of the adult children we surveyed made it into their adult years as Christians. But talking to them left us with this observation: Though all were Christians, many were not productive believers. They may have enlisted in the Lord's army, but a substantial number were nowhere near the front lines. Is that how you want your children to turn out?

We hope not!

You have to realize that the quality of your children's Christian lives and how active they are in their faith may be determined by what they see in you.

Do you want your children to have your love and compassion for those in need? Your attitude about church? Your desire to reach out to those who don't know God? Your ability to resist temptation? Your understanding of the Holy Spirit's work? Your love and obedience to Jesus? Your . . . okay, we'll stop.

We want you to realize that you are a *major player* in your children's lives. It's time to get your "game face" on—the one with a smile, of course.

Rather than producing unwarranted guilt, however, we want to try what the apostle Paul always did: that is, encouraging fellow Christians to "excel still more."

Here's one crucial principle we learned from those who spent most of their adult years raising Christian children: Passing the baton of faith is *more than a handoff.* Indeed, the Christian life has been accurately compared to a marathon, not a sprint. And we can't leave the coaching job primarily to others. We can't just put our children in Sunday school at age seven, sit back, and let the church do the rest. We have to be in this marathon relay race as a team—for life.

Kids, even adult kids, need to know that if they fall, we'll be there to help pick them up, pat them on their backsides, and send them on their way again. If they run too slow, we'll remind them to pick up the pace. If they run off the track, we'll point them back to the right lane. If they're discouraged, we're the first to encourage. If they quit the race, we'll tell them we still love them.

Not Just Values

Many parents believe that passing on biblical values is *the* all-important task—so important that they think, *If I can get them to behave like Christians, they'll keep the faith when they're older.* In fact, parents can be so concerned about kids' behavior that we may fall back on negative attitudes while our children are running around the spiritual track. We can be overly critical, always yelling that their efforts aren't good enough. We can discourage them by acting like we never failed. We can shut them out when they quit. All these scenarios tell our kids that they just don't measure up. Count on this: If your children feel they can never please you—or God—they'll quit trying.

Good behavior is not a bad target to shoot for, but it's not the bull's-eye. Think about what matters most to God. Is it being a nice person? Doing good works? Knowing the right "Christian words"? No, these aren't what God wants. He wants a clean relationship with us. He prefers that we zero in on following him because he created us and loved us enough to die for us.

In a similar fashion, we need to emphasize our relationship with our kids more than getting them to do all the right things. Ultimately, we want to pass on our relationship with Jesus Christ—not a code of conduct—to our offspring.

The Marriage Process

Let's back up a bit. What is the process people go through before they're ready to *follow* Jesus Christ? Most take these steps:

1. They hear about God and his love for them through Jesus Christ.
2. They learn more about the person who was born, died on the cross, and rose from the dead on the third day.
3. They count the costs involved in following him.

4. They accept his payment on the cross for their sins, repent, and begin building a relationship with him.

5. They continue to learn more about him and what he requires.

For some, the first four steps can take less than an hour. But for many of us, they take much longer. For all of us, number five is a lifetime proposition.

If you're tracking with us, you can see that this process parallels the one we went through for marriage:

1. We met our future spouse or heard about him or her from someone we trusted.

2. We started to spend time with him or her, with the goal of getting to know the person better.

3. We wondered if this was "the one." Deep down, we asked ourselves if we wanted to make a lifetime commitment.

4. We made the choice to be married, and later we recited vows to love and cherish our spouse for the rest of our lives.

5. We're now spending our days finding out new and wonderful (and not-so-wonderful) things about our spouse.

///

Stages of Faith

Researchers have discovered common stages in our faith development. Jay Kesler outlines them in his book *Energizing Your Teenager's Faith*.

1. Children in grade school who talk about God and Jesus are echoing the words they have heard from adults. It is an "experienced faith." Important patterns of spiritual development can be formed during these years.

2. Junior highers have an "affiliated faith" that sees

their beliefs in terms of a relationship. Jesus is their "best friend." Their faith grows mainly through church and youth group interaction.

3. High schoolers develop a "searching faith." Tough questions are asked to help them sort out whether to personally accept what they've experienced. This is the time parents need to spend hours discussing those questions.

4. Young adults begin to develop an "owned faith." Having freely accepted Christian beliefs, these adults incorporate biblical values as their own.

///

Okay, so that's a rough comparison, but here's the point: All relationships progress. They don't just happen and then stand still. Learning about the Lord, getting to know him, and eventually choosing to follow him is a process. We need to keep our children moving forward toward Jesus Christ.

Remember, picture what type of Christian you want your children to be when they've left the nest. You may even want to write down a few attributes and qualities on a piece of paper and slip it into the back of your Bible. Then ask yourself: *How can I get them there from where they are now?*

The priority of "lifetime baton-passing" is not only an attitude, but it also means implementing tons of creative ideas a busy parent needs. We want to start you off with some of the top ideas we gleaned from our surveys and interviews. After each vignette, we've included a "key thought" to keep in mind.

We're in This Together

"As our children got older," said a Philadelphia father, "I think they appreciated that we didn't pretend we knew everything about everything. We told them about occasions when we weren't disciplined, and we'd even ask them to pray for us so we could get back on track. Though we intentionally shared spiritual struggles and victories with our kids, I don't think that hurt our leadership in the home. We just emphasized that our journey had taken us a little farther than theirs, but we were both on the same road."

///// KEY THOUGHT
Make vulnerability a strength, not a weakness.

Building Spiritual Traditions

A number of adult children we talked with recalled fond memories of the traditions their parents attempted to build. "We lit advent candles, celebrated the church seasons, made a big deal about Holy Week, and sang a lot, too. The kids I see without any traditions won't have anything to pass on to their children," said a Dallas man.

Some other things you can do as a family: Sing Christmas carols to neighbors, eat lamb and bitter herbs at a Passover meal, attend Christian concerts together, give up a special treat for Lent, watch Christian videos together, or spend a week at a Christian summer camp. The ideas are limitless!

///// KEY THOUGHT
Boot up forty megabytes of great family memories that revolve around your spiritual life. If you do, the output could yield dividends for generations.

Battling with the Unseen

"Dad prayed for us every morning," one Oregon woman remembers. "We'd get out of bed and see him on his knees. Then when we left for school, Mom would put her arms on all of the kids together and pray over us before we'd walk out the door. It was an incredible feeling knowing we were under God's protection. I had a secure feeling that the day would go fine. I do the same now with my kids."

Another woman echoed that story: "My parents were big into prayer when I was growing up. Today, my friends would call me a prayer warrior. I've seen how prayer has worked in my mom's life. She would fast and pray for hours. What better role model than a praying parent?"

///// KEY THOUGHT

Spiritual battles need to be fought with spiritual weapons. If you don't think there's a battle going on for the hearts and minds of your children, you're wrong. Fervent prayer is the key from the moment God gives them life until the day you're called home to heaven.

Challenge Them toward Maturity

"Dad was always calling us to be men," a Washington minister relayed. "I remember standing in the garden with a hoe in my hand and Dad holding another in his hand. That afternoon, he told me a man stands up for what he believes and thinks his own thoughts. I learned to trust my dad with the deep things of my heart."

///// KEY THOUGHT

Have a goal in mind as you move them toward maturity. This will prevent you from making it up as you go.

Keep Your Word

I (Mike) made a promise to the kids one summer that I would take them fishing before we left on a longer-than-usual vacation.

We had never fished before, and we didn't have any equipment. During the last week before our departure, it would have been easy to trot out several of my tried-and-true excuses. But I remembered my promise, so one afternoon after work I drove the kids to a U-Ketch-Em lake in the Colorado Rockies. Along the way, I quietly reminded Andrea and Patrick why I felt it was important to keep my word.

///// KEY THOUGHT

Be consistent with your words. If they can't trust your promises, how will they learn to trust the promises of God?

Have a Faith Worth Imitating

"My parents were never the type of people who acted one way on Sunday and different on Tuesdays and Thursdays. They were the same at home and at work," said Doris Smith.

"Basically, if you're going to tell your kids not to lie, then don't lie. If you want them to be charitable, show it by giving to others. If God is real, do those things he wants you to do: worship, fellowship, and pray about everything."

///// KEY THOUGHT

You'll hear this from us again, but it needs to sink in: Hypocrisy smells worse than a dead skunk dipped in cheap perfume, and children have a very acute sense of smell!

Relating to Non-Christians

"I remember my dad when he was a youth pastor. He was involved in a church four days a week, but he always found time to be with nonbelievers," explained Jim Phillips. "He'd say, 'How are you going to reach out if you're around Christians all the time?' He did that by coaching basketball and refereeing football games. My home growing up was also a place where my non-Christian friends felt comfortable. That was important to me. It still is.

///

The Top Ten Ways to Hide Your Faith from Your Kids

10. Don't blow the dust off your Bible—let alone pick it up!
9. Limit their spiritual training to "Now I lay me down . . ." and "Romper Room" grace.
8. Leave child evangelism to the trained professionals.
7. If they catch you kneeling by your bed, pretend you're looking for a missing sock.
6. Always have your spouse say grace (or eat dinner in shifts so that everybody's on his own).
5. Offer simplistic answers to their heartfelt questions about life.
4. When the preacher says something that touches your heart and you start getting misty-eyed, pretend your contacts are bothering you again.
3. If they catch you with your Bible open, tell them you're doing research for the crosswords.
2. If the pastor calls during the week and asks if you'd mind reading Scripture or giving your testimony for the Sunday service, say, "Oh, uh, I think we'll be out of town that Sunday. In fact, we may be out of town for the next few months."
1. If the pastor starts talking about your thought life, tell the kids that you think you might have left the motor running in the car and you'd better go outside and check.

///

"I really appreciate the fact that my parents were willing to take chances. They didn't keep us from the big, bad world. They strongly believed in public schools—not because the education was always that great, but for the ministry value we could have as Christian students. They believed that if you took all the Christians out, who was going to do God's work? I guess they felt that part of being prepared for a life of service wasn't just the right amount of head knowledge, but a balance between knowledge and learning how to relate to the world. Now that I've been out of college and in full-time ministry for ten years, guess which one is more important?"

///// KEY THOUGHT

Many of us work with non-Christians all day, but once we go home, we crawl back into our little cocoon. We're either caught up in an array of church activities, or we socialize only with Christians. If non-Christians are a priority in your life, they'll also be a priority in the lives of your children.

Watch Out for Overload

"When I hit high school, my parents gave me some flexibility," a young woman from Minneapolis began. "I was going to a Christian school and was getting burned out on church activities. When you add up church worship, Sunday school, and youth group, plus my school—it was just too much. My parents took stock of the situation. They saw that Sunday school and youth group weren't interesting to me, so they didn't force me to go. That taught me that God's expectations weren't just to go to meetings, but that he wanted the daily life stuff just as much."

///// KEY THOUGHT

Find a balance between home, spouse, children, and outside interests.

Planned Relationship Building

Carl Thompson's oldest son used to leave at seven-fifteen in the morning to catch the school bus. Carl changed his routine so his son wouldn't have to eat breakfast by himself. As a teenager, his son needed that time to talk or just be with Dad.

"Evenings, I'd go in their rooms while they were doing their homework and spread my office work out on the floor," said Carl. "Sure, I didn't always get as much done as I would have liked, but it was a great chance to be there when they had questions about life, school, God—anything.

"My son filled out a school questionnaire one time that asked what a teen needs most from his parents. His response was quantity and quality time. Though he had never mentioned that to us before, his answer told us he still wanted our time."

///// KEY THOUGHT

If your bull's-eye is the relationship, then you'll do things to enhance it—no matter what the cost. If your bull's-eye is behavior or spiritual content, you may end up with good children who know the Bible, but they may not want to spend time with you.

Teach Basic Theology

From the time your kids are young, you can start relating biblical truths that will stick with them for life.

"We always stressed to our kids that a person is made up of three parts: your soul, body, and mind," said a New Hampshire mother. "Your soul is the foundation that your body and mind stand on. Then we listed all the things each of us has to do to keep all three parts healthy and growing. We just brainstormed around the table.

"We would say, 'Okay, your soul. What do you have to do for that?' The answers would come easily from the kids: love God, read the Bible, talk to Jesus, go to church, care about other people, and forgive those who wrong you. As they matured and got older, they were able to add a few more things to the list. Then we'd do the same with the body and mind.

"This helped our children—and us—to identify when we were 'sick Christians.' Soul maintenance and growth became natural to talk about. The temptation, of course, was to make Christianity something we *do* instead of something we *are*. We always talked about that, too. I don't think the kids ever felt they had to work to please God. That's because we always emphasized God's approval of us because of what Jesus did on the cross."

///// KEY THOUGHT

If you're perceptive, daily living can be the perfect classroom to teach biblical truths.

Make Sure They Know What Sin Is

Many Christian families are insulated from the darkness of sin. Consequently, it's easier for children to grow up without an appreciation for their own sin and the wonder of God's grace. One key to keeping children faithful is making sure they understand what sin is.

"Sin is an authority issue: wanting to be your own boss and be independent from others," said David Palmer. "I taught my kids to evaluate their own relationship with Christ by discerning whether they were complying with God's agenda and pleasing him. If not, that was sin.

"We talked hundreds of times about how they got away from the Lord, from prayer, or from church. When they could agree that they had moved away from those things, we were able to call sin *sin*. We did that from the time they were little, so it became a way of life. We would say, 'If you have stepped away from the Lord, the reason is that you want to run your own life.'

"The only things they could do at that point were to either admit their sin or stay in open-faced rebellion. Rarely did they choose rebellion as an option. Our relationship with them was too precious for them to want to pursue that."

///// KEY THOUGHT
To appreciate salvation it's important to understand what we were saved *from*. Without that knowledge, it's easier to take God and his compassion for granted.

They're Accountable to God

"As soon as they started doing things at school that they were afraid to tell us about, such as fighting, swearing, or putting other children down, we sat them down to explain how we felt about that," said Lisa Haubrich. "We'd say, 'Now, we can't be with you every second of the day to keep an eye on your behavior. And sometimes you're not going to feel comfortable telling us the bad things you've done. But that's okay.' Then we'd describe a few things we couldn't tell our parents to show them they were normal. 'While we always want you to have the freedom to talk to us—and you won't get punished for telling the truth—you need to realize God knows exactly what you've done. Your ultimate responsibility is to please him, not us.'

"Our goal was to build a certain degree of God-consciousness in them from an early age. It was tempting to paint God into a corner and make him the bad guy, but whenever we used that line, 'You're responsible to God,' we always explained what God thinks about us, even when we mess up."

Lisa and her husband often shared these principles with their children:

- God knows we're going to make mistakes and isn't surprised at anything we do.
- God's more sad than angry when we disobey him.
- He's quick to forgive when we ask him to.
- Above anything else, he wants a clean relationship with us.
- God loves us too much to allow us to stay the way we are, which is why he offers us his power to overcome temptation.

"We always wanted to make God the good guy," said Lisa. "It's tough enough for kids to follow someone they can't see. We saw no reason to make him the heavenly oppressor. We tried to emphasize his loving eye, not his judging gaze. We reminded them that since God was for them, who could be against them? Another one was: 'Nothing people do can separate them from the love of God.' I believe our children grew up with an accurate picture of God's character—and the knowledge that they were accountable to someone higher than us."

///// KEY THOUGHT

The earlier your children "own" their relationship with God, the better. From an early age, emphasize how personal God wants to be. Help them see that God is the greatest friend they could ever have. Give them responsibility for maintaining a close relationship with Christ by showing them how important your relationship with him is.

Never Give Up

What happens if you became a Christian *after* your kids were into their teen years? "Don't despair," said Andy Lange, a Southern California dad. "It's never too late to present Christ to your children, even when they're older and don't seem interested in your faith. The key is to admit your mistakes. Don't give them such a holy model to look at. Otherwise they'll give up even thinking about Christ. We saw a lot of folks in our church who felt intimidated by their children because they were rebelling. Though we struggled with our oldest son's rebellion, we never gave up. He eventually returned to his faith."

///// KEY THOUGHT

Our timetable isn't always God's. There is a season for everything, and for some, the season of faith may come later in life. Remember the apostle Paul's attitude about his past—years he spent persecuting the church of Jesus Christ: "Forgetting what is behind and straining toward what is ahead, I press on toward the goal to win the prize for which God has called me heavenward in Christ Jesus" (Phil. 3:13-14).

Perseverance is really what this parenting business is all about. God was tenacious with many of us as he showed us the truth and waited for our response. In fact, he can be downright unrelenting! Why? He paid too high a price for us—his only Son—so he's not about to let go of us easily.

To us, that's the example we need to follow. With the end goals of a growing faith for our children in mind, we must always press forward with our kids—reminding, exhorting, and praying. The only time we are ever allowed to give up on our kids is when God gives up on us. And that isn't going to happen.

Hopefully, these principles have given you a taste of what's ahead. The next chapter talks about how to handle two unpleasant parts of parenthood: conflict and discipline.

These battleground areas have tested the relationship between parents and children for centuries. Your response to these child-rearing areas could set the tone between you and your children for the rest of your lives.

CHAPTER 2

HITTING THE BULL'S-EYE, NOT JUST THE TARGET
Parents and Discipline, Part 1

Christy Davenport remembers when she went toe-to-toe with her two-year-old boy. Like Rocky Balboa's first fight against Apollo Creed, the bout went the distance.

One afternoon, Christy put Jake down for his regular nap. Jake sat right back up in his bed and grinned at his mother. *You're not going to get me to sleep*, his face of defiance said.

"Oh, yes, I am," replied his mother, who laid him back down in his crib. *Oh, no, you're not*, he replied, standing back up.

This tug-of-war of wills lasted an hour, with Mom returning every few minutes to lay him down on his back. Christy tired of this game, which isn't surprising, since two-year-olds have more energy than a trio of rap dancers. Nonetheless, something inside Christy told her to remain firm. They were locked in a battle of wills, and Christy *had* to win—for Jake's sake. Finally, her perseverance prevailed, and Jake fell asleep.

Did Christy celebrate with an end-zone dance?

"No, I sat in the hallway and cried," recalled Christy. "It really took a lot out of me. But you know what? Jake never pulled that stunt again."

Fast forward thirteen years. Jake has just been sent to his room for disobedience. When Mom went upstairs to look in on him, he yelled, "I hate you!"

Christy didn't lose her cool. She strode over to his bed and sat down beside him. "Jake," she began, "you probably do hate me right now, but I want you to know that your mother cares about you so much that no matter what you do, I will always love you."

That was probably the *last* thing Jake expected his mom to say. Years later, has Jake forgotten that yelling episode? Probably. But what remained was a feeling deep in his heart that he would always be loved by his mother. Why? Christy had constructed a solid ground floor when it came to discipline.

Can you see the pattern Christy set? From early motherhood—even during unpleasant conflicts that could have been ignored—she wouldn't give up on the relationship with her son, no matter what the short-term costs. Behavior was important, but relationship was the bull's-eye.

From Side to Side

The opposite ends of the discipline spectrum are "ultra-strict" and "Dr. Spock." That's a little joke. Actually, the other end is "ultra-permissive." The goal of the faithful parent is to find the middle ground that's best for *each child*. Yes, a hard-nosed method may have worked with the oldest, but that doesn't mean it will be the best approach for your youngest. "A parent's response to conflict with his child," said one father, "is the key that opens the front door of his heart."

Handing our kids the baton of faith—in such a way that they'll take it—means we can't make it up as we go. We need to have a long-range view regarding discipline and conflicts. For openers, don't fear it. Sure, there are times when you don't want to come down hard on your child's misbehavior. Other times, you're too *tired* to deal with it. But keep in mind that several of the adult children we interviewed pointed to their parents' discipline as instrumental in bringing them to Christ.

"It strengthened our relationship by reinforcing their love," said Dale, a twenty-nine-year-old man. "Their discipline showed they cared about what I did. When I was ten, I was in the barn playing with some equipment. I shouldn't have been there. I got myself in a precarious spot. I screamed, 'Dad!' as loud as I could. He came rushing in with this look of fear on his face. After pulling me down, he gave me a pretty hard swat on the rear. I knew I deserved it."

Another adult child remembered how bad her temper was as a kid. "I would smack my brothers and sisters hard if I was mad at them," she said, "especially my little sister. She still has a scar from a hammer blow I gave her once [yikes!]. My parents handled that situation very calmly. I was still so angry that their controlled response caught me totally off guard. If they had responded in anger, that would have just fed my fires. Their patient and firm attitude after that caused me to become a Christian. I knew I was a sinner and needed help. Instead of going ballistic for what I'd done, they used the situation to point me toward my need for a Savior. That was a big step in helping me understand what kind of God my parents followed."

How do your kids feel? Do you make it a point to tell them you love them? Do you separate love from performance? Do your children know that?

You and your children will butt heads off and on until the day they leave home (and beyond!). Perhaps they won't like your house rules because they're the strictest ones on the block. Maybe you make them do their homework before they can play. Perhaps you enforce a no-TV-on-school-nights edict. Maybe their curfew is earlier than their peers'. As you set rules in your house, you will have to decide where to train your big guns and when to hold your fire.

Early Sources of Conflict

From the early grades to the teenage years, there's not much new under the sun as far as how kids get into trouble.

According to the parents and kids we surveyed, these were the top sources of conflict *before the teen years:*

- wanting to spend time with their friends
- fighting with siblings
- not doing what they're told
- outright disobedience
- being selfish
- their will vs. your will
- trouble at school
- talking back
- not listening to directions
- breaking rules
- temper tantrums
- using "that tone of voice"
- telling lies or half-truths

If your kids are infants or in the cute toddler stage, you've got a few things to anticipate. (And you thought diapers, teething, and ear infections were a pain!)

Conflict with Teens

As kids move into the teen years, they generally become more responsible (no promises, though). But along with fixing their own breakfasts, cleaning their rooms, and doing homework without being reminded, they also become more . . . *sophisticated* in their ability to cause a parent grief.

Teenage conflicts offer whole new worlds for testing parents' patience—and their ability to respond correctly. Instead of moms (or dads) looking down to the child, they're often locked eye-to-eye with them over issues such as:

- using bad language
- fighting or loud arguments with siblings
- not getting what they want
- wanting to be out of the house and with their friends
- talking back
- deciding what they want to wear
- deliberately disobeying the parents' expressed wishes
- cleaning room, finishing chores
- displaying an adolescent attitude of disrespect and defiance
- fibbing and telling lies
- arriving late without a phone call
- breaking curfew
- going to church
- dealing with girls, girls, girls
- dealing with boys, boys, boys (like, duhhh)
- shooting at a train with a BB gun (easily solved: no BB guns)
- wearing makeup after Mom has forbidden it
- drinking or taking drugs (that won't happen to *our* kids, of course)
- hanging out with the wrong crowd of friends

WHEW!!!!!

Does this list make you wish someone would invent a time-warp machine so you could keep them at their cutest and most compliant age? Alas, there's no avoiding the inevitable—and perhaps you're already there!

Is it possible for your kids to end up in their twenties with a strong faith (and you still in your right mind)? Of course it is. It's not a bleak situation, it only looks that way.

///

What Were the Most Effective Ways of Resolving Conflict?
Asked of Adult Children

In grade school, apologizing for poor behavior was mentioned often. One woman said her dad always let her tell her side of the story before he responded. "I felt he really listened," she said.

In junior high, the children said they preferred talking things out with their parents. "I would tell parents to not respond to a conflict out of anger," wrote one. Another says his parents would explain why they were so strict, and that made him feel better. But a few respondents said their parents did a poor job of facing conflicts and resolving them. "In our home, problems were virtually ignored until the situation passed," said a Chicago man.

In high school, conflicts have a way of festering. The children said they *wanted* to be able to sit down with their parents and calmly discuss the source of the conflicts without the discussions turning into shouting matches. Some appreciated their parents letting them choose between options; others felt better if they could present their side. "I love you enough not to let you do this," one child remembers his parent saying. Another said, "They would withhold something until I did what they asked me to do. Then they would give in a little so I would have at least a *small* victory."

///

Taking Aim
In any era, moms and dads have wanted kids to act with good

behavior. But one parent who raised three strong-willed kids who never went through a rebellious stage (hard to believe, isn't it?) articulated the real goal we need to aim for: "Behavior wasn't the most important issue. Our *relationship* was." (Dozens of others we talked to agreed.)

"My kids didn't see an *authoritarian* home," he continued, "but they did see an *authoritative* home. We never had to dominate the kids; we just never lost control.

"Permissive parents eventually let their kids take control. A strict home simply means the parents stay in control. Being a strict parent isn't being tough or unreasonable. It means knowing that if you lose the leadership in the home, you're probably going to lose the kids.

"All my kids tried to get out from under the control of their mother and me. They pushed the boundaries and kicked the end out of the rules continually. It was like they were saying, 'If you're not strong enough to stop me, you'll lose the battle.' Today, they recognize that it's a godly thing for parents to lovingly and firmly stay in their leadership role."

There was obviously more to this home than staying in control. Both parents worked hard at building family unity through fun times, through communication, by staying involved with their kids at every stage, and by representing Christ accurately. They wanted their kids to know—without a doubt—what type of God their parents served. Though years of living a consistent faith was essential, one vignette occurred in each of the three kids' lives that none will forget.

"With all three, I took the punishment *for them* at least once," this faithful dad remembers.

Say what?

"A situation would occur where they were obviously guilty. After calmly and clearly establishing that they did deserve the paddle, I'd say something like, 'I want to show you what Jesus did for us. Now we agree that what you did was deliberately wrong and deserves punishment. I'm going to give you the paddle, and I'll take your punishment for you.'

"My two oldest kids couldn't do it. They broke down and cried. My youngest didn't miss his chance. He was tentative, though. I think he was in awe of the moment. It was like he was violating something sacred. After he smacked me a couple of times, we sat and talked about what Jesus did; what it was like to take our place even though he didn't do anything wrong. This happened before they were ten. I only did it once with each child."

Not only does something like this stick in the memory of each kid for the rest of his life, but it also accomplishes at least three other goals:

- It teaches a spiritual lesson: Kids will remember their sinful nature and what God did to initiate a relationship with them even though they are clearly in the wrong.
- It allows each child to see that he's only punished after establishing the guilt of deliberate disobedience or a willful, defiant attitude (as opposed to childish mistakes).
- It moves the parent/child relationship up another notch toward the *ultimate goal* of mutual respect and friendship.

///

What Were the Least Effective Ways of Resolving Conflicts?
Responses from Adult Children
- "I'm the parent."
- "Because I told you to."
- "When your dad gets home . . . "
- "I don't have the energy for this."

- "Don't sass me."
- "Go to your room." (One fellow likened this to being banished to "Outer Mongolia.")

Also, children *hated* being yelled at—this was the most common response. Others heard ultimatums every hour—which lost their impact. Lastly, one woman said her mom held her head underwater in a dishpan when she misbehaved. (This method isn't recommended by us, Dr. Dobson, *Good Housekeeping,* Dr. Spock, or Murphy Brown!)

///

Things to Keep in Mind

Former Chicago Bears head coach Mike Ditka has some explosive coaching habits. After repeated tirades with his quarterback one year, he was asked by reporters if he was worried about the player's relationship with him. His response?

"Relationship? What do I care about a relationship? I'm the head coach."[1]

When you're coaching forty-seven professional athletes, you can get away with that type of strategy. But when you're coaching precious sons or daughters to be lifelong followers of Jesus Christ, the quality of your relationship is a strong determiner of whether they'll respond to your faith the way you'd like . . . or resentfully pull away from you for a lifetime.

If you glance through the lists of conflicts again, you can see that many of the behaviors last for only a short while. For example, remember the parent who said her child shot a BB gun at a train? By taking the gun away, that specific behavior is stopped. You're now ready to deal with the next mishap—which is guaranteed to happen in about an hour!

What does last, however, is the child's memory of how you responded to his misbehavior. Though occasional instances of "over-disciplining" are easily forgiven by a child, repeated out-of-control responses by the parent leave their mark.

The parent who let his children spank him with a paddle raised all three kids to walk closely with the Lord. None have rebelled toward him or the church for more than a very short time. The man and his wife were strong-but-calm disciplinarians, especially when there was a battle for control. Their "bull's-eye" emphasis, however, wasn't simply right behavior but building a close relationship.

Now that you know what the bull's-eye is, you have the foundation for building a strategy on dealing with conflict and discipline issues . . . in the next chapter.

CHAPTER 3

A WINNING STRATEGY
Parents and Discipline, Part 2

Okay, where are we?

We've given you survey results in which parents and kids told us about the sources of conflict they each experienced. The next logical step is to talk about what parents did to discipline their kids, and then to ask the kids what they thought about *that*.

We're going to discuss discipline that drives a wedge between parent and child, discipline that's neutral, and discipline that actually *helps* the parent/child relationship.

Before we start, let's remind ourselves what the goals of good discipline are:

- To protect children from themselves. (Toddlers and young kids need to learn not to touch hot stoves and sharp knives.)
- To promote good behavior. (Who wants to be around brats?)
- To instill solid values. (Punishment helps a child learn right from wrong.)
- To help children become productive members of society. (Undisciplined kids have a hard time in school, buckling down to study, and developing good work habits.)

When we asked parents how they disciplined their young children (grade-school age and below), many simply could not remember any details! "Sure, we spanked our kids" was the typical response, but beyond that they drew a blank.

Fortunately, the adult children—not so many years removed from childhood—were able to recall Mom and Dad's disciplinary efforts. Here's what they said their parents employed:

Disciplining Grade-Schoolers

- spankings (As expected, this was a runaway winner.)
- spankings, followed by heart-to-heart talks and hugs (This was mentioned a number of times. Spanking alone is effective in molding behavior, especially in younger, defiant children, but not as effective as the child grows. More on this later.)
- time out (Again, another popular choice.)
- the "rod," or belt or leather strap (We asked the few who wrote this down if this method really worked. Yes, they replied, it was "effective," but they believed it didn't encourage respect for the parent. Instead, many said a parent who exhibited "controlled discipline" won their respect. When there was outright fear of Dad administering a "whupping," the punishment usually failed to help cement the relationship—especially when it was done in anger.)
- "Being sent to my room"
- "Mom telling me she was disappointed"
- verbal reprimands
- grounding

//

The Top Ten Worst Ways to Discipline Your Grade-Schoolers

10. Tell them they can only watch four hours of television per night.
9. Send them to their rooms (where their toys are).
8. Promise them a trip to McDonald's if they stop misbehaving.
7. If they're misbehaving at McDonald's, promise 'em Chuck E. Cheese's.
6. Tell them if they don't shape up, they'll have to go live at the pastor's house.
5. Hit them over the head with one of Dr. Dobson's books.
4. Dangle them over the lawn mower.
3. Threaten to tell Santa what they're like. Or, threaten to tell Santa not to come to your house this year.
2. Bribe them with ice cream. (That's like trying to extinguish a car fire with a gas pump hose.)
1. Just say yes.

//

There's nothing earthshaking in the above responses. You probably remember what worked best from your childhood. Plus, there are dozens of great books about discipline, including our favorite, *The New Dare to Discipline*. Dr. Dobson revised this classic parenting book in 1992, and you don't need to go any further than his book. We're not going to repeat Dr. Dobson's prescription for proper discipline, but we do want to emphasize the most effective methods.

An Oregon man relayed this about a childhood experience he'll never forget: "When I was in sixth grade, I lied to my dad about a homework assignment. I told him I'd completed it when I hadn't. When he saw my teacher at a parent/teacher conference, she insisted I had missed that important assignment. My dad stuck up for me, saying I had told him I finished it. When he found out the truth, he confronted me. He said, 'I stuck up for you tonight, and then I found out you lied to me. But I'm going to keep believing in you.'

"I didn't lie to him anymore. I couldn't. He believed in me. From that moment on, I did all I could to not let him down. My dad had one main theme for me: manhood. He told me real men don't lie; real men have integrity. He cemented this distinction by pointing out that some men aren't honest, some don't treat girls right, and some don't try their hardest. He said I needed to be one of the honest, respectful, and hardworking guys."

If you do your job right during the grade-school years, your teenagers may one day be able to give this type of testimony:

"My parents didn't do much disciplining when we were teens, but that's because they did such a thorough job on us as youngsters! Though they had four kids in five years, they were consistent with us, even with my youngest brother who was a terror. They insisted on prompt obedience. They never counted one . . . two . . . three, yet they didn't have to spank a lot, either."

A lot of parents (and kids) emphasized that consistency was the key. You can't have a "Rule of the Week" and then audible at the line of scrimmage. Parents need a solid front line. One parent said, "If one of us would discipline a child and the other disagreed, we wouldn't talk about it until later. We felt it was important not to undermine the way the other parent handled it."

By having a united front (and settling any differences out of earshot of the kids), we can discipline with grace and a "velvet hand." If not, that trust we so desperately want from our kids will take longer to build.

///// KEY THOUGHT

The things to keep in mind about discipline in the grade-school years are: be consistent, don't back down, follow through on punishments, and watch for times when your kids will test you. If you do your disciplinary spadework early on, you'll be able to trust your teens all that much more.

Junior High: Big Kids or Little Adults?

The teenage years bring a whole new dimension to discipline. Depending on their maturity level, kids are finally capable of abstract (and sometimes logical) thinking. Somewhere between twelve and fourteen, a bell should ring in your head. *Brringg! Time to start treating them like little adults.* Here's the reason: Though many kids accept Christ at a young age, most do not make a "lifetime" decision to follow him until their teenage years . . . and beyond.

Many parents chaperon their children to Sunday school and kids' church programs year after year, only to see their kids later walk away from everything they've been taught. Why? They never heard the bell.

Through my (Greg's) fifteen-year experience in teen ministry with Youth for Christ and *Breakaway* magazine, I'm convinced the key time that your kids are watching—and listening to your words—is right at the beginning of their growing independence. Without making a sound, many kids are wondering if they really want your faith to be theirs. Therefore, *mutual respect* (within limits, of course, and with a knowledge of who is still in charge) must be developed.

If you lose their respect by flying off the handle in the early teen years, it'll be an uphill battle to keep them on your team. If you continue to treat them like little kids when they're shaving their faces or legs, you've sent a strong signal that you don't understand. Instead of looking at you as a parent, they begin to see you as an opponent—and they'll want to win the arguments they start! In their mind, they assume that since you're on the other side of the line of scrimmage, your God probably is, too.

///// KEY THOUGHT

In the junior high years, it's time to start building mutual respect. Without abdicating your authority, begin to recognize your maturing teens' individuality and ability to understand the situation.

Disciplining Young Teens

With that in mind, here's what the adult children said were the most effective forms of discipline/conflict resolution during the junior high years:

- revoking privileges
- one-on-one conversations
- grounding (This method was mentioned most, probably because it molded behavior without demeaning their blossoming individuality.)
- "My dad's reprimanding scowl" (This one was mentioned by a lot of *guys*. We suggest the father of the house find a mirror immediately and begin practicing that curl of the lip. It could be a lifesaver.)
- limit on TV watching
- "Talking to me and expressing disappointment"
- social restrictions
- withholding allowance
- "Throughout my teen years, they avoided responding

out of anger. We listened to each other and talked things through."

- "We talked, and I obeyed. But they always explained to me why they were strict, just so I could understand better."

- "I don't remember getting much discipline in junior high and high school because expectations and respect had been developed when I was younger." (This came from a woman who had three other siblings who all turned out to be growing, productive Christians. We received surveys back from all four, plus her parents. What the parents did should be bottled and sold in stores, because all four said they had the greatest folks in the world.)

- "The best discipline was when my parents offered up what the punishments could be, then let me choose."

///

The Top Ten Worst Ways to Discipline Your Teenagers

10. Tell 'em you *really* mean it this time.
9. Only *threaten* to take away their MTV.
8. Shame them with stories of how your parents never let *you* get away with all the stuff you let them do.
7. Tell them you'll make them get jobs if they don't agree to stop terrorizing you.
6. Ask your spouse to do it.
5. Sic the dog on them.
4. Make them get really goofy haircuts.
3. Burn their music tapes. [Careful: the fumes could take several years off your life.]
2. Change the locks on the house.
1. Send them to *your* parents' house for the weekend.

///

Disciplining High Schoolers

"In my home," a Texas woman told us, "the punishment was always well thought-out, and it fit the crime. One time I came downstairs wearing a miniskirt on my way out the door to a rock concert. Dad took one look at it and told me to change. I did, but then I put the miniskirt in my purse and changed into it on the way to the show. I don't remember how he found out, but he did. Maybe he looked for it. Anyway, the next day he asked me if I changed skirts. When I admitted I had, he didn't fly off the handle. He simply grounded me from records and the radio for three weeks."

Transitioning into high school—and the last few years you're still an influence—should mean that you're adding to what you've built on during the junior high years. If trust and respect haven't been well-established, hold on to your seats. You're in for a wild ride.

One Minnesota parent remembers being buffeted in a church parking lot.

"I was standing outside church one night, talking to a deacon. All of a sudden, our son drove off and sprayed gravel everywhere as he sped away with the car. When he got home, all I said was, 'Son, put those keys on top of the drawer. You can use them again in a week.' He learned his lesson not to drive like a nut."

Had the respect not been well-established, the teen could have resented the punishment. When we talked to the son about the incident, he laughed. While he didn't intend to make the rocks fly (of course), he knew his dad handled the situation with fairness. "He was always reasonable with me, so I didn't see a need to do battle—especially since I messed up."

While a rebellious teen may cause more than a few problems, you definitely want to be on *clear and open speaking terms*. Why? Communication was far-and-away the top method in which conflict was *effectively* dealt with. If the limits are well-defined, many teens won't push them—well, too hard—because they know where the line is.

"Mom and I were close friends," one Orlando woman told us. "Though her parental role was well-established, she made it easy for us to approach her because she listened well. She knew what she stood for; she was very secure. But that attitude made us feel safe, and it was something we wanted for ourselves." Wondering when—or if—you'll become friends with your children? We've put together the responses from parents and adult children in appendix 8. Though each family was different, it serves as a good reminder of what our long-term goal should be.

///

"You Just Don't Understand!"

If you hear that once, you'll hear it a thousand times. The problem is, we *do* understand. We understand our children want their way, they want more freedom, they want to do what their friends' parents are letting them get away with . . . they're changing into little adults and want to be understood. Here are a few tips for getting along with that young teen who thinks you don't have a clue:

1. **When your child is picking battles with you on every front, save the big guns for the major battles.** Be emotionally prepared to handle the barrage by deciding ahead of time which areas are worth taking a firm stand over (grades, treating family members with respect, church attendance, curfew, etc.).

2. **Know when to lighten up.** If home is a fun place to be, the kids will view it as a refuge. They'll invite friends over and realize they have it better than a lot of their peers.

3. **If you have responsible children, loosen the reins.** That will help them mature faster and will decrease the amount of confrontation over their need to

establish their own identity. This strategy also hastens the process of developing *their own* faith. If your children are less mature, you'll need tighter reins. But always hold out for them the goal of more freedom when they prove themselves over time.

4. **Tell stories of your own adolescence when your kids are in the mood to listen.** That doesn't mean in the middle of a lecture, after they've done something wrong. Though kids will *say*, "That was the Stone Age," they're really thinking, *Maybe they do understand what I'm going through*. This is particularly effective if you've built a pattern of telling them about your life during the grade-school years.

5. **Respect their opinions even if you don't agree with them.** Don't be too quick to show them how childish they are. Learn to ask questions in a calm tone that helps children logically think through the consequences of their demands. If the decision can wait until tomorrow, suggest that you both think and pray about it overnight and discuss it the next day. That gives the Holy Spirit time to work—on both of you—and it shows that you're *trying* to be reasonable.

6. **Say yes whenever you can.** When you have to say no, think of alternatives.

7. **Never give as a reason "This looks bad" or "What would people at church think?"** Otherwise, kids learn that their requests are at the mercy of strangers from a building where they spend one or two hours a week. All it does is build resentment toward an institution you want them to learn to love.

8. **While your goal is a strong relationship, remember that you're the parent, not their best friend.** In the early teen years, they don't want you to be their best friend. They want a parent who will provide freedom within limits.

///

On the flip side, another woman admitted *deep* problems in the way her dad punished her.

"His harsh discipline was probably a symptom of where he was at," said Jennifer, from Arlington, Virginia. "The discipline was never delivered with the best intentions but out of anger. Belt whipping continued through the teenage years, sometimes with bruises. He left the family when I was seventeen. I had absolutely no respect for the man."

While most children will eventually come around and want a close relationship with their parents when they reach their thirties, more than 30 percent of the kids we talked to were estranged from their parents in their twenties. The reason? The way they were disciplined in their teens. So let's not waste a whole decade (or more) by getting stuck in an overdiscipline rut and refusing to change.

Some of the adult children were glad their parents kept a steady hand during the teen years. What worked, they said, was talk, talk, and talk.

"It seems we were always having a family discussion," said Tim Gallagher. "Though it was hard to swallow at the moment, I remember a safe feeling later on when I thought about it."

A young woman said her parents had a rule they tried to stick by: Never let the sun go down on your anger. "I remember Dad waking me up after he came home late from work one night. We had fought before I left for school that morning. He wanted to make things right before he slept."

Another woman said she and her parents talked about *why* things went wrong. That helped her understand even more why poor behavior must have consequences.

For some, knowing that discipline was part of the whole Christian equation helped them sort out their feelings. "I knew Dad and Mom were praying for me every morning," said Dick Inverness. "Whenever conflict came up, I knew their motives were good, even if the discipline seemed unfair at the time."

Others appreciated their parents' not turning up the decibel level when they disobeyed. "A calm, two-way conversation involved some vulnerability on their part," remembers a San Diegan. "I felt better about taking my medicine when they told me about something they messed up on . . . calmly."

Added another respondent: "Whenever I compared myself to someone who acted worse, my parents never let me get away with it. That was just me trying to divert the issue."

Realize, too, that there will have to be some give-and-take. "They withheld something until I did as I was asked," remembers a Montana man. "Later, after the punishment was decided upon, my parents would sometimes give in a little to let me have *some* small victory, like extending curfew a half hour. That was done frequently enough so I felt more respected, but infrequently enough so I couldn't count on it."

///// KEY THOUGHT

Begin a pattern of controlled consistency in the early teen years, and then build on that mutual respect by reinforcing your love—and authority—again and again. Stay on this track and you'll have a son or daughter who will want to be around you after leaving the nest.

Post-High: Fine-tuned

Many of the kids we interviewed didn't leave home right after high school. This presented challenges for both parents and children, as the children had one foot at home and one outside.

"One time, my oldest boy decided to head off to Boston with some friends," said a New England mother. "He wound up staying at a buddy's house, but he never called. When he got home the next day, I told him it wasn't a terrible thing to stay out all night [he was nineteen at the time], except that it caused me a lot of worry. I wasn't angry; I just stated the facts. All he had to do was call me. We worked it out, set a curfew he could live with, and after that, he never failed to call if he was going to be late."

This story illustrates the fact that if your kids hang around home past their high school years, you'll be faced with a dilemma: *I still need to have some rules, but I realize that they are, for the most part, adults. Yet, they remain my children, and they are not totally independent. They need to be treated like adults, even when they sometimes don't behave like it.*

The ideal is to trust them enough to treat them as you would another friend. But that's far easier said than done. The parent/counselor role will be ongoing, but the parent/disciplinarian role will be nearly over. On some matters, you may have to agree to disagree. All you can do is express your views and then sit back and watch how matters develop. The art of give-and-take will be sorely tested.

The Least Effective Ways of Resolving Conflict

We heard some grinding of teeth here. Many admitted that certain methods of discipline didn't work at all. Some reported mixed results: One method worked with the oldest daughter, but failed miserably with daughter number three. The reason: different personalities. Several wished their parents had recognized this and had been more creative. While *no kids* held this against their parents (unless the discipline was harsh and unreasonable), they all were doing things differently with their own kids.

Here's what the adult children had to say:

Grade School

- "All I heard was, 'I'm the parent.'"
- "I hated being forced to give my brother a hug after fighting with him." (While some believe forced apologies or signs of affection need to happen after discipline, several kids who experienced this thought it was wasted effort.)
- "Hearing, 'Because I told you to.'"
- "I don't know how many times I heard my mom say, 'When your dad gets home . . .' "
- "Yelling. Mom and Dad lost it occasionally."

Junior High

- "Mom would say, 'Just quit doing that. I don't have the energy for this.'"
- "Wait until your dad gets home; he'll give it to you."
- "Throughout my teen years, they responded in anger without any respect for me."
- "Telling me 'Be quiet and obey' or 'I told you to.' I felt as if my ideas and opinions were nonessential to them."
- "When they yelled," one woman said, "it was usually because they felt they were losing control. In my mind, even as a twelve-year-old, they had control *and* my respect when they were calm."
- "We found that anger on either part always caused problems."
- "They would say 'Don't sass me' when all I really wanted was an answer or an explanation."
- "I would often go to my mother if I had a conflict with my dad and ask her to resolve it for me. This was not a good idea!"

- "My parents wouldn't confront issues like normal people. They would either try to smooth them over or lecture me that I was wrong for being angry."
- "We were very poor at facing conflicts and resolving them. Therefore, I grew up thinking conflict was bad. Problems were virtually ignored until the situation passed."

High School

- "We never verbalized our thoughts to each other."
- "They screamed and lost control." (Fortunately, this method was used unsuccessfully by more kids than parents.)
- "My parents would just announce what their decision was. No discussion."
- "I felt pressure to bend to their ways. It would make me more rebellious. They never gave in, even on smaller issues. They always had to be in control."
- "I hated those arbitrary because-I-said-so rules."
- "It was still spanking, but by this time I loathed my father. The punishment was inappropriate, and I harbored much anger."
- "We did not resolve conflicts at all. Looking back, I feel it would have been good to explain life and the situation to me. I work well with reason and logic."
- "I liked giving my parents the silent treatment."
- "Mom was the disciplinarian. My dad didn't get too much involved in that. I feel like that hurt my relationship with men, because I saw them as weak and easily overpowered. I sure wish things would have been different. I wound up divorced because I followed my mom's lead of being the dominant one in the family."

It should be noted that eventually each of the kids who told us of bad discipline strategies by their parents made it through those years with their faith intact. While some harbored deep scars and resentments from unreasonable treatment, most were able to cut their parents some slack.

CHAPTER 4

WHEN PARENTS SHOULD NEVER COMPROMISE
Parents and Giving In

Show us a mom and dad who say they never compromised on anything and we'll show you a set of extremely rebellious children produced by the same cookie-cutter. But for many parents, compromising—or the art of give-and-take—becomes part of the parental landscape as kids grow up. Most parents learn to compromise fairly early because they can't know *everything* about *every* situation that comes up during the child-rearing years.

Besides, many of us *want* to compromise. As the kids enter the complicated teen years, the black-and-white absolutes start to get a little gray around the temples. Parents and their getting-more-independent-by-the-day teens often seek a middle ground. Moms and dads who understand that—but remain consistent in what's really important—should have fewer problems.

On the other hand, just because a sixteen-year-old asserts his independence doesn't mean that parents step back and let him go by like a bull passing through a matador's cape. Some things in life are not negotiable—and never should be. For many, the line in the sand is the authority of God's Word. The Ten Commandments, as pundits have noted, are not the Ten Suggestions.

Compromising: The American Way?

There is increasing evidence that many Americans believe Old Testament stuff like the Ten Commandments isn't relevant in today's high-tech, fast-paced society. The Gallup organization conducted a poll in 1991, asking respondents about moral absolutes. While more than 90 percent of the adult respondents said religion was very important in their lives, around 70 percent believed morality "depended upon the situation." On top of that, about two-thirds rejected the concept of moral absolutes—that is, the Ten Commandments.

The Gallup poll also revealed that 43 percent said their own individual experience is the most reliable guide to truth, while just one-third said they rely on the Bible or religious leaders. Sixteen percent said the teachings of their parents or other authoritative figures had decided truth for them. Seven percent looked to science, and only 6 percent to the media. (Now there's some encouraging news!)

This survey illustrates that we live in a society of moral relativism, where the line in the sand "wiggles." The average American of the nineties is in the habit of downgrading his view of truth and morals to fit his behavior, and we are already seeing the consequences of this misguided philosophy.

Since these same people will probably be trying to convince our children of their convictions (or lack thereof), Christian parents need to cast a wary eye toward those espousing the old mantra, "If it feels right, do it." Not only will parents have to work harder to establish what is truth, but they are also handed the delicate task of *presenting* biblical truth to their children.

That is where we believe the emphasis on the bull's-eye of relationship is so essential. The emphasis on the right truth and correct behavior must be made in the context of mutual respect. Remember, the goal is to make your values your children's values—without having them reject you or your faith.

So, what do parents value? What did our survey respondents value so highly that they were not willing to compromise on? We asked parents that question, and we also sought answers from the adult children. We categorized each response by grade school, junior high, high school and post–high school. We've led off with what the parents said they never compromised on, followed by the adult children. We hope this chapter will simply reinforce what you already know to be true.

Grade School: What parents said you should never compromise on

- "We taught them respect from age two or three. We were soft, but we were also firm. They learned early that Mom and Dad are the authority in the house. They were never allowed to sass or be rude, but they were allowed to discuss things." (This was the number-one response.)
- "Honesty." (This was the number-two response.)
- "Being consistent in discipline."
- "*Learning* to respect their parents."
- "I emphasized kindness toward others and keeping their eyes on Jesus."
- "Schoolwork, chores, respect, church priorities, and getting along together."
- "Small children should be taught to obey."
- "Making sure they're aware of who's in charge."
- "Reading material and videos that you allow them to see."

- "Sunday school attendance."
- "Movies and music."

Grade School: What adult children said parents should never compromise on

- "Obedience." (This was the most-listed response.)
- "Disrespect toward parents." (This was the second-most-popular answer. Most felt that if they didn't respect their parents in grade school, it would be hard to respect them during the teenage years.)
- "Bible basics and a foundation in a relationship with Jesus Christ, not a church or rules."
- "Basic values: no cheating, lying, or stealing."
- "Bratty behavior."
- "The authority of the parents."
- "Disobedience of agreed-upon rules."
- "Keeping tabs on what their children are learning about God."
- "Always being honest and requiring honesty from them."
- "Spending time with them and accepting them based on *who* they are, not on *what* they do."
- "Having fun and teaching what is right."
- "Letting them know they are loved, being honest with them, and no physical violence."
- "Time with their children, talking about God and salvation."

///// KEY THOUGHT

Parents were more worried about discipline and attitude than about spiritual matters. The adult children generally agreed, but added that grade school children should respect the advice and teaching of their elders.

Junior High: What parents said you should never compromise on

- "Keeping your word."
- "Not letting them do things just because everyone else is doing it."
- "Being watchful of how peer pressure is affecting them."
- "Schoolwork, chores, respect, church priorities, and getting along together."
- "Since older children are able to think more concretely, parents should develop their kid's ability to discern right from wrong."
- "Reading materials, TV, and movies."
- "Being careful to not let your kids go to unchaperoned events."
- "Being disrespectful and getting overly involved with the wrong kind of friends."
- "Continuing to develop your own personal moral standards."
- "The harmful effects of substance abuse."

Junior High: What adult children said parents should never compromise on

- "Time with the kids and being involved in their lives." (This was a close third in total number of responses for all levels.)
- "Talking with their kids about drugs and sex, especially in today's world."
- "Always caring enough to know where your children are and what they are doing."
- "Maintaining discipline, but acknowledging when they were wrong."

49

- "Spiritual values and spiritual commitments."
- "Sexual purity and abstinence."
- "Respect for authority and for the other person."
- "Truthfulness, openness, and honesty."
- "Building in an attitude and a desire to do right."
- "Church attendance."
- "Monitoring the crowd a child hangs out with."
- "Dating guidelines: when it should start and what it should be."
- "The importance of getting the grades that reflect the child's ability."
- "Learning the hows and whys of independence and responsibility."
- "Discipline standards that have already been determined or agreed upon."
- "Moral standards for themselves and their children."
- "Unconditional love for your child."
- "Praying for them. Keep talking and listening. Living your values."
- "Honesty and integrity, even if it risks your reputation."

///// KEY THOUGHT

Here, parents worry about influences coming from outside the home, while the adult children emphasized spiritual values and monitoring who the child is chumming around with.

High School: What parents said you should never compromise on

- "The rule at our house was that if you go out Saturday night on a date, you have to be in church and Sunday school the next day. No exceptions."

- "Giving the children as much freedom as their maturity can handle."
- "Don't allow the kids to get away with disobedience. We were strict on truth-telling. We didn't excuse sin and say they were in a bad mood."
- "Giving them a *choice* of whether to go to church or not."

//

The Top Ten Worst Excuses Heard for Not Going to Church

10. "If I went *every* Sunday, Christmas and Easter wouldn't seem quite as special."
9. "The people there are too friendly. They must be up to something."
8. "The NFL on CBS."
7. "I always feel guilty when I go."
6. "The time change is coming soon, and I'm afraid I'll go to church on the day I could have slept in an extra hour, and I'll be the only one there."
5. "Sunday is a day of rest. Need I say more?"
4. "If God had meant for us to go to church every Sunday, he never would have given us golf courses, Saturday nights, the NBA's Game of the Week, ten-course brunches, and cozy beds to sleep in."
3. "Why, those lying, cheating, hypocritical televangelists! They make me so mad."
2. "I always like to stay up late on Saturday nights, and I know that if I went to church the next morning, I would probably nod off during the pastor's sermon."
1. "I went last month when a friend got married."

//

- "Kindness, chastity, and being sure you know God."
- "I didn't let my daughter call up boys or go to their homes. She has thanked me for that now."

- "Teaching them how to handle money like a good steward."
- "Never get into a car with a driver who has been drinking."
- "If the child is still under your authority, discuss privileges. Don't make them automatic."
- "Perhaps this is biased, but I feel that a dynamic, spiritually alive youth group is very important. Also, it's important that parents model their commitment to the church."
- "Have a mind of your own, and try not to follow the crowd."
- "Abstinence from drugs and alcohol."
- "Dating non-Christians."

High School: What adult children said parents should never compromise on

- "Spending time with them, and keeping channels of communication open."
- "Being 'unequally yoked,' either with the opposite sex or with *best* friends."
- "Sexual standards."
- "The harmful effects of substances."
- "The harmful effects of pornography."
- "Fitting in with the crowd is not the most important thing in the world."
- "Including the teen in making the decisions."
- "If I missed curfew and got grounded for six weeks, it didn't end up at three weeks. They were firm on the punishment they doled out."
- "The thing I remember most was they never argued in front of us kids. They always had a united front."

- "Commitments. When you say you'll be somewhere at a certain time, be there."
- "Truthfulness and honesty with themselves and others."
- "Respect for family members."
- "Putting the finishing touches on self-discipline and reflective behavior."
- "Building on good communication established in the earlier years."
- "Getting a diploma."
- "Allowing your child to own up to his mistakes and face the consequences."
- "Parents should never compromise in their own relationship with the Lord. They should be consistent and walk their talk. My parents never compromised. Though I didn't understand why God allowed them both to suffer long, painful battles with cancer and then die (leaving four young children), I will never forget my mother's faithfulness, perseverance, and unwavering love of the Lord and his Word."
- "Encourage them and support them. Be honest. Decide limits together."
- "Not allowing daughters to date seriously their freshman year, especially older boys."

///// KEY THOUGHT
Adults believed this was the time that teens started "testing" their parents on church attendance and relationships with the opposite sex. Adult children saw this as a time for parents to still keep their fingers in the dike of adolescence.

Post–High School: What parents said you should never compromise on

- "Never let them give up when things get tough."
- "Bad relationships can have lifetime consequences."
- "While they live in our home, they follow our rules and attend church."
- "Never *live* with a person of the opposite sex until marriage."
- "Establish goals in life, and seek God's will in every decision."
- "Premarital sex and live-in relationships, drugs, and alcohol abuse."
- "Never—as a parent—compromise on values or what you expect of them."

Post–High School: What adult children said parents should never compromise on

- "Showing love to a college student who's not sure *what* he wants to do."
- "Sharing ideas and accepting one another's choices."
- "Establishing (or reestablishing) the marriage as the first priority."
- "No double standards. If the parents don't want kids to watch R-rated movies, they shouldn't either. The same thing goes for drinking."
- "Patience."
- "Encourage their own faith development. Keep talking. Help develop independence and responsibility."

///// KEY THOUGHT

This is the time for parents to be rock-solid in their stance for sexual purity and allow God to bring the

right mates for their children. For the adult children, these are the waning days they will be "looking in" for advice. As they settle into their own belief systems, they don't want parents who preach, "Do as I say, not as I do."

Ongoing Absolutes

Here are some attitudes and behaviors that parents and adult children said should be maintained throughout the child-rearing years:

- "Obedience, respect, moral values, and Christian principles."
- "Going to church. Having family devotions. Living their talk consistently. Spending quantity and quality time with each child."
- "The importance of basing life on biblical truths, not societal fads or opinions."
- "God's Word."
- "Belief in the sovereignty and grace of God. Belief in the principles of the Bible. The truth that Jesus loves me and has a plan for my life."
- "Although I may not always approve of what my children do, they are flesh of my flesh, and I will always love them, just as God loves us."
- "Being part of the family."
- "Physical violence has no place in or out of the home."
- "Affection to the kids, marital faithfulness, commitment to work out conflict."
- "Putting God first in their lives, and letting their sons and daughters see it in their lives no matter what age the children are. That's how children, who are continually watching their parents, pick up the Christian life."

///// KEY THOUGHT

Love the Lord your God with all your heart, soul, and strength. And love your neighbor as you love yourself. Get the picture?

BUILDING A STRONG RELATIONSHIP WITH YOUR KIDS

Parents are competing against dozens of outside influences. What do your children need from you? A nurturing atmosphere where they can discover their unique personalities.

////////////////////////////

CHAPTER 5

YOUR CHILD IS ONE OF A KIND
Parents and Molding Bents

We're not going to do it. No way. We want this book on Christian parenting to be a *little* different from other ones you'll find out there.

What are we talking about?

The "P-word"— short for Proverbs 22:6.

So we're not going to quote it. It's not that we have a beef with its author, King Solomon. Actually, we think it's probably *the* best thing Scripture has to say on parenting. But crack open any Christian parenting book or listen to any preacher expound on the subject, and there it is on center stage—Proverbs 22:6, the "super verse." (If you're not sure what Proverbs 22:6 says, go look it up now, since it is essential to understanding this chapter. You can also find it at the end of this chapter if a Bible's not handy for you.)

If you're the parent of two or more children, you're well aware of their differences. My (Greg's) two boys are twenty-seven months apart, and they're like night and day. Troy (the oldest) was born a jock. He has an athletic build and has had great hand-eye coordination since he was two. He's *very* competitive, which sometimes drives Elaine and me crazy. We can tell that he's already influenced by the crowd at school. His grades are good, but he'll probably never be a 4.0 student.

Drew is Mr. Creative. Though he likes sports, he's just as happy playing in his room, making a game out of twenty pencils. He loves to draw and is always asking questions Troy hasn't even thought of yet. His only *B* grade is for P.E. His math skills are nearly as high as his older brother's. Scripture memory comes easy, and out of the hundreds of baseball cards he has, he always knows whether he's got that 1988 Donruss of Cal Ripken, Jr., when he's at a card show.

No doubt you can outline dozens of differences between your own children. God's painting a picture, forming each child with certain gifts and abilities. He's preparing a life for each as well, one that (we pray) will be part of the body of Christ. As parents, we not only get to watch that life unfold, but we also get to help in the process!

How do we do that? Here are some things to keep in mind when molding your child's bents:

Kids Come in Assorted Packages

Boys and girls can be compliant or headstrong, easygoing or a handful. They can be artistic or math-minded, competitive or casual, sloppy or compulsive cleaners. A parent's responsibility is to round off the edges of the less-desired traits and encourage the development of the good attributes. It's important for children's self-esteem that they excel at *something,* so if you have to fork out hard-earned money so your teen can be the best clarinet player in school (and march in the school band at Friday night football games), by all means, sign him or her up!

Discover Their Interests

Sometimes you'll have to introduce your children to different sports, musical instruments, and outside interests before something will click. We like what Donna Warwick, a mother of three adult children between the ages of twenty-four and thirty, did when her kids were young. Donna was their Sunday school teacher, bowling coach, Girl Scout leader, and youth group helper. "I think I interacted so much with the kids that I always knew what they were thinking about day to day," said Donna. She was also discovering her children's interests.

Donna learned that her oldest daughter, Susan, was more the aesthetic type. She liked to read, draw, and socialize. School didn't hold her interest; her idea of fun was to be a good friend to her friends. If Donna had been a high achiever herself, she might have forced Susan into an A-student regimen. Fortunately, she didn't.

Sally, the second child, was an athlete. Today, she's a high school gymnastics coach. Gregory, the youngest, was always musically inclined, but when he expressed an interest in playing Little League baseball, his parents encouraged him to explore it. All three took piano lessons, but only Gregory expressed any desire to keep at it. He continued taking lessons for a dozen years and later auditioned at colleges in Texas and Oklahoma to become a music major. He didn't make the cut, however, so he entered premed—thanks to his mother's well-rounded input. Today, he's in his third year of med school.

Find the Right Sport

If your youngster shows an athletic aptitude, help him find his sport. Are your children better suited for team sports—such as baseball, football, and basketball—or individual sports, such as gymnastics, tennis, and track? Take a look at your children's ability and temperament. If they have better-than-average hand-eye coordination and the mental makeup to perform when the game—or first place—is on the line, they may be suited for an individual sport. Many other children, of course, enjoy the camaraderie of team sports, and can find that "something extra" when spurred on by their teammates.

Be flexible, because sometimes things won't work out the way you expect them. When Neil Broad was growing up in Seattle, his mom signed him up for soccer leagues when he was barely out of kindergarten. Neil continued playing all through junior high, getting good enough to play in a competitive city league program.

When he went out for the high school team as a freshman, however, the competition was suddenly a lot stiffer. Neil was cut. His mom encouraged him to try out for track; after all, wasn't he fast on the soccer field? Neil won a spot on the team and became an excellent hurdler.

Nudge Them in New Directions

Neil's mom, Diane, didn't raise her children haphazardly. Although all three sons were different (no surprise there!), she said, "I encouraged them to get into music. I bought each of them an instrument, and that wasn't easy because we didn't have a lot of money. You sort of have to push, because if you don't, they won't take advantage of the opportunities."

Another thing Diane did to encourage their bents was to have the boys make their own cards for birthdays, Christmas, and special occasions. "They couldn't just go out and buy a card for Grandmother," she said. "They had to draw their own cards, and today my oldest son, Chuck, is an excellent artist."

Watch for Signs of Stress

If you fill your children's schedule with Scouts, piano lessons, soccer leagues, and Awana club, you could be flirting with burnout for them—and *yourself.* Just as you have to learn to say no to opportunities in your own life, so you will have to say no *for* your kid.

Some children will be able to handle a lot more than others. Find your children's stamina level, but don't exceed it. No matter how energetic your kids are, every school afternoon shouldn't be taken up with activities. Children need unstructured time to goof off with their friends.

Teach Them Why They Are the Way They Are

Geoff Whitson teaches his kids that their personality bents and talents weren't given to them for selfish reasons. "I have one child who's shy and one who's outgoing. I let both of them know that God did that so they could reach friends just like them. It's tempting to mold a child's bents toward tomorrow's job market, but the truth is, God's more concerned with the 'soul market.' My outgoing daughter is also on several sports teams. I tell her that God didn't give her the talent just to get her name in the paper or receive an athletic scholarship. He also put her on the team so she could have a group of friends to share her faith with. There's a bigger picture to my children's personalities and talents that I want them to be aware of. If they're not thinking of others as they grow up, they'll be less likely to reach out during their adult lives," said Geoff.

Know When to Give In

Every child isn't going to make the varsity team or the honor roll. Debbie Pate's parents always expected the best from her. Upon high school graduation, she left home to attend an academic-minded private college, although she was an average student in high school.

From the beginning, she struggled. Never a good test taker in high school, Debbie "choked" during midterm and final exams. "College only worsened the problem," she said. "I got really stressed over it. I would work hard and then get a *D* in a class. That was really frustrating. There were times when I wanted to walk out, but Mom was always there to encourage me. She would write me a letter with a Bible verse or send me a card that would support me."

Debbie persevered, but in the first semester of her second year, she flunked a class she *loved*—psychology. The prof graded strictly by test results—and her anxieties finally got the best of her.

During the Christmas break, a disconsolate Debbie told her parents she didn't want to go back. There was just one little problem: The second semester was already prepaid. Her parents were at a crossroads. They could have *forced* Debbie to return—and shattered her self-confidence. Or, they could let her quit—and go through life as a "college dropout."

Instead, Debbie's parents chose a middle course. After sitting down with Debbie and talking through what avenues lay in front of them, they offered this suggestion: Could she return to school but back off on academics and sign up for some undemanding classes? And if she didn't want to go back to school in the fall, that was okay with them.

The idea appealed to Debbie. She totally reworked her schedule and filled her day with fun classes. "That ended up being my final semester, and though it's hard to live life without a college degree, my current job doesn't require it.

I'm happy doing what I am doing. I'm glad I went to college, but I couldn't have kept going."

Know That the Acorn Doesn't Fall Very Far from the Tree

If *you* hate sports and were always the last one picked in sandlot baseball games, chances are your boy will not be the next Jose Canseco. If you couldn't play "Chopsticks" on the piano to save your life, your daughter probably won't learn to play either (unless you spring for lessons). For some reason, your children will gravitate to things *you're* interested in. There's nothing wrong with that. In fact, it's probably part of God's design.

The advantages of allowing sons or daughters to follow in your footsteps are many:

- You become a better coach or teacher because you're aware of what it takes to succeed.
- You'll be motivated to spend more time with them, and thus build a stronger relationship with your kids.
- You'll be able to spot the dangers of overcommitment and help them find a balance between what they like and other essential priorities.
- You can apply spiritual applications to the lessons they're learning. For instance, an outdoorsman can point to the order of the ecosystem—God's marvelous creation—and the instincts of animals versus self-discipline for people. The possibilities are endless.

Self-Fulfilling Prophecy?

The only danger we see in recognizing and encouraging your children in the way they should go is to push them too much in one certain direction. It's easy to be tempted to do that when they excel in one area. We understand that to be excellent in anything usually demands a narrow focus and a total commitment that may prevent them from being more well-rounded.

Only a few children will make it to the top of their field; most won't. That's why we recommend giving children a wide berth when it comes to developing interests. Not only will that allow them to relate with more people about their faith, but they may also discover something at which they're naturally gifted.

In high school, Ron Wheeler was a great athlete but an average student who never pushed himself very hard. His junior year, however, his parents "encouraged" him to take Spanish. (We wonder how they did that!) Ron turned out to be a natural linguist. He somehow understood the intricacies of this foreign language in no time. Today, he's a Bible translator for Wycliffe, working in the Philippines.

The lesson, of course, is to *channel* your children's early bents or natural talents in much the same way as a river flows: As long as it's flowing in the right direction, there's no need to dam up the river or divert it to another direction. Go with the flow, but challenge your offspring to branch out as well. Remember, you don't have a lock on knowing which direction God wants that water to travel. You just have the responsibility to guide your children safely through the river channel.

///

Proverbs 22:6
Train up a child in the way he should go,
Even when he is old he will not depart from it. (NASB)

///

////////////////////////

CHAPTER 6

LIKE CATS AND DOGS
Parents and Sibling Rivalry

This will be a short chapter, right? Kids *never* fight with each other, and if they do get into a little scrap, they quickly patch things up and resume playing.

Only an adult who never had kids could make that rose-colored statement. Said one East Coast mother, "It's funny how kids fight growing up. They swore they would never talk to each other. It didn't happen that way, but they sure fought when they were young."

After interviewing the parents and children, we can draw several broad-based conclusions:

- Siblings who fight are close in age.
- Sister-to-sister combat can be brutal.
- The middle child sometimes resents the attention the older and younger siblings receive.
- Boys—but not many girls—have sports as a competitive outlet.
- After the kids become adults, a truce is declared.

Why are we covering this subject, you ask?

Because some parents don't make the same effort to develop a close relationship with each child. It's often easier for parents to spend more time with a child who behaves, who is an athletic prodigy, who is popular at school. But if a child is a troublemaker or perhaps not as good-looking as another, he could be on the receiving end of a parent's wrath more often than his brothers and sisters.

If you aren't already in the throes of the "battle of the brothers" or "struggle of the sisters," you'll want to be aware of what lies ahead—and know how to handle the kids so one doesn't feel he's getting the short end of the stick. Also, though sibling rivalry isn't a major reason for kids to fall away from the faith, it can be a factor.

Even-Steven

Several parents we interviewed had matter-of-fact attitudes. "Sibling rivalry happens between sisters," explained Ruth Ann Campbell, a mom of two grown daughters. "If I had to do it all over again, I wouldn't make everything so even. If Sharon got to do something, Linda got to do the same. I was always trying to be fair and square. If one of them had something special for her birthday, we would make sure the next birthday lived up to the same expectations. Sharon will still say she had to pave the way with clothes and makeup. Pierced ears were another big thing."

Ruth Ann remembers going through a period when Linda was sucking her thumb. Each time she stopped, she received a present as a reward. After starting and stopping ten times, sister Sharon began complaining that Linda was sucking her thumb to get presents.

I (Mike) can relate to what Ruth Ann was saying about wanting to level the playing field for her children. When I was growing up, my brother, Pry, and I would fight about *everything*.

If we were going to split a 7UP, we actually grabbed a measuring cup from the kitchen cabinet. If we were sharing the last piece of cake, whoever cut the cake in two had to allow the other brother first dibs.

We were only sixteen months and one school grade apart—and never the twain shall meet. We often acted like John McEnroe twins. One Christmas, our parents bought us an English surrey, one of those push-pedal carriages kids can steer around the neighborhood. We continually fought over who would get to drive the thing. I think my parents got rid of it by Easter.

My story sounded similar to what Lindsay Porter of Virginia had to tell us. "My sister and I didn't get along," she began. "I mean, I didn't like her. She kept a clean room, but I didn't. We were very different. She just bothered me. I think if you would ask my sister, she would say we fought too much. I don't have too many bad memories of fighting with my sister, but I think she will give you a completely different story because she exaggerates everything."

Did things ever get better?

"We did grow out of it, and we get along better now, but when we were children, we had to sleep in the same room. I think that's where our problems began. When we moved and got a bigger house with our own bedrooms, we started getting along better. Plus, we were growing older. We found other friends and stopped being each other's playmate."

We did hear from a mother who said her kids pulled together when the chips were down. Cheri Fuller explained she had a hard time when her teenage son and daughter (who were a year apart) competed in a bike race together. He bested her (advantage, Rick). Then they took an advanced French class together, but she *parlez-voused* better (advantage, Melanie). It didn't help matters that they both had leadership roles in the National Honor

Society and were often put in honors classes together (deuce again).

"It was hard to manage a good family feeling sometimes," said Cheri. "And yet, sometimes they managed to do that. I remember when my son wanted to go to France on an overseas study program, but he filed late. We no longer had the money we had earmarked for the trip. My daughter came in and pleaded my son's case. She said, 'If you were going to let him go back then, you should let him go now.' She won us over."

Once Cheri went to a teacher's conference for her daughter, and all the teacher wanted to talk about was Cheri's son, whom she'd had the previous year. Cheri said, "Wait a minute— I want to discuss my daughter's performance, too." At a teacher's conference with the French teacher, she told Cheri that things were going well, but that the brother and sister seemed distant. She added that there could be a problem with their grades, since the younger daughter was doing *A* work and the son was in the *B*-plus range.

"Many times they shared the limelight," said Cheri, "and that's why I'm glad they opted to go to their own universities and own directions. Today, our son is at Purdue and our daughter attends the University of Iowa. Believe it or not, they look forward to hearing from each other."

The tension sibling rivalry brings to a home can really affect the atmosphere. If kids are always at odds with each other, building family unity and traditions takes an extra amount of patience that some parents just might not have.

More Harrowing Tales

Ask adult children if they fought and you receive some sheepish responses. "I look back and feel sorry for my parents," said Bryan

Marquardt, who is in his mid-thirties. "My sisters and I put them through a lot. I did like to aggravate those girls. Usually, I did it by changing the TV channel to a football game, things like that. Other times, they had to actually separate us. Or they raised their voice and told us to be quiet. Things could get nasty and abusive."

When we talked to Bryan's parents, they confirmed how bad he was. "Bryan and Lisa were always fighting," said Mrs. Marquardt. "He loved to tease her. They still go at one another."

Sometimes sisters who are close in age don't fight; but like male baldness, sibling rivalry can skip a generation. A middle daughter told us when an older sister became a cheerleader, her younger sister *had* to make the yell team. "But all that bickering between them wasn't for me. I don't remember fighting with my sisters. My daddy wouldn't have allowed it. I can remember he would snap his fingers, and that would be it. Dad was never a disciplinarian, but he was an authority figure."

If you move a lot, that may actually *help* the sibling rivalry problem. "My older sister is my best friend," said Jennifer Brown, "and that's because we had to move so much since my dad was in the Air Force. Once I got to know people, we had to move again. But my younger brother and I were bitter rivals because we were close in age, and he was a major tease. Now that we're older, things are fine, but there was a time that we fought an awful lot."

When we talked to Jennifer's mom, she said Jennifer felt threatened by her brother. She didn't do as well in school. The accolades didn't come her way. "I told her she was such a sweet person, and that was a nice quality to have, but she wanted to be like her brother. And that caused a real chasm to develop between the two."

It wasn't until high school that Jennifer and Paul took steps to bridge the gap. "They studied the Bible," said the mother, "and learned what Jesus would have us do. Today, the kids love each other dearly. It's important for a parent to keep working on that, but it's not something that happens overnight."

Some parents, believe it or not, will never have to work on getting brothers and sisters to live in harmony. "Our kids never fought at all," claimed an Arizona mother. "She was a little mother to him. Now we regret that we didn't have one more child. It's too late now."

What's the Answer?

To let the petty—and not so petty—arguments between siblings pollute the cheery family atmosphere isn't healthy. Parents can easily get so worn out from refereeing the bouts between teenagers that they don't have the mental or physical energy to plan those family times they need. Plus, if the kids are sent to their rooms for fighting, it's tough to reconvene the family for a devotional time.

What's the answer?

Ah . . . um . . . ah . . . we're not sure we have any ideas you couldn't think of yourself. Oh, well. Give these a shot:

- Start curbing the fights in the early years. Create a family attitude that says you won't tolerate disrespect for another sibling.
- If you can afford it, live in a home where each child has his or her own bedroom.
- Never compare your children with each other. That only reinforces a climate of competition.
- Don't come to the rescue every time your kids have an argument. Make them work it out together. By

encouraging communication, you're setting a good pattern for the future.

- Try "stress-building" activities where they have to rely on each other. When they're older, have an experienced rock climber take the family rappeling down a cliff. Go on a white-water river ride together. Explore caves. Give them work projects where they can only succeed by teaming up.

CHAPTER 7

WHAT MY PARENTS DID WRONG
Parental Miscues

Guess what? Your parents weren't perfect. Not by a long shot. Not one of them made it through twenty or more years of child-rearing without making a mistake.

Oh, well. As playwright Oscar Wilde once wrote, "Experience is the name everyone gives to their mistakes." Or, as the old saying goes: "How do you gain experience? By making mistakes. How do you stop making mistakes? By gaining experience."

With few exceptions, the adult children we interviewed and surveyed really wanted a clean, long-term relationship with their parents—no matter what problems they had in the past. Luckily for us, children forgive easily, especially if we will sit down and talk about what went wrong.

The adult children, however, had no trouble recalling mistakes their parents had made. Some of those mistakes did have long-term ramifications. If your attitude is, *It's my way or the highway* or *I'm not going to be the one to change around here*, your kids will probably tune you out, Daddy-O. And when they leave home, don't expect much of a relationship—or input into their lives. But it's never too late, and you can change if you want.

Don't be so insecure that you fail to hear what your children are saying—or thinking.

Do you recognize any of the following stories?

Christian Upbringing

"My parents were more interested in raising kids who behaved well than in having us develop strong characters. They emphasized salvation, but later on, it seemed like Christianity was an outward thing," said one young man.

Many adult children expressed frustration that their parents never really sat down and talked about their faith or how they felt about it. "They didn't teach us how to have a personal relationship with Jesus. All they taught was how to go to church," echoed a Texas man.

When Anita Hernandez became a teen, all she received from her parents was a laundry list of rules and restrictions—not guidelines on what Christians *should* do. Consequently, she grew up believing Christianity was a negative thing, that her "job" was to please God, even though she felt in her heart that he would never be quite satisfied, knowing she was imperfect. This woman later rejected the faith in a *big* way, but she eventually returned when she heard Christianity explained correctly.

Others expressed regret that they hadn't been told about Christ earlier in life, which could have spared them some adolescent grief. Others were disappointed to learn that their parents had feet of clay, all because their spiritual foundations were weak. "I heard very little emphasis on Christianity in my home," said Jennie Smythe. "We attended church, but my parents never discussed their faith. Mom had a lot of control on me, which I resented. Dad lacked firmness and never set limits."

On the other hand, some parents overdid it when it came to

being *in* church. "I got burned out going to services so often," Karen told us. "I had athletic talent, and I also wanted to be in the drama club, but we had church on Wednesday nights, and I could never miss that. So instead of track, volleyball, or going out for cheerleading, I did nothing. When I moved out after high school, I quit going to all these services except Sunday mornings. This still hurts because it didn't need to happen. They could have let me miss Wednesday nights for a few months, and I would have turned out just fine. That type of tight control forces people to go out and try things once they're set free."

It's been said that a child's way of relating to God the Father is interconnected with the way he sees his father here on earth. "I think I still have a problem with relating to God because of the way Dad related to me," said Bill Hawkins. "He was very loving to us kids, but he was also uninvolved. Sure, he'd be there for the easy stuff, like playing with us when he got home from work. But homework and discipline, forget it."

///// KEY THOUGHT
Lead your children to Christ; don't push them there.

Parenting and Communication

Some parents aren't born communicators. Many are the products of parents with poor communication skills themselves. But that shouldn't let reticent parents off the hook. "Both of my parents were not great verbal communicators," said one young man. "They didn't have an interest in some of the things we were interested in," said another.

"My parents were poor problem-solvers and communicators," said Christopher Harris. "Much was swept under the rug. I just tried to avoid conflicts."

Some parents didn't avoid conflict in front of their kids. "The thing I wish never would have happened is something Mom did out of frustration because Dad was so passive," said Francois Gavallett. "She would belittle him in front of us kids. 'You're just like your father!' she'd scream at him. If she could have handled things God's way with a gentle and quiet spirit, she could have prevented a lot of things. For a long time, her attitude caused me to lose respect for my father and men in general. I looked at them from her eyes instead of my own. Now I'm in a situation where I want to maintain a relationship with my dad, to accept him and love him. But Dad feels he can't relate to me because he thinks he's too small in my eyes after what my mom said."

Some complained about the autocratic rule that defined their households. A few typical comments:

- "They laid down the law, and it couldn't be questioned."
- "Dad created a fear of discipline and confrontation in me."
- "Dad didn't teach me things he knew, didn't communicate, and didn't warn me about guys. Mom never allowed me to disagree."
- "I felt like my dad was always verbally attacking me. If the report card was poor, he said I was a dumb, stupid kid. With a good grade, the praise wasn't as meaningful."
- "Mom screamed a lot and didn't show a lot of interest in what I was doing."

Several adult children told us how their parents never let their guards down. "Not once did they share their struggles with us," said Sharon Hackett. "They always seemed to do what was right even though I knew they struggled deeply with different situations. I resented this when my mom expected me to communicate openly with her. Even today, my parents have a hard time communicating openly with my brothers and sister. After running through the local news, we run out of things to say. I have tried to discuss deeper subjects, but I don't get too far. I think it's all because my mom came from a very conservative Dutch Reformed family, where almost everything was considered 'too personal' and shouldn't be discussed. My dad is more open, but I rarely get to talk to him without Mom being there too."

We also heard from a young woman who wishes her parents had had access to Christian parenting books and videos when she was growing up. "My mom told me she yelled too much and didn't instill a good self-image in me," said Gloria Plummer. "She said she was taught that if you praised a child too much, it would make him vain. She wishes she had had the resources available to raise kids better."

A North Dakota woman wishes her father had taken a more active role in raising her and her brothers. "Dad was brought up as an only child and hadn't been taught how siblings interact, or generally how to express love and emotion."

A Los Angeles woman said she was parented "out of sheer ignorance," but she felt she came out of the experience all right. "Although my parents meant well and tried hard, I am amazed that God's grace covered so much."

///// KEY THOUGHT

Words wound deeply, and it could take years before the scars fully heal. Listen to what the parenting experts—or friends you admire—have to say about raising kids. If your children complain about what you're not saying, don't brush it off as childish thoughts. They're trying to say something to you:

**"I want to get closer, but you're not cooperating."
If you think you can't change, you won't. If
you don't want to change, don't expect a close
relationship with your children.**

Other Parenting Mistakes

"My mother and father didn't act like they loved others; they
were too judging," expressed a frustrated Ginger Mittermiller.
"With us kids, they never tried to understand the reasons behind
our behavior. With our friends and others at church, they never
said stuff like, 'Some people act this way because they don't have
Jesus in their life. They need our prayers and understanding.'
Instead, they just condemned. I became just like that in high
school, and it cost me a lot of friends."

///// KEY THOUGHT

**Condemnation is a disease of sick Christians. Be
healthy; look for the good and comment on that.**

Several adult children recalled what it was like to grow up
without an involved family. "I feel we would have been a stronger
family if they had had a real interest in my brother's and my
activities. My parents were supportive, but not involved," said
Wayne Townsend.

///// KEY THOUGHT

**If you're too busy to attend their extracurricular
activities, you're too busy.**

We heard a preacher's kid say, "Dad stopped giving me affection when I started becoming a woman. That hurt. I think it
scared him."

///// KEY THOUGHT

Girls need appropriate affection from their fathers. Without it, they'll feel something's wrong with them—or they'll search for it elsewhere.

One young woman, whose parents didn't discipline her consistently, said, "Today, I think that inconsistency tells the child you don't really respect him. Plus, it doesn't create in your kids a respect for the parent."

Those who received corporal punishment in their teens greatly resented that treatment. (Spanking days should be over by the time the child reaches nine or so, says Dr. Dobson.)

"I got the belt until I was fourteen, and Mom spanked me nearly every day between the ages of six and eight," said Carmen Robinson. "It got to the point where I wet my pants because she hit so hard. Her whippings drove a wedge between us."

///// KEY THOUGHT

Discipline that demeans a child is always inappropriate. Sadly, many parents overdiscipline out of fear and ignorance. The proverb admonishing to "discipline diligently" is not always tempered by recognizing that children do childish things.

Correct discipline provides a way of escape for some kids who are caught in the traps of selfishness or peer pressure. Sometimes you simply must save the child from himself and rebuild the relationship after he calms down. Most will thank you for it later.

Some parents never taught the values of learning from mistakes. "Whenever I would run late in getting to high school, my mom would somehow bail me out," said Alice

Miller. "All through my growing-up years, she didn't think I should experience pain. I lived in a fairyland. My parents wouldn't let me make a wrong decision. If I had a paper due and I'd procrastinate, my mom would stay up until two or three in the morning and type it out for me. In my twenties, when life wasn't always going right, I questioned God because I thought that everything was supposed to be okay since I was a Christian. After a while, I realized that just because you're a Christian doesn't mean you can't have problems."

///// KEY THOUGHT
Allow your children to fail when they're young and they will be more motivated to succeed when they're older.

Sue Mendenhall says her parents were afraid of her messing up because it would make *them* look bad. "My folks were fearful people," she said, "especially about what would happen to their reputation if I got pregnant out of wedlock. That's what happened to them. When I developed breasts, they made me wear smock tops. They never told me when I could date, they just said, 'We'll let you know.' The crazy thing was, I was very committed to the Lord. Their fears blinded them to that commitment. All they went on was their own past."

///// KEY THOUGHT
Don't let your past totally determine the way you parent your children in the present. They will grow to resent being overprotected.

Another daughter of a mother who became pregnant before her wedding said, "Mom got married young—she had to—and never had the chance to do things she wanted to do. As I grew up, she absorbed herself in tons of outside projects because she was trying to fill a self-esteem vacuum inside of her. In the meantime, the home and the kids needed her attention. She wasn't very nurturing."

///// KEY THOUGHT

Many adults have experiences that make them get "stuck" at a lower maturity level. If you're trying to make up for lost time or relive your past, raising healthy, adjusted children will be a much tougher job. If necessary, see a counselor who can help you adjust to your present life circumstances.

Here are a few more notable comments:

- "They had a weirdness about sex. And they didn't let me make mistakes and suffer the consequences."
- "They didn't agree on dating rules or rules, period."
- "They never showed weakness. They almost seemed super-human. Also, they didn't allow me to learn from my mistakes. They forced me to conform before I got a chance to 'blow it.'"
- "They should have followed through with discipline a little more. I can't remember how many times I heard, 'If you ever do that again, you'll be punished.' The next time I did it, I would hear the same phrase again."
- Finally, a boatload of adult children complained that their parents never talked to them about sex. (We've got a whole chapter on *that* coming up.)

///// KEY THOUGHT

Parents are only human, and we are subject to the foibles of character. Can you take small steps

toward improvement? If you fly off the handle, can you control the next outburst? Can you think before you yell?

Parental Regrets

As you've just read, the kids we talked to had *plenty* to say about what their parents did wrong. But we already know we're not perfect, right?

We posed a similar question to the parents. They were equally as candid. Here are a few responses:

- "I handed out too much criticism and not enough praise."
- "My wife and I weren't always together on discipline."
- "I paid too much attention to the small stuff."
- "We should have encouraged them to memorize more Scripture."
- "Our great fault was not showing them our love and friendship."
- "I was too busy sewing, helping other neighbors and doing good things that others could have done, instead of concentrating on my kids as I know they wanted."
- "Since my husband did not attend church, sometimes I sided with my children against him. This caused problems until I rectified my position as a wife and his being head of the house."
- "I did not always trust the Lord with the outcome of our children. I felt it was my responsibility that they grasped all the teachings of the church."

Do You Need to Change?

It happened, didn't it? You spotted some things in the last few pages that mirrored what is occurring in your home. What are you going to do about it? What *can* you do about it? Are you committed to being the best parent you can be?

These three areas are the main problems we need to avoid:

(1) *A critical attitude.* When unconditional love isn't expressed to your kids, they grow up thinking God's love is conditional, too. Children have always messed up—that's Job Number One for them—but they need consistent, appropriate discipline. At the same time, they also need to know the compassionate, forgiving heart of God.

(2) *A legalistic faith.* We are defining this as the overemphasis on nonessential laws *not* expressed in the Bible. These legalistic rules may give the appearance of spirituality, but they are more closely tied to a particular church's tradition.

When the Bible or the person of Jesus Christ are used as rule givers, instead of as something or *someone* to lovingly obey, children aren't seeing the true nature of God. Consequently, they go through life thinking Christianity is a bunch of killjoy rules. They don't see it for what it should be—a relationship with a Person who loves them no matter what. When kids finally reach the point where they realize they can't obey every single rule (high school is when they usually get clued in), they assume they're not cut out to be Christians.

(3) *Lack of communication.* Admittedly, many of the parents we talked to grew up in an era when feelings were not expressed and emotions were not displayed. But with so many tough choices our children are facing—at earlier and earlier ages—parents need to help them sort through life. Dad can't afford to be silent anymore when his son could get AIDS by getting involved with a promiscuous girl in high school. Mom can't be overbearing if she wants her daughter to understand that some guys have

one-track minds (and they're not thinking about their next trip to McDonald's).

If these three "biggies" don't describe you, you're probably on target. Good work! Keep it up. And if you discovered a few areas that need fine-tuning, you can probably implement those changes fairly quickly. If it's a major item—like finding time to have one-on-one conversations with your kids—you're going to have to make it a long-term project. Remember:

- Pick only one thing to work on at a time.
- Inform your children of upcoming changes. If necessary, apologize to your children.
- Talk with a few friends, read a few books, and watch a few videos on how to get it done.
- Find someone you can trust to hold you accountable for the changes you want to make.

CHAPTER 8

YA DONE RIGHT, MOM AND DAD
Parental Lessons to Live By

Like most high school kids, Gary Rossberg liked to collect stuff. His thing was beer bottles. Every weekend, he brought home a different brand to place on his bookshelves. Talk about ninety-nine bottles of beer on the wall! One evening his dad came into Gary's bedroom to say goodnight. His eyes swept the room before he sat down on the side of his bed.

"When I was a kid your age," he said softly, "I used to collect models."

Gary's dad let the comment hang in the air for a moment. Then he got up and left the room without saying anything more. As soon as he shut the door, Gary fell into his pillow and cried his eyes out. His dad hadn't come down hard on him. Instead, he had stated what was important to him, what he *valued.*

///// KEY THOUGHT

Verbalize your values. While you don't have to nag your children, your subtle reminders—especially with older children—need to be interjected at the appropriate moments.

"For the first time, I realized I was disappointing him," said Gary. "The next day, I got up and threw all those bottles in the trash. Then I went out and bought a couple of car models. My dad knew what was right and pure, and he showed those attributes in a very loving way. His low-key remark moved me more than any lecture or icy stare ever could. That night was a turning point in my life. He loved and respected me enough not to treat me like an immature kid—even though I was one."

///// KEY THOUGHT

Try to treat your children according to their maturity level. While many don't necessarily deserve that type of privilege (like Gary), it's always best to "challenge up" rather than assuming they're not up to the task.

Not long after that incident, Gary began hanging out with a new crowd. He also began attending an active Young Life club at his school. The summer before his junior year, he finally understood the message of Jesus Christ at a Young Life camp and became a Christian.

Sorting Through

You don't have to be a nuclear physicist to sort through what Gary's dad did right and wrong. Let's look beneath the surface a bit:

In Gary's case, a lack of correct spiritual training probably led to poor choices. Without a strong father-son relationship, Gary could have gone off the deep end—and not resurfaced.

Perhaps you know young people who had an excellent spiritual upbringing, but now they are living *far* away from the Christian life. Why? Perhaps one (or both) of their parents didn't know how to have a close relationship with them. Maybe one of the parents didn't *want* a close relationship. Sitting in church every Sunday is no guarantee a child will walk with Christ for a lifetime. *Spiritual training is important, but like behavior, it's not the bull's-eye.*

Most kids now following Christ—and those who are actively involved in ministry in some form—said they had good spiritual training from their parents *and* a close relationship with them. They added that their mothers and fathers worked together as a team. Their parents were involved, consistent in discipline, and saw child-rearing as a call from God to be good stewards over the "gifts" the Lord had given them. If we could diagram a formula for success, this would be it.

Dozens of kids we surveyed said they received spiritual training and had a *pretty good* relationship with at least one parent, but they never saw their parents model a consistent Christian life. Consequently, those children made it into their adult years as Christians, although many rebelled or were estranged from at least one parent for several years. But many we spoke with admitted that they were not active participants in the kingdom of God. Instead, they were filling a pew by rote every Sunday morning.

There's Always Time

No matter what stage you're in as a parent, you can improve your parenting. The kids we interviewed gave us dozens of stories about the most memorable things their parents did right. Some were very specific; others were more general. Many were downright simple. We'll pass along some of those now.

As you read, pick out stories you'll want your kids to repeat when *they're* talking to a stranger about what *their* parents did right. If you've got a pencil handy, put a check mark by the ones you feel match up with you. Put a star by those you *could* be doing but aren't.

Parenting

"I had a friend whose dad got *Playboy* in the mail," said Louie Mack. "Once, I 'borrowed' a copy and hid it in my room. Mom found it but didn't say anything. When I got home, the magazine wasn't in the same place where I'd put it. I had been found out, and I knew it must have hurt my parents deeply. I threw the *Playboy* in the trash the next day. I sat in my room and waited for Dad to come home and let me have it. But nothing happened. After thinking about it for a day, I came home from school and said, 'Mom, I'm really sorry. I know better than that.'

"She looked at me and smiled. 'Thank you for saying something,' she said, patting my head. 'I wasn't worried about you; I was just disappointed.' That type of wisdom gave me more respect for them than anything else could have." A deft touch, Mom.

///// KEY THOUGHT

Give God time to work on your children after episodes of misbehavior. Repentance—and change—is far more genuine when your children admit faults and resolve not to make the same mistakes again.

Some of the adult children expressed appreciation that their parents held to the important points but didn't hassle them on minor ones. They encouraged their children to do things, like sports or taking trips with friends. "They were there for me no matter what," said Lynn Hart. "They came to everything I was involved in: cheerleading, band, choir, orchestra, track and field, drama plays. I was really involved in school, so it was quite an effort on their part."

///// KEY THOUGHT

Many children pursuing outside activities crave affirmation from their parents. No matter how high or low your interest level is—be there! Uninvolved parents communicate loud and clear that their children aren't worth their time.

Many of the adult children now understand what it meant for Mom to *be there* when they arrived home from school.

"Mom was there every day when I came home from school," said Nina Henry. "Back then I thought it was a pain, but now I'm really glad. If I had a bad day, no big deal. I could talk to her about it."

"Mom never worked," said a Montana woman. "She was always there for us with cookies and a kiss when we got home from school." Added another woman, "Mom didn't work outside the home except in rare incidents when we needed extra cash. She was always there, and she liked it that way. It was a bedrock for me."

Several young parents looked back and realized their home was a haven just for them. "Often at dinnertime, we used to have 'What if?' conversations. For instance, 'What if you met Jesus? What would you say?' That's how they got their points across to us," said an Oregon man.

"In our home, Mom and Dad put the family first," said another young person. Other adult children wondered how some parents can go on holiday without taking the kids.

///// KEY THOUGHT

Children want parents to connect with them. If the parents abdicate this role, they will resent it and search elsewhere—and usually find it with their peer group.

Larry Ledingham said his parents lived their lives as an example. "I remember when I was five or six, and we were the first house in our development. My dad filled a pitcher of ice water and went down the street to where the bulldozers were and gave the cold-water jug to the construction guys. He said it was the Christian thing to do. Dad told us he tried to witness to them but fumbled his way through it. It impressed me that he would go out of his way to do that."

Kids certainly look up to their fathers. "Though Dad was the leader and final decision-maker, he would listen to what we had to say," said an Arizona man.

One woman recalled her dad's decision to leave Ft. Lauderdale when their beach neighborhood got too violent in the 1970s. He left a lucrative dental practice and moved the family to a small town in central Florida.

We were also impressed with a story relayed by Jim Northrup: "I heard speaker Larry Crabb once say, 'A father walks ahead of his children on the path. He looks back to see how they are doing. But with his arms and his words, he beckons them to follow him, always with a goal of manhood in mind.' I've learned that a friend will walk beside you as you follow others, but a father always leads his son toward manhood. That's what my dad did. He was totally invested in my growth toward appropriate Christian manhood. 'I'm treating you like a man,' is what he would say. I learned that the only person who could tell you you're a man is your father."

///// KEY THOUGHT

You may never realize how your leading by example has long-term benefits. Telling your children what they need to know calls for constant repetition— but don't be a nerd! Showing them creates a picture in their memory that may never be forgotten.

Said Corinne Busslinger, "In Campfire Girls, we had father-daughter weekends that my dad always attended. I was proud to have him around to show my friends. I knew my parents were proud of me, but there was never pressure to do things to get their approval."

///// KEY THOUGHT

While good behavior is important, "performance parenthood" is out. If your children don't hear often that they are loved "no matter what good thing or bad thing you do," then they most certainly will try to perform to win your approval. This leads to insecurity—about themselves and the way they relate to God.

Here are a few other comments that we felt were worth noting and, if possible, following:

- "We only lived in two houses growing up. That provided a lot of security for us."
- "They were very loyal to me. They stuck with me during the hard times of junior high."
- "Dad gave me real responsibility early; I drove a tractor when I was ten years old. He also gave me a small motor boat at age twelve."
- "They shared everything that was appropriate to our ages. We had very few secrets in our house."

- "They supported what I was interested in. They told me as long as I did my best, my grades didn't matter. They trusted me."
- "They told me they loved me. They also developed my talents. For instance, Mom worked with me on singing. And they willingly sent me to sports camps so I could get more experience in things I liked to do."
- "We decorated the house together for every holiday. Traditions built family unity and have been a great example for things that we do with our families. We always had a Christmas Eve service in our house. Dad would read the Christmas story. We took family vacations to the same place in Indiana every year. We still go there together, even though all five kids are grown and live in different parts of the country. Somehow, everyone makes it."
- "Dad loved my mother and always showed her by doing the little things."
- "Dad talked to us while hunting, working on cars, or in the shop. He used those 'classrooms' to impart horse sense and spiritual wisdom."
- "He was constantly coaching me on what he was doing—and why. One night, we were caught in the middle of a lake with a dead motor. He said, 'This is the point that I feel like throwing the motor in the lake. But now is the time to be patient. Are you in this with me?' I replied yes. Then he said, 'You hold the flashlight, and we'll get this thing done together.' He taught me common sense and kept me out of a lot of trouble."

Spiritual Training

Parents who set a spiritual example in the home—by taking the family to church, reading Bible stories just before lights out, praying on their knees with all the family, and rousting the family to church on Sunday mornings left huge impressions on their children. "Dad and Mom, every single night of their marriage, knelt and prayed for each child," one man told us. A Louisiana woman told us, "The Bible was the center of our family. Besides my dad, my heroes were David, Daniel, and Joshua. What held our family together was our faith."

Many recalled having the Bible read to them. "My mom grounded each of us in Scripture," said Sue Lewis. "We had daily devotions and memorized verses."

///// KEY THOUGHT

Actions definitely speak louder than words when it comes to convincing children that there's a rock-solid core to the home that can never be shaken—your belief in Christ.

Many of the adult children lit up when we asked them to tell us what their parents did right when it came to creating a Christian home. One Indiana woman said her parents took her to the local nursing home every few months, not just at Christmas and Easter. Once a month they'd visit a minimum security prison, where they talked with inmates. "That's where I learned what true Christianity is—reaching out and serving others—especially to those who have no one," she said.

///// KEY THOUGHT

Centuries ago the apostle James said, "Faith, if it has no works, is dead" (James 2:17, NASB). Homes that only teach a "belief-oriented" faith will likely

produce children who can mouth the right words, but could care less about acting on them in a Christlike way.

"My mom always encouraged me to read the Bible and come talk with her about what I'd read," said Nancy Newburn. "Mom rarely gave me the answers, like 'This is what the passage means.' Instead, she encouraged me to search for my own answers. She would say, 'What does this Scripture mean to you?'"

///// KEY THOUGHT

Parents who don't challenge their children— and allow a few tough questions to come their way—are only postponing questions that will arise later in life, questions that may come from someone who is not a believer or doesn't have their best interests in mind.

Here are a few other statements:

- "I never heard my parents complain about going to church."
- "They entertained missionaries and Christian speakers in our home whenever they could. We heard their stories of how God had worked in their lives and could see that Christianity wasn't confined to our church."
- "They emphasized a Christian faith strongly and consistently. We had family devotions—not every day, but regularly."
- "They set a godly *example* for me to follow."
- "Dad taught me to think for myself, be observant, and think about others. He also gave me multiple opportunities to hear about Christ from different people."

- "My family did a lot of camping and fishing, sometimes with other families from church. Those memories are sweet. We learned to value family time and nature. We memorized lots of Scripture and learned to worship with other believers. They taught us the importance of knowing what you believe and standing up for your values."

Doing Things Right, or Being Right?

After reading through these I-could-never-live-up-to-all-that lessons and stories (don't worry, neither can we!), it's tempting to feel frustrated and overwhelmed.

Please don't.

Performance parenthood is like performance Christianity. It leaves no room for God to cover our mistakes and get the credit for doing the job. There is a huge element of trust that needs to take place. God is in charge, and he'll use the good things we've done *and* our mistakes.

We detected a sequential order to parenting. While the kids we surveyed didn't pick up on the sequence, most would agree it looks something like this:

(1) *God is first.* A husband and wife team who establish a pattern *early on* of loving God and serving him without complaint will speak that message loud and clear to their kids, probably without saying a word. *Be a committed follower of Jesus Christ.*

(2) *The marriage is second.* The Bible doesn't tell us we're "one" with our children, does it? There's a reason for that: the marriage needs to last longer than parenthood. At times, it's certainly tempting to put those little rug rats ahead of our spouses. They "need" us more, right? Well, in the long run, what they need is

to see a healthy, stable, loving and affectionate marriage. A firm commitment between Dad and Mom provides the security, consistency, and modeling necessary for our kids to develop into healthy, Christian adults (which inevitably produces healthy marriages—and healthy grandkids!). The legacy we want to hand down for generations begins when a husband and wife are totally committed to the marriage—above the kids. *Be the best husband or wife first. Then be the best mom or dad.*

(3) *Children are third.* Yes, we've been given incredible stewardship. But if God's going to entrust children to us, he wants us to keep them in the right perspective. They are "loaners" at best. *He* gives them life. *He* is at work in their hearts. *He* has to draw them to himself. *We* have to be faithful to "train them up." But it's up to the kids to respond.

Just as Abraham was willing to sacrifice Isaac on God's command, we have to be willing to "give them back" to him daily. It is God's ultimate responsibility to bring them to maturity. *Be a committed parent, but realize who really owns them.*

CHAPTER 9

MAKING THEM FEEL SPECIAL
Parents and Their Wonderful Gifts

This is the Morris home. Come in and go downstairs.
—sign outside the back door of Steve and Donna Morris's house in Waltham, Massachusetts

You don't see many simple signs like this one anymore. Most families perceive the home as a refuge from the stresses of everyday life, a place of retreat. There are still a few homes in a few neighborhoods where kids are welcome to play or hang out, but for kids growing up in this Boston suburb, the Morris residence was *the* place.

"We had kids come to our back door all the time," said Steve Morris. "One Sunday afternoon, my son Zachary invited some kids from the church over, and he lit a fire in the fireplace. He forgot to let out the damper, however, so the room filled up with smoke. What makes the story funny is that he got out our vacuum cleaner and tried to suck up the smoke!"

Another time, one of the Morris daughters hosted a party downstairs, but after running herself ragged all evening, she had a different outlook.

"It's *hard* being a hostess," she said.

"Welcome to the club," her father replied.

It was also hard to put the welcome mat out as often as the Morris clan did, but Steve and Donna didn't want to shut the front door—or the back door—to their children's world. They wanted the neighborhood to come on in.

Spend Time with Your Kids

Adult children who told us their parents were the type to buy a pool table for the rec room, play touch football on a cold day, build an oversized doll house, organize whiffleball games in the backyard, or take the family on long camping trips were often the same children who said their parents are their best friends today.

I (Greg) am always trying to think of things that will create lasting memories. That's why I put a few extra dollars into a cement slab and basketball hoop in the backyard. The hours spent rebounding free throws, playing horse, and getting beat by my boys in one-on-one is stuff that will stick in their memory banks their entire lives. As often as I can, whether it's trips or toys, I want to put my family entertainment and gift money into things we can do together.

Some of the adult children waxed nostalgic about the "little things" their parents did, like Dad driving them to youth group weekend or Mom chauffeuring the volleyball team to an away game.

You aren't being nerds, Dad and Mom. The kids *love* it.

Give Your Kids Individual Attention

What were some other ways parents made their kids feel special?

"Well, we always gave our children their choice of sandwiches," said Rita Hedley, a Montana mom.

Really?

"When you have five kids to make lunches for, and everyone

gets a peanut butter sandwich, they are one in five. In our house, they got to choose. That was their chance to feel different, to feel special. My sister-in-law gave me the worst time. 'I can't believe it. Have you lost your mind?' But she didn't understand. You have to find little ways to make them feel loved."

In the Hedley household, the five children also took turns being "King for the Day." The "king" could ride in the front seat to school, choose what he wanted for dinner, and generally catch all the breaks that day. But that child also had to empty the dishwasher, set the table, and be Mom's gofer. Another royal task was helping prepare dinner. Rita says it's no accident that her adult boys are very good cooks—and good eaters.

Gina Benedict, a young woman who called herself a "big-time Daddy's girl," said she loved it when her father would come into her room to chat while she was studying. Often her father traveled to Saudi Arabia (he worked for the Air Force) on tours that lasted several months. While he was fifteen thousand miles from home, he would write individual letters to her and everyone else in the family. "That made us all feel special," said Gina. "Sometimes only I would get a letter, but Dad always P.S.'d 'Say hi to Mom' on the bottom. He would also return from Saudi with little trinkets, such as a key chain or jewelry."

Establish Routines and Traditions

Parents can also make everyday routines, or once-a-year traditions, into special occasions. Sally Olin said her parents always reserved Sunday just for "family day."

"None of my friends could come over or even call," she said. "After we went to church, we'd take family walks along the train tracks. We'd talk, and Dad would teach us stuff as we walked. Then we'd go home and make pizza. The treat afterward was to watch 'Walt Disney World' after dinner. Our family days lasted until high school. My parents worked very hard on creating traditions in our family."

So did the Clarke family, who invited strangers, students, and friends of friends to their annual Thanksgiving feast. One November, they had a dozen countries represented around the living room. The day after Thanksgiving was always reserved for making Christmas wreaths. It was an all-day affair: gathering the branches, shopping for ribbons, and constructing the wreaths. On Christmas Eve, the Clarke parents passed around the family "grab bag," or little presents and white elephant gifts that the family could open up—and then trade.

Parents who supported their children's school activities also received high marks. "Mom came to a bunch of my track meets, while my dad came to a few," said Lee Mathis, whose father is now separated from his mother. "I appreciated what time I did get to spend with him. I miss him now. He wasn't a verbal guy, but he tried, and I'll never forget our hunting and fishing trips together."

I (Mike) can certainly attest to the value of parents' attending their children's sporting events. I played a lot of baseball growing up, and many seasons my father was in the third base coaching box. That made me feel more confident. And my mom was *always* in the stands, often huddled under a blanket. What I liked best were the postgame discussions, talking about the games and reliving the victories.

Making Grade-Schoolers Feel Special

- Leave notes in the lunch boxes. Buy a joke book, write down a funny one, and stick it in the lunch pail. Pretty soon, your child's friends will be looking forward to the joke-of-the-day!

- Always boast how intelligent your children are (without overdoing it, of course).
- Give a nice present at the finish of a school year.
- Walk them to the first day of school.
- Show up any time they are involved in a school function.
- Volunteer to be a teacher's aide in a child's classroom.
- Attend the back-to-school and teacher-parent conferences.
- Once a year, pull them out of school for a day and make a special trip to the lake, a local ski area, or an amusement park. Be sure to tell them *why* you're taking them out of school. I (Mike) grew up near a family that did just that. In May, when the surf was up and the Pacific Ocean was starting to warm up, the mother took her two boys to the beach. But it happened with the understanding that the boys couldn't stay home from school on other days unless they were *really* sick. The day trip was a reward for excellent attendance.
- Help with homework. Not only will your children learn more, but they will also sense that education is important to you—and more important than the TV.
- Make a big deal over birthdays. It's a lot of work to put together a birthday party, but kids will always remember them. "We let our daughters pick the menu for their birthdays," said Mary Ann Campbell of Gary, Indiana. "They usually wanted chocolate cake with grease frosting. I know it sounds horrible, but they loved my grease cakes for twenty years."
- Arrange treasure hunts. These days, my (Mike's) kids are at the age where they love my little hunts. I make clues and hide them around the house. They have to find each clue, which eventually leads to a piece of Swiss chocolate.

- Take plenty of photos, and when they come back from the photo lab, don't consign them to the nearest shoe box. Put them into photo albums with captions (very important). Your kids will *love* seeing how they were when they were younger.
- Touch a lot; give hugs, and make good eye contact. If you don't start now, your kids won't be approachable in high school.

Making Teens Feel Special

- If your children are gifted enough to play on one of the athletic teams, be there! If your son makes a great tackle to save the Homecoming Game, you don't want to shuffle your feet while the whole town talks about it.
- Before an evening contest, take your young charges out for a special pregame meal.
- Give your children a "key ring." (We talk about this in the chapter on sex education in the nineties.)
- Take your children to a pro football or baseball game. If there are none nearby, attend a big collegiate contest. Sitting with 106,000 others at the Michigan-Ohio State football game, for example, is one of those bigger-than-life spectacles.
- Go on a college-hunting trip the summer before their senior year.
- Ask what their favorite meal is, and serve it often (as long as it isn't cheeseburgers!).
- Take them to see a Christian music artist you both like.
- Take pains to praise their good behavior.
- You can still touch a lot, give hugs, and make good eye contact.

///

The Top Ten Worst Ways to Spend Time with Your Teenagers

10. Checking out the Fox TV network's fall lineup.
9. Staying awake in front of the TV set.
8. Sleeping in front of the TV set.
7. Trying to convince them that *your* music was much better than theirs.
6. Playing video games—and losing to them every single time.
5. Letting them drag you to a movie that requires your presence in order for them to get in.
4. Bailing them out of jail.
3. Trying to influence their taste in fashions or hairstyles.
2. Driving them around town and getting only one-syllable responses to your comments and questions.
1. Nodding off while they tell you about their day.

///

Making Post–High Schoolers Feel Special

- If your children leave home to attend college, be sure to write regularly. "Mail call" is a big event for a homesick freshman, especially during the fall quarter. As they make new friends and settle into college life, the mailings can taper off.

- Ditto that advice for sending "goodie" packages in the mail. After a steady diet of dorm food, homemade chocolate/coconut cookies (even though they are crushed by the mailman) taste great.

- If the university is not too far, attend "Parents' Weekend." Then you and your kids will have more in common when you talk about campus life.

- If you live two or three hours from each other, meet halfway for a restaurant meal.

- If you eat out in a restaurant, always pick up the tab. This is probably done in all households, but there's something "all right" about Dad picking up the check.
- Call often on the phone. Again, be sensitive to overdoing it, but steady contact builds healthy communication.
- Think of reasons to ask *your* children for advice. Your little ones are now little adults. Are you still "talking down" to them? It may not be an easy habit to break, but you can start with something innocuous. Perhaps your son is a huge Chicago Cubs fan. Ask him if this season will be the first year since 1945 that the Cubs win the National League pennant. (If he says yes, you know you have a die-hard Cubs fan in the family.)
- Help them pay for college, but also help them understand the sacrifices you're making. Tell them you're dipping into savings, you had to cash in a life insurance policy, or Mom went back to work. Don't make them feel guilty, but explain that you're doing it out of love.
- Help them get that first job. Adult children do need to learn how to stand on their own feet, but contacts are sometimes everything in the business world. Tell them they are on their own after that, however, and that you won't bail them out for poor performance.
- Show your children how to balance a checkbook and open bank accounts. Also explain the dangers of credit cards and what their proper use is.
- Serve their favorite meal when they come home.
- If a child graduates from college, take him or her on one of those "once-in-a-lifetime" trips. One mother told us she took her son, Jeff, on an around-the-world trip following graduation. (Must have been nice). When I

(Mike) graduated, my grandmother took me to Hawaii for ten days. (That was *really* nice!)
- They are never too old to touch a lot, give hugs to, and make good eye contact with.

Finally, we heard from parents whose children made *them* feel pretty good. "Recently," said Kathy Mosher, "one of my girls cross-stitched this sentence from Scripture for me: 'I have no greater joy than to know my children walk in the truth.' That was something special."

//

Stay in Touch

We asked parents how they stay in touch with their adult children. A large majority said they telephone often, which is hardly surprising, given the trend for adult children not to live where they grew up and the availability of inexpensive calling plans these days.

In second place was visiting, and corresponding by mail was a distant third (sorry, Mr. Postman). Families that live close to each other mentioned sitting down for Sunday dinner together or taking vacations *en famille*. Others mentioned taking care of grandchildren while the parents worked.

Finally, we heard from parents who remain *really* close to their adult children. "They're still at home!" exclaimed one mother of two children, ages twenty-two and twenty.

Guess that old parenting job never ends, does it?

//

COMMUNICATION: WHAT TO TALK ABOUT, WHEN, AND HOW TO DO IT

If you think peer pressure begins during the teen years, you're wrong. We must work extra hard to guide them through the struggles they'll face.

CHAPTER 10

TALKING WITH YOUR KIDS
Parents and Communication

The communication habits of the families we interviewed was the scariest information we gathered. *In a high percentage of Christian homes, parents and children aren't learning to communicate until well after high school or, in many instances, after college!*

Only about 20 percent of the adult children stated they communicated well with their parents during the high school years and below. In fact, the teenage years were the worst. (A complete list of responses is in appendix 1.)

Ladies and gentlemen, we can't let this continue!

The swing from the end of the twentieth century into the twenty-first will not be a return to "Happy Days." Our society has made an about-face on morality over the past twenty-five years, and the waves of poor (okay, *rotten*) values will continue to pound the beach. Not only will the surf not abate, but it assuredly will *intensify.*

Now would be a natural spot to quote several "bummer" statistics on teenage pregnancy, sexually transmitted diseases, alcohol consumption, casual drug use, vandalism, and suicide. But since you've probably heard them all before, we've decided not to waste the space. What's discouraging is that most of those stats—including those for premarital sex—are nearly the same for Christian teens and unchurched teens!

Who's to blame? Surely we can point our finger at Hollywood and assign the entertainment industry a high percentage of the responsibility. Whereas adults will look at movies with jaundiced eyes, teens will buy into a film's premise much more easily. In addition to Tinseltown, we can name record companies that release dirty albums, news media that support them, a government that won't enforce antiporn laws already on the books, and a godless public school system—all these are easy targets. And to a degree, it *is* fair to point out these institutions as culprits. They're certainly not reinforcing Christian family values these days. But then again, that's not their job—it's ours!

Can we change any of those influences? We can certainly voice our views and participate in our democratic society. But we can have the greatest influence in our homes, with those precious kids God has entrusted to us. Frankly, society is already on a downhill course. We don't believe an all-out assault against popular culture holds the golden key. These days, because of the sway of our legal system, whether one votes Republican, Democrat, or Independent doesn't make a huge difference. Having the "right" political leaders is no insurance policy against immorality touching our homes.

Are There Answers?

Besides hiding your kids away from the world—which a few concerned parents have chosen to do—how can you prevent the influence of a sick society from entering your home? Is it the TV? How about the magazines you subscribe to or the books you bring home? You can and should monitor what comes into your home and teach your children to use discernment about such things themselves. (We'll discuss that more fully in chapter 18.) But an essential first step is to promote open communication with your kids *inside* the home. Being able to talk with our kids—and knowing they feel free to talk with us about anything that comes up—is the foundation for everything else we can do to raise faithful kids. Unfortunately, there are a lot of "communication killers" lurking about that make healthy communication a challenge. We'll try to unmask the most deadly ones here.

Communication Killer #1:
Not taking the time for each other

Two parents made these confessions about why they failed to have quality communication with their children:

- "During the upper grade school years, we were busy and took them for granted."
- "Whenever I would allow myself to get deeply engrossed in my work, communication would screech to a halt."

Remember what Jesus said one job of Satan is? "The thief comes only to steal and kill and destroy" (John 10:10). Even in Christian families, the dark one is allowed to steal the time that a parent and child spend together.

Here's the no-brainer of the day: *If you're not with someone, you can't communicate very well.*

We're not sociologists, but you don't have to be an expert to detect some trends here. Families are chasing after the American dream, with split-level homes, two shiny cars in the driveway, and the latest fashions. To afford all this stuff, Mom and Dad have to be *away* from the home earning money to pay for the goodies *inside* their home. And when the parents *are* home, they're often home only in body!

Mom? Well, it's no longer "fulfilling" to be a homemaker. Needing to feel "productive," she heads off into the work force, content in knowing that day-care centers and the school system can do a "pretty good job" of nurturing and educating her children. "After all," she tells herself, "we do need the money."

For all too many homes, this is true—they do need the money! Some laid-off dads must work six-dollar-an-hour jobs until something better comes along—but often, nothing opens up for several years. So Mom reenters the work force to keep the mortgage paid and groceries on the table. It's not a sin to be a double-income family when you're trying to make ends meet.

Nor is it a sin to live in a better neighborhood or drive a late-model car. But if "nicer" things are the goal, and your family needs a double income simply to pursue the aforementioned life-style, don't blame God, the church, or our culture when you can't communicate with your children or they've opted to stop going to church. The best way to invest in the future and plan for a happy retirement is to raise kids who follow the Lord with all their hearts.

Besides a tragedy in the family, what could possibly bring more regret and grief to a parent than having children who rejected Christ or are only following him halfheartedly? And that's something parents will have to deal with for the last thirty or forty years of their lives.

Expensive furnishings, stocks, bonds, and mutual funds— could they really provide *any* sense of fulfillment if your own children weren't on track with their faith?

Not to us.

That's why we wrote this book. Nothing else we could

accomplish will compare to the satisfaction of having faithful children raising faithful grandchildren. Nothing.

Okay, sorry about the sermon. Where were we? Oh, yes. Time.

In these days of unparalleled immorality, our kids need our time . . . from the day they are born until they leave the nest.

Examine your life and decide whether your relationship with your children could benefit by a few more hours a week. Then do something about it. You may have to do some radical re-arranging. If so, do it soon.

Communication Killer #2: The thing everyone stares at

The "one-eyed monster" deserves a trainload of blame for stifling communication between parents and kids. Sure, TV is an easy target to load, lock in, and fire on, but no one can deny its effect on families. Not only can it pump 100 percent pure filth into your home, but it can also rob literally months and years of valuable time away from talking, listening, and playing with your kids— stuff that cements relationships for life. One woman knew exactly what effect the TV had on her household. "The TV was a demon that destroyed our ability to talk about anything meaningful after six o'clock every night," she said wistfully. TV can make everyone in the family act as if they've just had a frontal lobotomy.

True confession time: I (Greg) own a TV set. (So does Mike's family.) Actually, I have two televisions hooked up to my cable system. No, I haven't lost my faith. Do I make poor viewing choices? Sometimes, without a doubt. But every now and then, I sit down and take a hard look at our family's TV habits. If the few hours we do watch don't allow for wholesome, fun times, we'll make adjustments to get back on the course *we* want to be on.

I applaud those families who have trashed the tube altogether, like the San Diego father who picked up the family TV, calmly walked out to the garage, and then heaved the set against the wall. But I've discovered that families *can* have a balance, and they can even use TV to enhance family togetherness. TV sports have definitely allowed my two boys and me to enjoy "bonding" times. And recently, I organized an "Ernest Film Festival" for the three of us. It consisted of two "Ernest" videos, pizza, pop, and a sleepover together in the basement. The boys will never forget it—and they can't wait for the next one! (Mom can't either. She got the night off!)

If the TV has hurt our home in any way, it has probably been in preventing me from thinking about more creative times of communication we could have as a family. It *has* numbed me to initiating family talks. This hit home when one woman told us about the "family councils" they used to have at her house.

"Though we'd always complain about them," Jennifer Dorner said, "we were always glad we had them. We'd leave the dishes on the table after a Sunday meal, go into the living room, and talk until we were talked out. Then we'd have a little Bible study. My dad would ask us what our favorite verses were. We'd have quizzes, and then Dad would find three passages on the same subject. We'd do little things like that to keep it fun.

"Often we'd go over problems that came up during the week. My parents were really good at gauging the temperature of the family. Do you know why? *They asked us what we thought.* Especially when it came to discipline issues. They wanted to know how we felt about what they were doing. They asked us what discipline meant to us. We, of course, thought it meant punishment. They'd explain it was much bigger than that. Our longer discussions about these types of issues usually happened in high school. Sometimes it would go for two to three hours. Today we're all married and have our own families, but nearly every Sunday we go over to their house for Sunday supper, and we still have those long talks with the dishes on the table."

Communication Killer #3:
Little children growing into obnoxious teenagers

Three things are inevitable as kids grow up: puberty, peer groups, and pop culture.

We're simply not the only influence screaming for our children's attention. One's yelling from the inside, one is whispering in his ear, and the other is tantalizing his thoughts by what he looks at and listens to.

Since we can't prevent puberty, protecting them from the next two is tempting. But really, do we want to overprotect them forever (or, as Mark Twain once suggested, lock them in a barrel and feed them through a hole)?

How realistic is it to try to insulate them from every negative influence out there, be it a billboard or a heavy-metal friend down the street? Not very. A better strategy is teaching them "discernment skills" from their early years. (Remember, we'll get to this in chapter 18.)

We've talked to parents who really seemed to do everything right in trying to establish a close relationship, yet because of the "three Ps," their kids still got off track for a while. We heard confessions like these:

- "In high school, she knew everything."
- "When they hit high school, they began to rebel against our authority, trying to be more independent."

- "Even in the junior high years, our communication was terrible because of the changes they were going through. They just preferred talking to their peers."
- "Ages thirteen to nineteen were tough times because they thought Mom and Dad knew nothing. They didn't understand that the freedom they so desperately desired came with more responsibility than they wanted."
- "In high school, the children wanted to do their own thing without interference from me."
- "They weren't reachable during the difficult developmental years of high school."

Even the adult kids admitted their parents weren't to blame for their poor communication habits.

- "I thought I had all the answers in high school. I always could talk to my parents; I just didn't think I needed to."
- "I was a strong-willed, very emotional high school girl. Those years were hard on my parents. I really tested them."
- "During the high school years, I was trying very hard to become my own person, but I didn't feel I had many freedoms."
- "In junior high, I closed up. My parents didn't attempt to 'force' themselves on me, which was a good plan. I eventually opened up."

For nearly all the adult children we talked to, good communication eventually returned. Some teenagers, however, are susceptible to peer group pressure and being influenced by the popular media myths of "coolness." No, it's not genetic; it's a learned insecurity. Sometimes it's brought on through unstable grade school years where one or both parents are uninvolved due to time constraints, divorce, or fatigue. Often, other circumstances beyond the control of the parents—like those "exploding" hormones—affect children.

The answer? Keep your head, ride it out, and don't overreact every time they act moody, are moderately disrespectful, or want to spend more time with their friends. Stay involved, keep trying to program fun activities together, and definitely be interested and uncompromising in your love *for* them and belief *in* them.

Communication Killer #4: Not respecting your kids

Sometimes parents can be real dorkbrains. (Just ask us!) Being head of the home doesn't make us infallible. When we are nerds, we need to admit it quickly.

I (Greg) took Troy, my oldest, to school one November day and walked him to his fourth-grade class. I started talking with a teacher while Troy went off to play hoops with the older boys. When I was done, I wanted to say good-bye, so I walked over to the court. Troy gave a faint wave, turned away, and hoped I'd take the hint. I didn't. I went over, gave him a hug, and kissed the top of his head.

Bad move, Dad!

Later that night, I asked if I'd embarrassed him. He sheepishly nodded his head, trying not to show how disappointed he was. So I immediately told him he was being childish and that since I was his dad, I'd kiss him anytime I wanted!

NOT!

I apologized and told him I'd try not to do it again. Then I looked at Troy a long time and realized, *My little boy is growing up. I should remember to respect his space when he's with his peers.*

When we realize we're irritating our children, we need to cut it out and remember what it was like when our parents irritated us. Loving them enough to respect their growing individuality is hard work, especially when it seems it was just yesterday that we were the only significant people in their lives.

As our children grow older, it's even more imperative that we learn to respect them. Here's what a few adult kids had to say about the respect issue:

- "In high school, because certain priorities of mine were not treated with respect, I shut my parents out."
- "My interest in boys wasn't taken seriously in grade school. It was made light of. I clammed up. In high school, secrets I held dear were disclosed by my mother. I vowed to never open up to her again."
- "They got on my nerves in junior high. Dad teased a lot, and Mom always made me feel guilty because I spent all my time with friends."

Another respect issue that crops up especially during the teenage years relates to the way conflicts are resolved.

"One thing I really didn't like," a woman told us, "was not being able to go to my room and be alone to think. If anything was wrong, we had to talk it out, talk it out, and talk it out. I feel there are times when kids need their space. We never got ours. My mom grew up in a home where her parents would get mad and not speak to her. As a result of that, she overcompensated with us. Her strategy was to talk things through, but she went too far the other way."

The message: Learn early to treat your children with

appropriate respect. Give them some elbow room once in a while until they're ready to talk. Don't tease them if they're bugged by something—especially the opposite sex. And don't ever blab secrets they've told you in confidence. That will come back to haunt you.

Communication Killer #5:
Failing to invite them into your world

"When our children were in about fifth or sixth grade," one Seattle father told us, "we really made an effort to treat them like fellow human beings. On many occasions, we'd talk to them, ask them questions, and relate to them as if we weren't their parents. We acted like—and really desired—to have fun with them.

"When we treated our oldest son as we would another best friend, the change was amazing. The person inside just came out and met us. It takes a lot of time with each child for this to happen, because you've still got to parent. But we placed a high value on developing a deep friendship. I learned this from my own father. He showed his love for me from an early age. He was proud of me. He preferred my company to the company of others. He talked to me about things that troubled and puzzled him. I remember when I was eight, we were out looking at the stars. He started talking about the limitations of being human. 'We are so tiny compared to the stars,' he said. He let me into a man's world. He let me think his thoughts. I remember just being in wonder of all the realms my father had. I didn't understand everything, but it was such a privilege to be let in."

Are you curious about the legacy of this man's father (a Wisconsin farmer)? He raised two sons who became pastors. His two daughters married pastors. All four adult children have raised children who are strong followers of Christ, a number of them involved in significant ministry. Why? One reason this man points to was his dad's commitment to taking the relationship to a higher level of friendship.

Communication Killer #6:
Not understanding the changes kids go through
Sadly, many parents figure that the day they graduated from school, they received a lifetime deferment on learning. Others promised themselves they would never read another book to *learn* something, even though they sure enjoy flicking the pages of a potboiler novel. But we trust that you're far from the madding crowd (how's that for a literary reference?), and that you're reading this book to expand your knowledge about parenting.

Fifty years ago, new mothers and fathers often lived in the same town as their parents and siblings. Having family members close by meant young parents had models to watch and see how it was done. (They also got some baby-sitting help!) Today, because families are so mobile, we often live hundreds—more like thousands—of miles from parents or older siblings who could mentor us. Others, like me (Greg), were raised in broken homes. We don't have any *good* childhood memories to fall back on when difficult—or routine—parenting situations arise.

Even though I've worked with teenagers for fifteen years, I still can't afford to make it up as I go. The youth culture is changing too rapidly. I have to stay current with the pressures they're facing. The greater my knowledge of *their* world, the greater chance I'll have to understand them.

When your teenagers start making statements that you're out of touch and have no idea what they're going through, they might be right. Here are a few samples of what adult children said their parents didn't understand:

- "In junior high, Dad wasn't home much [he was a pastor]. His authoritarian way of handling things didn't sit well with my struggle for independence. I needed someone who took the time to explain things, not just bark orders."
- "Because the teen culture I was growing up in was so different from my parents', my high school years were terrible. They were clueless to the pressures I was under."
- "In high school, I felt my parents were always telling me what to do."

What can you do? Read and listen to materials *addressed* to your teens to discover the world they're living in. For instance, parents would do well to glance through *Breakaway* or *Brio*, our publications for teen guys and girls, respectively. The topics we write about—peer pressure, changes in their bodies, relating to the opposite sex—will open a little window into their world. Of course, there also are plenty of other materials worth seeking out (books, tapes, and videos) by those specializing in teen ministry.

Communication Killer #7: Parental insecurities

It's tough to admit, but some parents are more insecure than their kids. Somewhere along the line they never gained the confidence necessary to parent—or stand up to an unruly teen. When a parent is unsure of his role, he will either overcompensate and be authoritarian, or he will undercompensate and get walked over. The adult children we talked to easily identified this phenomenon, and they knew the damage an insecure parent could bring:

- "My teen years were the worst because my parents felt challenged. If we didn't automatically agree with everything they did, we children were automatically wrong! All my father wanted to be was a dictator with an obedient family."
- "They didn't admit when they were wrong, even when we both could see they had made a big mistake."
- "After college, I was living at home trying to get a good teaching job. One time, I was invited out to a bar with friends. I was twenty-four, and I wanted to go out with them. I knew I wouldn't drink, but my dad threw a fit. 'What will people from church think?' he asked. I shot back, 'What would they be doing in there?' It was just another example of how they wanted to control me and the appearance of things instead of letting me grow up."

Because today's society is so much different from the one in which we grew up, some situations and fears are legitimate. Our kids, however, will bolt if we give place to unrealistic fears that cause us to be unreasonable. If at all possible, we need to express confidence and trust in our children, as this next woman's father did years ago:

"Once when I was set to go to a church youth event at a hotel, my dad sat me down to talk," said the young woman. "He said he knew there would be guys and gals in hotel rooms, and he mentioned that a boy and a girl could find themselves in a room alone. He said, 'I remember what it was like to be in high school at your age. There's a possibility you'll end up alone with a boy in your room. If it happens, I know you'll do what's right.'

"I didn't give it a second thought because I knew it wouldn't happen to me. But that weekend I somehow ended up with a guy in my room! I couldn't believe it. I quickly told him good night and left. It would have been easy to make the decision the other way, but I didn't want to violate that trust and respect my father showed for me."

Secure parents trust their kids. Secure parents raise secure kids. Secure kids can be trusted.

Communication Killer #8: A know-it-all parent

"If my parents had asked our opinions on things," one Wichita woman said, "we would have been friends earlier. Instead, we lived in an atmosphere where if the kids said anything, we got in trouble. I remember saying, 'Other kids don't have to go to church every Sunday night.' Dad said, 'You're not other people's kids.'

"Another time he said something in anger to my mom. My brother and I told him he shouldn't talk to her like that. He turned around and told us to shut up and stay out of the conversation. We both bit our tongues and kept quiet. If we had pressed it one more time, he would have gotten even angrier."

Know-it-all parents have to win every argument, often invoking either high decibels or their God-ordained role as head of the family. If their goal is controlling behavior, they will rarely admit defeat.

Frankly, we don't think it's unscriptural for parents to back down once in a while. In fact, it actually draws children closer to their parents when the parents admit a mistake. It brings us closer to their level.

All of us, throughout our lives, learn to either respect or not respect people we've come to know. With me (Greg), my "Respect-O-Meter" goes off the scale when I see someone who can, with humility, admit his faults. I want to hang around that person because he showed he was human . . . just like me.

125

We have to fight the self-righteous urge and take time to talk things through when there's conflict.

"Unfortunately, when I got upset and angry," one parent told us, "I started preaching! That usually shut off the communication valve pretty quick. I had to make my point, and then I had to be right."

Robert, a Phoenix man, looks back sadly to a family that couldn't talk because his dad always had to have the last word. "We never have communicated. On this subject, all of my siblings and I agree: Our family did not communicate—especially serious feelings. My father was a visionary leader, and only his thoughts and feelings were important."

Communication Killer #9: Differences in values

Along with the three *P*s mentioned on page 117—and sometimes because of the three *P*s—our kids won't always accept our values. Their decision *not* to adopt the attitudes and behavior we'd like them to have is sometimes due to a lack of consistency in our own lives. Children are the first to notice if a mom or dad says one thing and does another. And they're not too keen on following in those footsteps. (Who would be?)

Most often, however, an adolescent in an emerging adult body is simply testing the values he was taught to see if he wants them as his own.

Here are a few examples:

- "From ages sixteen to eighteen, I found it difficult to live their degree of morality. I was the oldest, and I was charting a new territory of independence."
- "I met a guy at work and fell crazy 'in love.' The relationship grew rocky because his parents were from a

completely different denomination. My parents, especially Mom, made it clear they were opposed to this relationship. They couldn't condone a nominal Christian dating their daughter."

- "In junior high I got into the wrong crowd and was influenced by the other kids with things that were not acceptable to my parents."

As much as we'd like our kids to believe something because we said it, that doesn't always happen, especially if there are other voices whispering different things . . . and there are MANY!

Communication Killer #10: Poor relationship skills

We heard it time and again:

"My dad was the quiet one of the family." "My mom always lectured and never asked me what I thought."

We realize not every parent has the interpersonal relationship skills of a professional counselor, but that's no excuse for not making an effort. One pastor who has watched dozens of children rebel against their families points to this issue as a major contributing factor.

"You can't justify the lack of relational skills as a parent," he says. "No matter what you were taught or how you were raised, you need to work hard at communicating to all your kids. Too many parents settle for the status quo and don't realize what they're creating in the process."

Whether it's an overbearing dad and a mom who can't speak her mind or vice versa, poor relational skills by one or both parents—especially those raising teens—can be devastating. I (Greg) read letters every week from *Breakaway* guys lamenting how their moms or dads don't understand them. What they're really saying is this: "They won't spend time listening and talking with me!" If these parents would talk to their children with some degree of empathy, they *could* understand!

In these days when so many issues need to be bounced off caring and involved parents, we simply cannot be unapproachable because we're convinced we don't have the skills to invite them into a heart-to-heart discussion.

On this one, we recommend that parents who are timid seek out a counselor and learn some skills in interpersonal communication.

Communication Killer #11: A dad who's not there

"I'll be home at five-thirty," his dad said on his way out the door. For the rest of the day, the son waited dutifully for the magic hour to hit. But all too often in his home, Dad didn't keep his word. What this son learned was that dads don't come through for you when you need them.

Though kids are forgiving, it doesn't take them long to realize their dad can't be trusted to do what he says. Children in single-parent homes (where only the mom is present) learn this one quickly. But even kids in two-parent homes figure out, by their parents' actions, that there are often more important priorities than playing catch or doing errands with them.

It's not just a dad's physical presence that's important; it's also what he does when he *is* home. When a child hears a mom say, "Don't bother your father; he's had a tough day," he'll learn that dads are unapproachable after work. Dad may be there in body, but he's not available.

Then on the weekends, Dad chains himself to his easy chair and flips on the ESPN college basketball triple-header. What the child learns is that on weekdays, dads go slay dragons. On weekends, dads cheer for the Bruins, Hoyas, and Orangemen. Oh yes, if you want to get anything done (like asking permission for something), go find Mom. That's why it's important for dads to "engage" when they're home, to "click in" to the family rhythms.

"My dad never complained about work when he got home," said Joseph, a young man from Atlanta. "He'd come home from a week-long trip and immediately dive into whatever we wanted. The impression I got was that when you were in trouble, call your dad—he can handle it. He won't run from it. He'll walk down and face the grouchy old neighbor whose window you just broke."

Being there also means responding genuinely and promptly to your kids' overtures. Betsy Smithhouser told us she wrote her mom and dad a note from college. "It was a real heartfelt letter, thanking them for paying my way and reminding them how I felt about them. They never responded to it. It took years for me to risk anything else."

Willie Brown still remembers when he left home for college. "I'd never really seen my dad cry much, but when I left for school, he cried in front of everyone. He wasn't ashamed to do it. That taught me that it's okay to display emotions."

Communication Killer #12: Conditional love

"When I was nineteen, I started dating a non-Christian guy," an Austin, Texas, woman told us. "My parents objected, and a rift grew in our relationship. But I didn't want to break up with this guy, even though I knew we could never get married.

"I quit going to church for a year, even though I still lived at home. Each time the subject would come up, my parents made it clear they couldn't condone what I was doing. But they always told me they loved me. It was very clear to me how they felt—on both subjects.

"When I finally broke up with the guy, it felt good not to worry about upsetting my parents anymore. They never manipulated me, and that let me see how much I valued their love above someone else's—especially another guy's who wasn't interested in Christianity."

Conditional love would have made the daughter's *performance* the litmus test in determining how her parents would treat her. Children can mess up—sometimes for long periods of time. When a child exhibits bad behavior, or when conflicts in values arise, parents need to take the high road and not let it affect their expressed feelings for the child.

Quite a list! Every parent bumps up against some of these "communication killers" sooner or later. Examine your style of parenting—even your own personality—to see if you're shutting off the flow of quality communication between you and your children. If you are, work to make the necessary changes.

CHAPTER 11

THE MAJORS AND MINORS
Parents and the Essentials

I (Mike) was nine years old when the Beatles appeared on "The Ed Sullivan Show" on February 9, 1964. I can still remember bouncing on the living-room couch to the beat of "Twist and Shout," the opening song for John, Paul, George, and Ringo. My parents, who weren't squares, nonetheless wondered who these four "mop tops" were.

"They look like girls," my dad harumphed. My neighborhood buddies and I didn't agree. We thought they were the greatest; all we could talk about that spring was the Beatles. We even formed our own "band," using tennis rackets as guitars and lip-synching to 45s of "Please, Please Me" and "She Loves You" in Andy Harrah's backyard.

Each of us had his favorite Beatle, and I was the "John Lennon" of the band. Naturally, I wanted to grow my hair long like his. (Have you looked at any of the old Beatle album covers recently? Their hair length would be a *joke* today.)

That idea didn't sit well with my parents. Dad was still cutting my hair in those days, and he knew only one style: the "brushcut"—white sidewalls and some hair on top. I did get him to let me grow my bangs out some, but that was it.

When my bangs reached my eyebrows, I started "swishing"

my hair with a jerk of my head. Naturally, this drove my father nuts. One night he said he had had enough and hacked off my bangs.

So much for being John Lennon.

These days, their sons' hair length isn't a big deal for a lot of parents—it's earrings. But back in the mid-sixties, long hair was the leading edge of a cultural change sweeping the country. Mind-altering drugs like marijuana, LSD, and speed were soon to follow, but I didn't know anything about *that*. I was just nine years old.

Measuring your child's spirituality by his hair length, or how many holes he has in his jeans, or how many pierced earrings she wears—we don't think is right. By emphasizing the outward appearance, you're passing a baton of faith based on looks, not a heart attitude. The truth is, parents often make this a major issue because it reflects on *their* spirituality to church friends and neighbors. Kids could care less about how their looks affect *your* reputation. Frankly, most are too busy just trying to survive the teenage years with their self-image intact.

Is there a balance? Sure, there is. I once heard a parent tell his son, "Look, if you're growing your hair long to rebel against what I stand for, then we're going down to the barbershop today. But if you're growing it long because that's what everyone is doing, then I will allow it."

Did this dad cave in to the whims of his child? Hardly. He firmly established the motive for the change in appearance and stood his ground.

One mother I interviewed said her son's hair length wasn't a big deal to her, even though she thought it looked awful. "When is Charlie going to get a haircut?" all her friends at church asked. *I don't know. Why don't you ask him?* she thought.

I wondered just how long her son's hair was, imagining this

guy looking like Axl Rose. "His hair touched the top of his ears," the mom told me. "We didn't make him get it cut because his hair wasn't that long [no fooling!]. Besides, *we felt it was a phase.*"

Bravo, Mom! You were right, and because you didn't go overboard, your son got a trim all on his own just before he left home to attend a Christian college.

What Goes Around

The old cliché is that parents should "major on the majors and minor on the minors." If that's true, what are the big-ticket items on which parents should dig in their heels? While hair length (actually, it's hair*style* these days, what with all the Mohawks and purple dye going around) is still topping the charts in a few households, most parents we interviewed bulleted spiritual matters on their hit parade. Attending church on Sundays, raising their children in the knowledge of Jesus Christ, teaching them how to pray, telling the truth, remaining sexually pure before marriage—all these were mentioned often.

"The most important thing is to have a personal relationship with Jesus Christ as your Savior," said Jerry, an Oklahoma father. "Be true to God and his principles."

Added Bill Butler: "Accepting Christ was number one in our family. We wanted our children to pray and read God's Word daily. We steered them toward Christian friends, but we wanted them to be kind to non-Christians."

That's why you should emphasize reaching out in your household. Neighbors will watch the way you interact with one another—and talk about it amongst their social set. Will they be able to see Christ in you?

A Texas mother also urged her five children to be the right kind of example to others. "I told them, 'You are judged by the type of company you keep or run around with.' I've always encouraged my kids to associate with people who have something in common with them; that have the same beliefs as them. If they run with a crowd that's rough, they'll get in trouble. They need to run with people where their light will shine and people will see Jesus in them."

On the other hand, we were glad to hear from parents who weren't dogmatic about spiritual matters. "When our kids were in high school," said Mary Beth, "they didn't want to go to Sunday school, although they still went to church. They always felt that their Sunday school classes were cliquish, so they didn't like it. My husband and I talked about it, and we went along with them."

Normally, you should insist that your children attend Sunday school, especially if that's a family habit. But in this case, the children were attending a Christian high school during the week. Were they receiving enough religious instruction outside the home? Of course. Did they *really* need that Sunday school class? No.

From the Other Side

What did the adult children say about the "majors"? Their observations matched up fairly well with their parents'. Many said their fathers and mothers stressed church attendance, seeking God, and knowing his Word.

Others said sexual matters were key topics in their homes. "I heard my parents say that I should save my virginity for marriage," said one daughter. Another young woman said she remembers her parents saying, "Boys will get what they want and then drop the relationship. They always told me not to have sex, but they never told me why and how it would affect me." (We feel the issue of premarital sex is probably *the* biggest major for high-school-age teens, and we'll talk about this in much greater detail in chapter 14.)

Certain things your parents say have a way of sticking out in your mind, even decades later. When we asked the adult children what were the major issues their parents emphasized, they were quick to respond. Here are a few others that haven't been mentioned yet:

- "I should serve God to the best of my ability."
- "Spending time with God, being involved at church, having my actions meet my words."
- "Keeping peace in the family."
- "When choosing a mate, make sure he or she is a Christian."
- "Stand up for what you believe in. You are a servant on earth, so work hard and be honest. Treat others better than yourself."

We've covered a few of the majors, but we're going to leave the real upper-end issues for later. We believe any area that could put a relational wedge between the parent and the child deserves its own chapter.

How to Discuss "Gray Areas" with Your Kids

Was everything black and white in your home when you grew up? It wasn't in mine (Greg's).

Not only did my parents smoke and drink, but after Dad left home, Mom didn't run a very tight ship: My brother and sister were allowed to smoke in the home in early high school (which naturally made them very popular with their friends). By the summer of my junior year, I was smoking dope—with my dad, no less!

My buddies really thought he was cool. One time Dad asked me, "Are you guys going to drink tonight at your poker party, Son?" When I stammered for a minute, he said, "Then just have your friends come over here. I'll provide the beer and wine—but you've got to promise to stay in the house."

That parenting style is called "freedom, with limits," right?

Your home won't harbor that much liberty, but that doesn't mean you won't struggle with certain issues. School dances, movies, rap music, French kissing, makeup, clothes, penny-ante poker, earrings, MTV—this is a short list of issues facing today's parents. Should you slap a "major" label on all of them and enforce the rules at any cost . . . even though the Bible does not speak *directly* about them?

Take a look at Romans 14, in which Paul recommends what to do regarding eating meat sacrificed to idols. It was one of the early church's first gray areas. Paul's conclusion was that we don't do anything that makes us or someone else stumble.

The first time you're hit with a gray area, calmly sit down with your child and read through Romans 14. That's right, have a little Bible study. Find out *together* what that chapter's saying. Locate the principle of not causing someone else to stumble; then help your child apply it. If your son really believes an earring isn't going to cause anyone to reject the faith—and if he's not rebelling against your authority—it looks like a minor issue to us.

Then, as other gray areas hit the fan, you can refer back to Romans 14 for further guidance. This will reinforce the Bible as the ultimate source of wisdom and build a respect for God's Word.

Down to the Minors

So what were some of the minors—the child-raising issues that parents didn't get too worked up over?

"For me, it was how my four daughters were dressed," said Sandy. "One time, they all wanted to wear short miniskirts, but I cautioned them about wearing them too short. But those are minor things compared to what kids have to face these days. We didn't have the problems back then like they do today, such as sexually transmitted diseases and AIDS."

Here's a list of some things that parents considered minor:

- trivial rules
- clothes
- an occasional bad grade and whether or not they finished their food
- breaking dishes and other material things
- winning in sports
- dressing in the latest fads
- condition of their bedrooms

We also recorded this answer from the winner of the stick-in-the-mud award: "I can't think of anything that I would say *wasn't* important."

Come on, Dad, lighten up!

CHAPTER 12

COOL, MAN, COOL
Parents on Popularity

My (Greg's) oldest son, Troy, is a fourth-grader and already knows the difference between "cool people" and "uncool people."

"Cool people have more friends, Dad," he explained to me in a matter-of-fact voice. "They say funny things, and all the girls chase them around the playground."

Innocent stuff, right?

Perhaps.

When I was a sixth-grader back in 1967, I was voted the "Most Popular Guy" out of three sixth-grade classes. While I would have settled for "Best Looking" or "Best Athlete," I still felt good about myself. The recognition meant people noticed me. I had friends, and yes, the girls loved to chase me around the playground.

But when my parents got divorced a couple of years later, being cool took on a whole new level of importance. We're talking survival time for my self-image. During junior high, my athletic ability kept me near the upper-cool crowd. But high school was a whole different ballgame. There, the real cool people were athletes who *drank*. And if you wanted to be really, really cool, you smoked dope, too. By the end of my junior year, I was trying to be really, really cool. Instead, I got really, really messed up.

Would things have been different if my parents had stuck together?

Maybe.

Could I have been strong enough to turn my back on dope if I had known how cool God was—and how cool he thought I was?

I'll never know. But now that I've been a Christian nearly twenty years, I can make an educated guess that things would have been different. Had I known how special I was to God— and that he had a purpose just for me—I think that would have given me the power to make better choices.

Father/Son Challenges

Since Troy knows the definition of cool at his school, we have some challenges before us. They can be boiled down to these questions: Will Troy seek out the cool crowd or stay on God's path (which most of the time may not seem that cool)? Will I teach him the dangers of the cool crowd? Will I show him how cool God is in a way he can understand?

The answer to the second question is easy. Because of my work with teens, I can tell dozens of stories about kids who made their lives miserable by jumping into the cool crowd. Many of them were church kids, too.

But the answer to the first question isn't necessarily determined by my diligence to the second question. The pull of the crowd is strong, especially in public school. This is where your choice of schools comes into play. Christian schools can sometimes head off negative peer pressure, although, as we found in our surveys, that isn't always the case. Home schooling has its advantages and disadvantages as well.

Besides, I'm the type who wants his kids to learn that strength and character come by attacking the fire, not by escaping it (so far, that is!).

Why? Well, I want my boys to be fire fighters who will lead others away from the flames. They may get scorched and even burned, but I hope they'll develop a real love for God's frontline work. I don't want them to end up being teenage Christian pew-sitters like so many hundreds I've seen.

To accomplish this, I'll have to be involved in their lives more than ever. I have to patiently answer the same questions over and over and be prepared to talk things through. I need to remind my children constantly of their worth to God, of their uniqueness, of my pride in their accomplishments (big and small), and finally, of how much I love them. If my boys feel secure about themselves and their relationship with God, they'll be able to resist when the pressure mounts to "be cool." We're hardliners when it comes to talking with children. Childhood pressures need to be addressed early and often.

The Cycle of Insecurity

You need to be aware that this battle isn't won without diligent prayer and an understanding of the pressures kids face on their road toward maturity. Here's what happens to kids toward the later grade school years:

Your children are living in a secure home where they are given an accurate picture of themselves and God. But through a series of low-key confrontations among friends at school, in their minds, being cool will be presented as a favorable option.

Two choices face the parent at this juncture. Ignore their desire to be cool and think it's a normal part of growing up (secretly hoping they'll wind up in the cool crowd), or help your kids to see the struggles they'll face if they *pursue* the cool crowd. Both lead to natural conclusions.

The results of ignoring the pressure your kids feel to "be cool" will be:

- Children will think being cool is the way to go.
- Coolness will lead to greater "peer pressure" (i.e., doing things to maintain a level of popularity).
- Your kids will face internal struggles. They will be faced with the choice of stepping over the line of what they know you expect.
- They *will* succumb to those early challenges and may not suffer any consequences (either through punishment or their consciences).
- Their friends will then offer "popularity rewards." They'll be part of the gang.
- The value of being cool will then rank higher (and give more rewards) than the values they were taught.
- Their newfound popularity begins meeting their immediate self-image needs. It feels good to be accepted.
- As they grow, maintaining their popularity will be contingent upon accepting and participating in the behavior of those who are popular (often drinking, drugs, premarital sex).
- Ultimately, they will make potentially scarring or life-threatening mistakes.

It's a ten-year cycle that's tough to break if not caught early, when children start noticing the difference between "cool" and "uncool" kids at school.

But look at the results of rationally addressing "being cool," often and at an early age:

- Children will see the conflict in following Christ versus following the crowd.
- Unconditional love, reasonable limits, and proper discipline will be in place, and they can learn to see the value of following Christ and the folly of following the crowd.
- Kids' values will be constantly reinforced through discussion, limits, discipline, and love.
- Your kids may soon become the influencers and not the influenced. Why? Their insecurity (which leads to choosing to succumb to peer pressure) is nullified.

It all sounds psychological, but it's really simple: There's a battle raging for the hearts and souls of your children. Satan's strategy is to convince them that they have no worth apart from the crowd. If Satan can lure them, during their formative years, into pursuing the crowd to feel accepted, he can keep them in that self-destructive rut for a long time—perhaps for a lifetime.

The parents' role is to stand in the gap, to be there for biblical direction and unconditional love. This *will* yield a knowledge of their worth to God (something much greater than the crowd can ever offer), and hopefully, a desire in them to pursue the God who has proved his love to them.

Well, this all sounds good on paper, doesn't it? But what happens when families split? When the picture of God is distorted? When "appropriate discipline" isn't used? When parents don't communicate with their children? When there isn't a united front in teaching God's values to the kids?

The answer is that the "failure" rate is increased exponentially. Yes, the kids have a free will, and that's why there aren't any 100 percent guarantees. But what the diligent parent wants is to put the family in the *best possible situation for success.*

Anything less could bring a tragedy that would haunt them the rest of their lives.

While most of the adult children we interviewed were raised in the sixties and seventies, the pull of the crowd hasn't changed over the years. Here are some of the things they felt pressure to do in the junior high and high school years, followed by some of the ways their parents handled them.

Junior High Pressures

- "I felt pressured to look cool. My parents tried to make me feel good about who I was."
- "Even though I had friends who did everything I wasn't supposed to, they never pushed me." (That's unusual!)
- "I was in the rock music scene. My parents would occasionally comment, but they never dropped an iron fist."
- "I wanted more than anything to be popular. Little did I know the price that exacted. I was morally narrow and straight."
- "I listened to rock music with bad lyrics. My parents explained the harmful effects."
- "I wanted to go to dances badly. They said absolutely not. I'm glad for that today—I think."
- "I wanted to go to parties, swear, date guys, and be physical with boys."

High School Pressures

- "I was pressured to have sex, but I credit my folks for helping me stay pure."
- "I wanted to have sexual intercourse with girls. But I couldn't because of fear and my morality."

- "I remember refusing to smoke pot, but my friends made me feel guilty and left me out."
- "My parents responded well and kept control when I had boyfriends."
- "Drinking at parties was the biggest pressure, I believe. They never knew, but neither did they ever talk to me about it."
- "Drinking. My dad offered $1,000 upon high school graduation if we could abstain from all alcohol and tobacco."

About 40 percent of the children who made it into their adult years as close followers of Christ admitted they drank or took drugs on more than one occasion. That means 60 percent experimented only once or never tried the stuff. That's a good sign. Predictably, the kids who did try it more than once had parents who occasionally drank socially at home.

A friend of mine (Greg's) awhile back told me the story of what happened to him on his son's tenth birthday.

"We have a tradition in our home where the kid gets to choose the restaurant he wants to go to on his birthday. Jason picked a pizza place. We asked him why. 'Me and David can have fun drinking all the root beer we want, and you and Mom can have fun drinking all the beer you want,' he explained.

"Jason was ten years old, but he'd already made the association of alcohol with fun. We weren't drunks or even social drinkers, but we did like beer with our pizza. That's when my wife and I decided to abstain from all alcohol."

That decision to stop casual beer drinking speaks volumes about parental choices. Our children are watching—and learning. No matter how responsible we are, they'll hear about their buddies drinking or see ten zillion beach-and-beer commercials.

It seems wise not to even give a wink to something they could struggle with later on, then justify by thinking, *Mom and Dad always get a pitcher when they have pizza.*

Of course, there are exceptions, but it's been my experience that drinking is often the first negative behavior a teen succumbs to in his search for peer acceptance. (Stealing, smoking cigarettes, and vandalism are a few of the others.) For the junior high set, alcohol is usually combined with something else that seems "harmless."

For girls, their first sips of booze usually happen at slumber parties in homes with well-stocked wet bars. For me, it was in high school at "harmless" poker parties. Pop and chips got boring.

Left unchecked, teens can easily progress toward drugs and partying. In addition, alcohol drops a teen's inhibitions to sex.

This downward cycle has some variations. But the real message you should be aware of is that *the seeds of teens' finding their self-image needs met in their friends are germinated during the grade school years.*

As we said, there are no 100 percent guarantees, but parents should do all they can to break this cycle early. Present the clear choice that pursuing God offers many more benefits than following the crowd.

CHAPTER 13

WHAT'S OFF-LIMITS HERE?
Parents and Taboo Subjects

My (Mike's) mom was a young bride, and one day when I was two and my brother, Pry, was an infant, another mother rang our doorbell. Mom answered it with Pry in one arm and me wrapped around her right leg.

The neighbor looked at her, then turned her gaze at my brother and me. "Is your mother home?" she asked, thinking Mom was the baby-sitter.

I told you my mother was young! My brother and I were both born before she was twenty. Lots of times as I grew up, other children would impertinently ask Mom her age. "Oh, I'm sixty-two," she would reply when she wasn't a day over twenty-eight. Age wasn't something we talked about. For Mom's fortieth birthday, we weren't allowed to do a *thing*. No "over-the-hill" surprise parties, no black crepe paper, no friends to share the occasion. I think we watched a "Laugh-In" rerun that night.

Mom's gotten better about her age, but for years it was one of those subjects we had to tiptoe around. It's not as if she was alone. We're a nation with a lot of hang-ups, the pundits tell us, and most of the time we don't want to talk about it.

"Dad, what's sex?" the second-grader asks.

"I'm busy; ask me later," comes the reply from the La-Z-Boy.

"Mom, how much money does Dad make?" asks the junior high student.

"That's none of your business, and don't ask your dad or he'll blow his stack," replies the mom.

"Dad, do you ever pray?" asks the vulnerable high school student.

"My religion is personal, Son. It's tough for me to talk about it."

You get the idea. And kids will catch your drift: You're not up to a certain situation or discussion, so they steer clear of certain topics to keep you happy.

The generation of parents we talked to—and the kids they produced—lived by this rule. Important issues that should have been talked through in an open and honest way weren't. Instead, parents placated their children until the kids caught on to their strategy. By high school, teens *knew* which subjects to avoid in the home.

While most of the kids we interviewed didn't hold it against their parents, they also knew that their parents' unwillingness to address issues was a barrier to the relationship.

"In my home," one woman told us, "we *never* talked about sex. It touched too close to an issue. You see, they always lied about their anniversary because I was born four months after they really got married. When I was a teen, I once said, 'Mom, you're so funny about this subject, it's almost abnormal.' She came unglued and went upstairs after a mad, embarrassed yell."

Sex was a taboo subject in most homes. In fact, because sex was *by far* the hugest taboo, we're going to spend a lot of time talking about this "silent subject" in our next chapter.

For now, we want to talk briefly about two interrelated dangers inherent in most parental species:

- Allowing your kids to say things you want to hear (the Eddie Haskell Syndrome).
- Avoiding subjects you don't want to talk about.

Saying the Right Things

You can still find "Leave It to Beaver" in syndication. Recently, we watched an episode begin this way:

"Where are you two going tonight?" June Cleaver asked as Wally and his friend Eddie Haskell were walking out the door.

"Oh, thanks for asking, Mrs. Cleaver," Eddie said in his trademark sickly sweet tone. "Wallace and I are first heading to the library to do some studying. After two or three hours of hitting the books, trying to get our grades up even higher, we're going over to Clarence's house to watch his dad tie flies. We should be home well before nine o'clock. My family has church tomorrow, and I want to be wide awake."

Ward Cleaver rolled his eyes. June eked out a half-smile as the two teenagers headed toward Eddie's car.

"Gee, Mom, Dad, why does Eddie always say stuff you want to hear and never stuff that's true?" asked the Beaver.

The answer: Probably because Eddie's dad trained him to say things to keep the peace.

We don't have any way of proving this (Mr. Haskell was never on camera), but it seems that he mirrored an entire generation of parents *and* kids. It was almost as though our moms and dads made it their job to let certain things pass without notice; to let their teenagers say whatever was necessary to keep them at bay while they went out and did what they wanted.

These days, sitcom dads regularly play the village idiot. Confronting bad behavior and dealing with major moral issues isn't cool. What's cool is the teenage son getting away with everything.

Here's how today's parents train their kids to say what they want to hear: *Change the subject whenever your kids bring up an issue they're "too young to know about."*

Within the past year, my (Greg's) grade school boys have asked some tough questions. They heard on TV that Mike Tyson was sent to prison because he raped a beauty pageant contestant.

"Dad, what's rape?" asked Drew, a second-grader at the time.

A few months later, one of their favorite basketball players suddenly retired. "Magic Johnson quit the Lakers because he has the HIV virus," I explained.

"How did Magic get sick, Dad?" asked Troy, who was in fourth grade.

Whew, that's a toughie. Drew was seven and Troy was nine, and it would have been easy to say, "Ask me tomorrow"—hoping, of course, they would forget. But I didn't. I answered their questions in a way that was biologically accurate. I also used those uncomfortable teachable moments to talk about God's plan for a man and a woman, describing their mom and dad as examples of two people who waited until marriage for sex. (We'll tell them *later* about the close calls we had . . . unless they ask sooner, of course.)

Did the boys understand everything? Hardly. In fact, because of the number of questions I've received since then, I doubt they remembered a thing. But I've deliberately set a pattern in our relationship that no question is too tough for Dad to tackle, no matter how unpleasant. It gets pretty uncomfortable sometimes, and they don't always ask at convenient times, but my strategy is working. They're not holding back.

One mother mentioned that the subject of sex came up quite often with her three kids. When their oldest was around ten, she and her husband had a formal sex talk with him. "He felt good about asking questions," she says. "It was all news to him. But his reaction was, 'You mean you did *that* three times?'"

The goal, of course, isn't to gross out our kids with information they're not ready to handle. What we want to do is set a pattern of communication that will carry over to their teenage years. I want my boys to be able to say what one rare adult child told us about her mother and father: "I had smart parents. They never placated me. When I had something to say, I'd say it. I knew I could go to them with anything."

If we wait until our children are mature enough to understand every answer, we'll probably never hear them ask the questions. One parent I talked with had the best strategy. "I try to stay one step ahead of where they are," she said. "I don't wait until anything is old news. I want to be the first to address whatever issue is the topic of conversation with their friends."

Set the pattern early, and don't back down from *any* question. That doesn't mean that if your six-year-old son asks what "being gay" is, you launch into an anatomical discussion of what homosexual men do to each other. Instead, honestly answer his question *according to his maturity.* Then, when the subject comes up again, you can build on that foundation.

Selective Parenting

Another issue that emerged from our interviews was the notion that *Mom raises the daughters and Dad raises the boys.* And never the twain shall meet. Though it's usually never a stated assumption, one grown daughter told us her dad did have the gall to actually tell her that.

"Dad once told me he felt more responsible for my brother, and that Mom was responsible for my upbringing. Even back then I thought it was weird. I think it was rooted in some of his own feelings of guilt for not spending enough time with us."

Several female respondents mentioned that as soon as they hit puberty and started to "develop," their dads pretended they were no longer there. It was as if they were embarrassed their daughters were becoming women.

What a tragedy!

Instead of being their daughters' first date, letting them know how they should be treated and explaining how guys and gals are different, these fathers abdicated those precious moments because they felt uncomfortable.

If a daughter has the courage and openness to ask her dad personal questions about anatomy or boys, and the gruff response is "Go ask your mother," the girl has just been trained to stay superficial with him. Instead of a lifetime of warm and open communication with his little girl, he has settled for chit-chat about the weather, the grandkids, and where they're going on their next vacation. And it will never get deeper than that.

As we wade into the two toughest issues parents face with their kids—sex and dating—examine your own style. If you're not open and available for anything . . . CHANGE! The nineties are not the decade to avoid sensitive subjects. The stakes are too high.

CHAPTER 14

SEX (EDUCATION)
IN THE NINETIES
Parents and The Sex Talk

Imagine this conversation taking place not too far into the next century:

"Well, Joe," says Randy Carter as he hands his oldest son a soda, "seems like you and Bonnie are getting pretty serious."

"Now that you mention it, Dad," says Joe with a smile, "I've been thinking about some preengagement counseling for us."

"You two have talked about marriage?"

"Yeah, a couple of times. I really think I could spend the rest of my life with her. Now that I'm out of college and working a regular job, I feel I'm ready to make a lifetime commitment. I've dated quite a few girls, and from everything I've seen in Bonnie, I don't have to look any further."

"What does she think about that?"

"Well, she got a big smile on her face when I told her about the preengagement counseling idea. I think she's waiting for me to pop the question."

"Wow! Sounds like she might be the one."

"I sure hope so."

"That means you guys are probably ready to go to the doctor and get tested, right?"

"I haven't brought that up yet. You know how it is . . . How do you bring it up with a girl? I mean, we've had some close contact, but we're committed to staying virgins until marriage. Are you really sure it's necessary?"

"Son, this is 2005. Everyone gets tested."

"Yeah, I know. But I've known her for over two years."

"But you met her in college, Joe."

"Dad, she's grown up in a Christian family! I'm pretty sure she's never . . ."

"Pretty sure? If you really think she's the one, Joe, an HIV test isn't an option. Especially since you didn't know her in high school. I'm sure she's been an upright girl. She does seem committed to the Lord. But when it comes to your life, Son, I don't want you to take any chances. You've heard the statistics. Twenty-five percent of your graduating class is probably HIV-positive right now, and most of them will have full-blown AIDS by the time they're thirty. You've already attended the funerals of five classmates who died of AIDS. And the Harper boy from church has it now."

"You're right, Dad. Mark and Susie both got tested before they got engaged. I think I'll make an appointment with Dr. Weston, and when I get the results back, I'll show her the doctor's clearance. Then I'll suggest she go. I'll even offer to pay for it. I suppose neither of us can afford to have any doubts."

"Sounds like I raised a pretty smart son."

The Future Is Now

Will such a father-son talk ever happen? Not in the next few years, but certainly in the twenty-first century, when even Christian couples will have to take every precaution to insure they're not walking into a death trap when they walk down the aisle.

With three-dozen sexually transmitted diseases being passed around like party favors and the specter of AIDS hanging over every incidence of sexual intercourse, Christian couples aren't immune from catching a *bad* disease in the heat of passion. *But not my son or daughter,* you think. *They're good Christian kids.*

Actually, Christian teens are nearly as sexually active as their non-Christian counterparts. According to a major survey conducted by the Josh McDowell Ministries (of the "Why Wait?" campaign), 43 percent of churched youth had engaged in sexual intercourse by the time they were eighteen, and another 18 percent had fondled breasts or genitals. (By comparison, a Lou Harris poll several years ago found that 57 percent of the nation's seventeen-year-olds had had sexual intercourse.) And catch this: one-third of the youths said they were *not* able to state that sexual intercourse was morally unacceptable before marriage!

Yes, not everyone is "doing it," but by the time your children reach their senior year of high school, they will be in the minority if they're still virgins. That's why you need to talk about sex *long* before they start dating.

How will we—as part of this generation of parents—talk to our children about sex? The cliché is that most people parent as they were parented. If that's the case, we're in BIG TROUBLE! Nearly *80 percent* of the adult children we talked to received *little or no help* from their parents on the subject. In fact, we can confidently state that this is where yesterday's parents blew it. Want some anecdotal proof? Here's what passed for "sex education" in a few homes:

"When I was a senior in high school, I had been seeing one girl quite a bit. One night, before I walked out the door, my dad said, 'I want to talk to you for a minute, Phil. You know, when you're with a girl, sometimes things get warm, then they get warmer, then they even get a little warmer. You know what I mean?' I replied yes, and that was the extent of our sex talk!"

Here's another guy's story:

"In third grade, Dad sat me and my brother down for a talk. 'Well, boys, I guess you know there's a difference between boys and girls.' We said we noticed. Then he said, 'Well, . . . we'll talk about it later.' We're still waiting!"

And another:

"My mom sat down with me when I was in grade school and showed me a cartoon book. The next time she talked about sex was the night before my wedding! She wondered if I had any questions."

Okay, one more:

"My dad wrote me a letter (typed by his secretary) regarding the dangers of STDs when I was at summer school in Mexico City. I was seventeen at the time."

We could go on, but it gets worse. If you want to read a few more responses, turn to appendix 6.

Many of these stories would almost be funny . . . if they weren't so sad. Where were our parents' heads?

- Some were stuck back in the fifties, when you didn't *have* to talk about sex or it wasn't considered the nice thing to do.
- Many trusted their school districts to teach the biology and teachers to emphasize chastity. (Forget that these days.)
- Some followed the example of *their* parents—which means they didn't utter a word.
- A number felt they didn't have a platform to speak from since they weren't virgins when they married.

- Some were too embarrassed to talk about it. They quickly changed the subject when their kids brought it up.

While any of these "reasons" for keeping quiet on sex may have let *your* parents off the hook, if *you* fail to talk about sex and instill God's teachings, it may be the biggest regret you will ever have.

It's Not All Bad News

While many of the adult children expressed bitterness, even anger, at the way their parents left them in the dark (literally) when it came to the opposite sex, we did see *some* hopeful signs. A few parents did do the right thing with their children, and the results were predictable: The kids whose parents talked to them about the facts of life early and often were the ones who experimented sexually far less than those who learned it from sisters, brothers, neighborhood friends, or the old-fashioned American way—the gutter.

What were some of the ways they did it?

- "When I was ten, my mom and I were watching an episode of 'Little House on the Prairie' that dealt with rape. That's when the subject came up."
- "My parents, especially Mom, talked openly about sex from the time we were little. I could always ask questions."
- "At twelve, Mom discussed my body and the changes ahead. At fifteen, my dad talked to me about the differences between men and women and how they respond sexually to each other."
- "Before I was a teen, my father and I went on a camping trip, and we talked about sex. I later found out the trip was for that very purpose."

- "Whenever I asked sex-related questions of my mom, she tactfully covered them."
- "It all began at six years old and continued at approximately every year and a half until I was seventeen."
- "My dad talked to me in tenth grade. He said, 'Marie, make sure that a kiss always stays special. As soon as it isn't special anymore, you've gone too far.' I had no idea what he meant. But I remembered his words. One time, I knew that I'd gone a little too far because kissing my boyfriend wasn't all that special anymore."

My (Greg's) first attempt at talking about sex with my two boys occurred when it was over 100 degrees on a smoggy Saturday afternoon at our southern California home. We had the kiddie pool filled, and I was cooling off with my two boys, who were seven and five at the time. Out of nowhere, my oldest, Troy, said, "Dad, how do you do sex?"

After losing my balance and nearly drowning in a foot of water, I quickly regained my composure. I needed to stall for time, so I asked Troy, "Do you really want to know?" I was secretly hoping he'd say no. But both chimed in, "Yeah."

With a smile on my face, I started talking about how good a gift sex is, and how God has reserved it for marriage. Then I briefly went through the biology of it, using anatomical terms. I explained sex's dual purpose of pleasure and having children, and closed by asking if they had any questions.

After hearing a chorus of "yuckies!" I got their attention one more time. "Guys, I want you to know that whenever you hear something on the playground or have a question you want answered, you can feel free to ask Mommy or me anything. No question is too dumb. I want you to always feel you can talk about this stuff. Okay?"

///

The Top Ten Reasons Not to Give Your Children a Formal Sex Talk

10. You're not too sure what the right answers are yourself.

9. They would sense your anxiety about the subject, and it would probably give them some deep-seated hang-ups.

8. They probably know more about the subject than you do.

7. Your spouse already took care of it.

6. They've already heard the TV sitcom dads give "The Talk" a few dozen times, and you can't think of anything else to add.

5. Perhaps they haven't thought about s-e-x yet, and as they say down on the farm, "If it ain't broke, don't fix it."

4. It would only encourage them.

3. They might ask if you and your spouse still do that.

2. The story about the stork still works for you.

1. They will never be old enough.

///

That incident happened almost four years ago at the time of this writing, and since then we've had a dozen follow-up conversations. Sometimes they initiate the discussion, and sometimes I do. But usually after every "episode," I end with an open invitation to ask me more. I want them to know there are no taboo subjects in our home.

When the Opposite Sex Is on Their Minds

In my work on *Breakaway* magazine, I've read hundreds of letters from teens and preteens asking questions about the opposite sex. These are questions they really should be asking their parents, but for one reason or another, they can't or won't. In the magazine, we try to be appropriately frank about the subject, but we can only go so far. Parents who can relate all the physiological information *and* scriptural truth will build security and morality in their children far better than a magazine editor.

Those are twin goals every parent should strive to reach. If we allow schools, friends, books, magazines, or videos to usurp our parental role, we can't be sure our values and opinions on the subject of sex are registering. We *must* take the lead, which means bringing up the topic *before* they ask. Why? Because they usually *won't*. An opening line like, "Do you have any questions about sex?" may seem to suggest you're doing your job, but most children, especially older ones, will always answer no. Your next response should be, "Well, let's talk about it for a little bit."

Here's a game plan you can follow as the kids grow up. The first three points are things to start talking to your grade-schoolers about. Then, as your kids get into junior high and high school, continue working your way through the list. Of course, each child will have different questions at different ages, so be sensitive to their particular maturity level. But don't put it off! The earlier you can start talking with your kids about these issues, the easier and more successful it will be.

The Physical Differences between Boys and Girls

Before they reach puberty, your children should have a good understanding of the physical differences between boys and girls. They don't have to know *everything*, and you can expect them to be too embarrassed to ask for more details. For smaller children, a picture book comes in handy.

Why God Made Men and Women Different

If you can get across the idea of the "wonder" of it all, how creative God is, you're laying a great foundation. You should emphasize that sex was God's idea.

The Facts about Intercourse

After you've talked about the physical differences and how sex is part of God's plan for families, you may think your children don't need to know about *this*, too. But they're going to hear about it somewhere, so it's better if an explanation comes from you. This is an excellent time to reinforce the fact that God has told us to save sex for marriage.

The Emotional Differences between a Man and a Woman

It's a good idea to have the father explain to the daughter how a man's mind works, and for the mom to explain to the son how a woman's works (since the father couldn't explain that one anyway!). This should be done just after the children have started noticing that the opposite sex doesn't have "cooties."

One woman recounted how that very thing happened to her.

"My dad told me that boys are more visually activated sexually and that looking at a girl turns on their motors. He also said that women are driven more by touch and emotions. I'll never forget the afternoon he took the time to tell me that."

Building Friendships with the Opposite Sex

An often-asked question at *Breakaway* is, "How do I start and keep a conversation going with a girl?" Dads, teach your sons how to talk to girls! If they know how to develop friendships with the opposite sex, they won't have to "resort" to physical contact when the conversation slows to a standstill.

Physical contact builds a false bond of attachment. Kids are so experiential that they'll start equating sex and love. If you've been married for a while, you know there's a BIG difference.

As adults, we've learned that the key to any relationship is communication, right? An important skill moms and dads can teach their children is how to talk to the opposite sex. Show them how to ask questions to discover a person's values and interests. And emphasize (to a fault) that the purpose of dating in the teen years is to learn how to be friends with each other—not to form mini-marriages.

What Real Love Is

Emotional attachment to the opposite sex shouldn't be swept under the carpet, even though kids can't be expected to know what "real love" is in their early teen years. But adolescents do know they long for certain boys or certain girls more than others in school. Those feelings shouldn't be laughed at. "Puppy love" is the first step to real love—and it can be healthy. Their struggles shouldn't be downplayed. Instead, use them as further opportunities to build your relationship with your children.

You can start by explaining the difference between "emotional love" and "committed love." Relate your own experiences, but never be condescending about theirs. Talk about the benefits— and the downside. Don't say, "I had a crush on a girl when I was your age, but I grew out of it in no time." Instead, be a listener when your kids confide in you. It's at this point in their lives that they need someone mature—and trustworthy—with whom they can talk.

What you want is for them to come to you when the big questions arise as they enter new situations. Remember, they're just beginning to travel these relationship roads.

Having a "Key Talk"

One of the biggest responses we ever had to a *Focus on the Family* magazine article occurred several years ago when we published "A Promise with a Ring to It." It was the story of Richard and Renee Durfield, who came up with the idea of having a private, personal, and intimate time with each child to explain the biblical view of marriage and the sacredness of sexual purity.

This is done between father and son or mother and daughter (same sex is preferable but not mandatory) at a nice restaurant, as befits a special occasion. When Richard Durfield took his son Jonathan for his "key talk," they dressed to the nines and went to one of the best restaurants in their town.

Shortly after they were seated, Richard told his son that no question was out of bounds and that if he had been thinking about one of those awkward questions about sex, well, this was the night to ask it.

In such a setting, you can imagine the special father-son communication that ensued. Richard capped off the evening by asking his son to make a covenant before God to remain pure until marriage. Then he presented him with a specially made gold ring to symbolize that commitment.

"You wear that ring until you're married," explained his father, "and then on your wedding night, you take the ring off and present it to your new spouse—that night when a life of sexual experience begins."

What a wonderful idea! Apparently, the *Focus on the Family* readers felt the same way, and more than twenty thousand parents wrote in requesting more information about the Durfield's "key ring" brochure. They later elaborated on the idea in their book, *Raising Them Chaste.*

What's Expected When You "Go with" Someone

Each household needs to have its own rules in this area. If you're going to be a hard-liner, please have some good arguments mapped out and ready. "Because I said so" won't cut it. When your children are in fifth or sixth grade—before they're actually interested in pairing off with someone—a good statement might be something like: "Do you know how some kids hold hands and spend time with the opposite sex? Well, we'd really prefer that you wait on that until we talk about it beforehand. We know it might be tough to talk about it when the time comes, but we'd like to help you think through everything before you dive in. Okay?"

At *Breakaway*, this is the number-one question: "I'm trying to get Mary to go with me. How do I do it?" Kids are going together as early as fifth grade! Don't deny it exists. While most young teens aren't allowed to date in junior high, some will still want to "go together." When that issue arises, ask them why. When they reply, "Because I like her," recall some of your own memories. Tell them you understand how it's the popular thing to do, but you'd rather that they slow down the guy/girl thing until high school, when they will be more mature. Don't expect these discussions to go very smoothly. Give them a day or two to think about it.

As teens get older, you won't be able to do much about long-term relationships. As you talk about the challenge of keeping standards high, remind them that you're praying for them often. You don't want to quench your relationship with them—or their natural tendency to spend time with the opposite sex. But you *do* want to make sure your sons and daughters are ready to treat the opposite sex with respect.

What Pornography and Masturbation Are

When a boy's hormones start to kick in, Dad and son need to have a *long* talk. Fathers should build three things into their sons: (1) respect toward women; (2) respect for themselves; and (3) having a thought life free of guilt.

Talking about masturbation—and the role porn plays—will earn your son's respect for tackling the *tough* subjects. Describe how the world has completely corrupted sex into merely a physical act of pleasure. While these subjects will be the toughest to address for dads—mainly because of their own lack of success—personal failure shouldn't keep you from bringing it up. You need to be careful in divulging too much about the past, however, in order to maintain your son's respect for you. This is a subject you can speak about in generalities, and one that can be a tool to keep the lines of communication open.

A young man told us this story, which happened when he was in his twenties and engaged to be married: "I was living in Los Angeles when an old girlfriend called me out of the blue. We met at the Disneyland Hotel for a friendly lunch, and we had a fun time. I was a Christian and committed to my soon-to-be wife, but thoughts of pursuing something I shouldn't crept in. I asked Dad, 'Did you ever look at another woman?' He said, 'Son, when you're engaged, there are no other women.' That's all he said.

"My dad was the type who loved to tell stories about his victories in World War II, but he couldn't talk to me when I needed a man-to-man discussion. When he was quiet on a subject like this, or others like pornography or masturbation, I now know it was because he wasn't successful. What would have cemented our relationship for life would have been if he just would have told me of the few times he wasn't perfect. I would have loved him all the more because I wasn't perfect and needed someone who'd struggled with the issues I'd been struggling with."

We highly recommend Dr. Dobson's book and tape series *Preparing for Adolescence*, because he tackles this subject forthrightly.

For the women reading this, we don't have a clue how you should talk with your daughters about masturbation. We didn't have the courage to broach the subject with the moms we interviewed. (We were too embarrassed.) Can you talk to someone you respect about how she handled this ticklish subject?

How to Respond When Someone Is Getting Sexually Aggressive

You're probably aware of the dangers of daughters dating older boys, boys they don't know very well, or boys who aren't Christians. It's best to rehearse these situations before they come up. Older boys can "hit on" vulnerable girls, using age and experience to get what they want. Boys your daughters don't know well can turn into Mr. Hyde in a parked car. Non-Christian boys may think premarital sex is okay, as long as they "love each other."

On the flip side, if your son is dating a non-Christian girl (or even a churchgoing one), *she* may come on to him. Here's one story we heard:

"I went out with one girl one time," he said, "and all of a sudden she stripped down and said, 'Let's do it.' I said, 'Sorry, you've got the wrong guy.' I kinda think she did that to test my faith. Everyone in the school knew I was a Christian and didn't fool around. I really believe that if my dad hadn't taken me on hikes to talk to me about sex, making sure I knew what I needed to know, it would have been easier to give in."

Sheesh, that incident happened in the early seventies!

Now that feminism has put the sexes on a more-equal footing, some girls aren't waiting for the guys to take the sexual lead. You should role-play potential situations with your children. For instance:

- You're parked in a car, watching the city lights, and Roy reaches over and begins kissing you. He puts his hand on your breast. What should you do?
- Billy announces a change in plans. Instead of going to the movies, he tells you about a great party at a friend's house. "His parents are gone for the weekend," he says. What should you do?
- You go to the lake with your girlfriend, and it's pretty secluded. She takes her top off, saying she wants to get a good tan. What should you do?
- You're kissing your boyfriend when he takes your hand and starts to guide it where it shouldn't go. What should you do?

Giving your teens advice *before* these tests happen will increase the chances that they'll pass with flying colors.

The Purpose and Dangers of Petting

From an early age, where their hands can go should be discussed. A good rule we heard is that kids' hands shouldn't touch "anything a swimsuit can cover." While many said they didn't stick by this rule—dozens admitted having "done everything but . . ."—it should be the standard.

"I was heavily into dating by seventh grade," an Indiana man told us. "I don't think my parents knew the dangers. My mom once told me petting was okay, but I think it was because that's what she did. I kept up an unhealthy pace physically, and I was lucky to be a virgin by marriage."

Most of us can remember starting the engines too often and too early. One Louisiana man told us something that's not often discussed.

"Since we were both Christians," he said, "we were committed to being virgins until marriage. But during courtship and engagement, we had trained our bodies, especially my wife's, to get to a certain point, then stop. After two years of this, marriage made everything legal and okay in God's sight, but our minds had been programmed to get to a certain point, then stop. Instead of enjoying the fun of clumsiness for a while, we struggled for three years to retrain our bodies that it was okay to finish what we started."

That's the type of story we hope he tells his kids. Our bodies just aren't meant to start and stop, since sex is progressive. Once the train starts rolling down the hill, it's hard to put the brakes on.

//

What Schools Are Teaching

Nearly all fifteen thousand public junior high and high schools in the country have a sex education curriculum, but few teach the concept of abstinence.

What some sex education teachers are pushing these days is the concept of "outercourse." It's an extremely explicit method of teaching students how to have sex without penetration. Techniques about mutual masturbation and oral sex are taught, along with how to use sex toys.

School districts have also authorized teachers to:

- use films that show actual intercourse
- teach how "healthy" it is to have sexual fantasies

- allow homosexuals to speak to classes about their sexual orientation
- show, in detail, how condoms and other forms of birth control are used
  Underneath all this sex education is this message: It's up to the individual to determine if he or she is mature enough to enter into a sexual relationship. If your children are in a sex ed class this year, we strongly urge you to read the curriculum beforehand. You may decide that this is one subject in which you will want to home-school your children.

//

There Ain't No Such Thing as "Safe Sex"

You will need to convince your teens that condoms don't work very well, nor do they make sex emotionally safe. According to a study published in the *Family Planning Perspectives*, condoms failed an average of 15 percent of the time during twelve months of use among unmarried, sexually active young people. The HIV virus is one-tenth of a micron wide, but the holes in condoms are five microns wide. Put another way, HIV is *450 times* smaller than sperm.

Dr. Malcolm Potts, one of the inventors of the modern-day condom and president of Family Health International, says that telling a person who engages in high-risk behavior to use a condom is like telling someone who is driving drunk to use a seat belt.

A Los Angeles mom who works as a registered nurse would come home from work and talk to her two daughters about what went on at the doctors' offices. "I would explain the effects of bad choices," she said. "I would tell them about the fourteen-year-old girl who came into the office after being involved with a boy, and look what happened. She has this, and she has that, and now she must deal with the consequences of her actions. I don't make it sound scary, but just show the fallacy of her choice. They heard this in junior high. Talking to kids about sex in the pre-junior high years is not too soon in this day and age."

//

A Few Facts on Teenage Sex

- According to the Centers for Disease Control, one in four teens will contract a venereal disease before finishing high school. Teens are currently contracting 2.5 million cases a year.
- Today in the U.S., AIDS is the seventh-leading cause of death among those aged fifteen to twenty-four. An estimated 21 percent of all AIDS patients contracted the disease as teenagers.
- Adams City High School in Commerce City, Colorado, was one of the nation's first schools to begin distributing condoms to students. After three years, the birth rate among students was 31 percent higher than the national average.

//

What to Expect in Marriage

Most guys think marriage is spending every spare moment in bed with a willing and passionate mate. You'd better burst that balloon early. And please, give them realistic expectations about what happens on the honeymoon (assuming they're virgins, of course). You don't need to explain everything, but a few pointers might make their first nights better than yours. Don't be embarrassed, and don't wait until they ask. They may think they know more than you do, but they probably don't.

God's Heart when It Comes to Sex

Throughout all your children's growing-up years, remind them often of God's views on sex:

- First of all, God is for it! He created sex, it was his idea, and he did a nice job arranging things in the right places. All for our maximum enjoyment, we might add.
- Second, God made sex a powerful drive—but not an uncontrollable need. Explain the difference between satisfying a need (such as eating, drinking, and breathing) and channeling a drive (such as sex). Sex must take place in marriage to be experienced the way God intended—without regret or fear. That means our most-important sex organ is the mind. God wants us to develop self-control, and he wants us to do that before marriage—not during. (Tell them learning self-control *in* marriage is not too fun!)
- Third, abstinence until marriage is God's best. Anything less is less.
- Fourth, he understands our sinful nature, and he will forgive anything if we repent. If your children confess that they've blown it and gone "all the way," pray with them, and after they repent, tell them about the concept of "secondary virginity."

As Richard Durfield explained in his *Focus* magazine article, teens who have fallen short can become virgins again in the sight of God. Once they're forgiven, it is as if they never sinned. Isaiah 43:25 says, "I, even I, am he who blots out your transgressions, for my own sake, and remembers your sins no more."

Also, this would be a good time to let them know *you'll* forgive anything, too!

God needs to be presented as the Good Guy throughout all these discussions. He not only created this wonderful gift, but he's also told us when we can open it. Even better, he still loves us if we mess up and open his present early.

CHAPTER 15

JUST LIKE ROMEO AND JULIET
Parents and Guy/Girl Relationships

Richard Harris is nearing sixty, the season of life when he can downshift to a lower gear. One of the joys for this southern California grandfather is watching his grandchildren grow up—and quietly grinning while he watches *his* adult children gingerly tiptoe through the mine fields of child-raising.

"It is nice to have the grandkids for a few hours and say, 'Here, take them home!'" said Richard. "But it won't be too long before those kids will start going out. My son Mike said his daughter isn't going to start dating until she's twenty-five!"

That story draws a rueful shake of the head from Richard. Fifteen years ago, he locked horns over the dating issue with his oldest daughter, Sandra, a high school senior at the time. He's still not sure if he handled the ugly confrontation very well.

It all began when he grounded her for missing curfew. The following Saturday evening, the doorbell rang. Richard opened the front door and saw a gangly sixteen-year-old boy standing before him, shuffling his feet. He mumbled something about taking Sandra to a party.

"Gee, didn't Sandra tell you? She's on restriction," Richard said, sketching in a few details for the lad. Then, while he was in midsentence, Sandra busted right past her dad and told her date, "Come on, we're leaving."

Richard stood there, jaw on his chest, and watched the couple jump into the car and peel rubber down the street. His daughter's direct disobedience crushed him. A younger son, Gary, witnessed the confrontation.

"Dad, I can't believe you let her leave," he said. "Why didn't you lay down the law?"

"What do you want me to do?" pleaded Richard. "Do you want me to kick her out of the house and ruin our relationship? She knows we don't approve of her behavior."

Richard faced a tough call that evening, but today's parents know the stakes are even higher. Even if you're fairly certain you're raising good, solid Christian kids, those offspring are growing up in a culture that says, "Teens are going to do it anyway" and "Party hearty, dude."

Before we go much further, let's look back at this teen dating phenomenon. A hundred years ago, a young man and a young woman "courted" under a social system tightly managed by their parents. Things began to loosen up—some would say unravel—in the twentieth century, especially as teenagers discovered the automobile. Today's adolescents live in a society where the social mores of teen dating have changed *a lot* since you were dating in the sixties, seventies, or eighties. Here's an example:

Scene: *Early evening, circa 1971. All Frankie has been thinking about the last hour is whether he should ask Lisa out next weekend. He sits next to her in trigonometry, and they often leave class together and walk to her locker. Finally, he dials her number.*

Frankie: Hello, Mr. Robinson? This is Frankie Rys. May I please speak with Lisa?

Father: Sure, Frank. Let me get her. I think she's finished with her homework.

Lisa: Hello?

Frankie: Hello, Lisa? Hi, it's Frankie. How are you doing?

Lisa: Fine. Wasn't that trig homework tough? Did you get yours done?

Frankie: Yeah, I did. But I had to ask my dad for some help.

They make small talk for ten minutes, and then Frankie makes his move.

Frankie: Umm, Lisa, I was wondering if you're doing anything Saturday night.

Lisa: This Saturday night?

Frankie: Yeah, this Saturday.

Lisa: I don't think I'm doing anything.

Frankie: Well, I was wondering if you would like to go to the movies with me. We could go see "Love Story." I hear it's a really good movie.

Lisa: Sure, but let me ask my parents if I can go.

A few moments pass.

Lisa: My parents said it's okay.

Frankie: Good. The show starts at 7:30. Shall I pick you up at 7:15?

Lisa: Better make it fifteen minutes earlier. My father, you know, always likes to meet whoever's taking me out. I have to be back by ten o'clock. You know how parents are.

Frankie: Yeah, I do. I've got two of them myself. Well, I'll see you in math class tomorrow.

Lisa: Bye, Frankie.

Now contrast that with this conversation from today:

Scene: *Toby's bedroom, 10:30 p.m. on a weekday night. Toby is listening to his favorite heavy-metal group, Slayer, on his CD player. It's a bummer that he can't turn up the volume the way he does after school. That's when he has the house all to himself (except when his bratty brother isn't over at J.J.'s place). His mom and stepdad are never home anyway. They're always working. The only thing they seem to care about is how loud he plays his music.*

Toby's telephone rings. His parents got him his own line last summer after he monopolized the family phone during his junior year. He picks up the receiver.

Toby: Talk to me.

Voice: Hiiiii . . .

Toby: Who's this?

Voice: Chantel. Remember me? We met at that kegger at Palmer Park last Saturday.

Toby searches his memory bank. His recollection of that night is pretty foggy.

Toby: Ah, ah, yeah, sure I remember you. You were wearing black leather that night.

Did he guess right?

Chantel: My, you have a good memory. You were looking pretty hot yourself.

Toby: Well, ah . . .

Chantel: There's another big party Friday night. It's over at Gina's house. It's such a cool place. Her mom is away on business for the weekend, and nobody's going to be home. It should be really rad.

Toby: What time does it start?

Chantel: I don't think much will happen before eleven. Are you going to come?

Toby: Sure, why not?

Chantel: Good, and I'm going to be looking for you, Toby.
    You know, I've had the hots for you since last weekend.

Toby: Really? I barely . . .

Chantel: All my friends think you're really cute, and so do I.

Really cute.

Toby: Ah . . . well . . .

Chantel: I hope you're going to come prepared Friday night.

Toby: Prepared?

Chantel: You know. Gina's house has a lot of bedrooms.
    Maybe you better bring some of those you-know-whats.

Toby: What . . . ?

Chantel: You know what I'm talking about. Those little
    packages you can get from the school health clinic.

Toby: Oh, *those.*

Chantel: I knew you were a bright guy, Toby. See you at the
    party Friday.

Toby: Yeah, sure.

What was her name again?

Girls Are More Aggressive

In some parts of the country, that's what we're up against, folks.
And it's not just non-churchgoing families who are facing it. The
"rules of engagement" between the sexes have changed big-time
since we were prowling the high school halls. These days, girls
call guys on the telephone—and leave risqué messages on the
family's answering machine. Guys don't bother picking up their
dates; they meet them at the party—if they don't change their
minds at the last minute and go somewhere else.

But there is hope. If you treat dating like any other aspect of
child-rearing (in other words, give your children early training
and emphasize what type of behavior is expected), chances are

greatly enhanced that the "dating scene" will be a positive experience for you and your teens.

An Indiana mother of two daughters made sure her children understood what was expected of them. "They knew that they had to be home at a reasonable hour, and that they were expected to act appropriately."

///

What If Your Teen Doesn't Date?

We talked to plenty of adult children who said they never dated in high school. "I cried; it was hard sometimes," said Wendy, who was given permission to start dating at sixteen. Just one problem: The phone never rang. "Maybe I scared them off," she said. "I have a wonderful husband now, but at one point I thought I would never go out."

Wendy's parents handled the situation well. All along, her mother assured her that the right guy would come along. She told her that guys just didn't appreciate her good qualities yet. Mom was correct: When Wendy went off to college, her social life improved dramatically. It's certainly all right for kids to be late-blooming daters.

One father told us he agonized over the senior prom. "Like it or not, the prom is such a status symbol. I had to sweat it out—whether my daughters would be asked to go. They both were, but I would have bribed someone if I had to. The way kids are, if you weren't going to the prom, you were nothing." What should you do if your child doesn't get the bid? Make it a fun getaway weekend for the family. Leave town. That way your sons or daughters will have their *own* memories of a special occasion, even if it wasn't at the prom.

///

A Florida father said he and his wife took pains to explain what dating was to their four daughters. "They heard us tell them that dating was to create friendships," said Raymond, "and we encouraged them to have their friends over at our home. We wanted to know what was going on. We allowed them to go to school functions, but they couldn't stay out past midnight unless it was a special event."

Kim Spring said she'll never forget going on a country drive with her father when she was around fifteen. He pulled off the road and said he wanted to talk to her about dating. "Kim, you'll be dating soon, and you should know that boys are more activated sexually by looking at women, and that women are driven more by touch and emotions," said her father.

"My dad didn't talk a lot, but he really impressed me that afternoon," remembers Kim.

Patty Culver also emphasized to her six children that boys work from a physical aspect and girls from feelings during the dating years. In addition, she wasn't afraid to tell her children that she and her husband started going out with each other at age fifteen. Although they started dating early, their relationship led to a happy marriage. But they quickly point out that young dating couples should be careful, especially as they get older, since every dating experience could bring them closer to finding a mate for marriage.

It also helps if teens know *beforehand* when they will be allowed to start group dating, double dating, or one-on-one dating.

Sandy Black told her two daughters and one son that they had to be fifteen before they could go out on group dates (like meeting friends at the pizza parlor). "We also told them they had to wait until they were sixteen before they single dated," she added. "We didn't compromise on that. Our youngest daughter, Eileen, wanted to date earlier. She wasn't the kind to have a knock-down, drag-out fight about our stand, but she really enjoyed the boys. She had her eye on a couple of them, and those in her peer group were already dating."

Age or Maturity?

At *Breakaway*, I (Greg) am constantly put in the middle between teens and their parents. I get letters like this every week:

"My dad says I can't start dating until I'm sixteen. I don't think that's fair. My friends are going out with girls right now. What should I say to my dad to change his mind?"

Yeah, right. Like it's a good idea for me to step on that land-mine in front of ninety thousand guys—and their parents!

Seriously, though, my advice to young guys is this: "Your parents know you best. They'll decide when you're ready." (*Whew!* I dodged another potential explosion.)

What's going to be the determiner for you? If you set an arbitrary number like age sixteen, you might be headed for trouble when they hit the magic age and have the maturity of a thirteen-year-old. What if they're mature and responsible at fifteen? Now what? Do you stick by your rule for the sake of the rule, or do you make adjustments based on good performance?

Each family has to set its own standard, but it's always smart to hedge your bet. Whenever your kids bring up the subject, be a little vague. "When I see that you are responsible here at home with your homework, chores, and curfew, I'll know you're ready to treat the opposite sex the right way."

Don't form a strategy based on what *your* parents did. Develop your own game plan based on each child's maturity level. That way, you'll help your kids learn that dating is a privilege, not a right.

We feel comfortable, however, with this advice from a Chi-cago-area mom: "We felt it was best for our daughter to wait until her sixteenth birthday. We explained our reasons for this: her ability to drive; her ability to choose a good date; and, of course, her ability to handle any sexual advances that might come her way. She really needed maturity before stepping into that arena."

Popular speaker Jay Carty once told the following wonderful story at a Focus on the Family chapel. (He later included it in his book *Counterattack*, as well.)

"Nobody," said Jay, "can be trusted when it comes to sexual temptation. That's why God tells us to *flee* those situations. Knowing that, many high school girls—when attempting to get their way with their parents during the dating years—will often resort to the time-honored plea, 'But you don't *trust* me!'

"Guys are more defiant," continued Jay. "They'll stand in front of their fathers and say, 'Hey, Dad, why don't you trust me? Huh? Huh?'"

This is how Jay summed it up: "When it comes to sex, I want my kids to know something absolutely for certain, for sure: I DON'T TRUST 'EM! I don't trust them because they *can't* be trusted. And neither can you. That means there should always be a few precautions taken to protect relationships from sexual compromise."

Sandra Aldrich, who is senior editor of *Focus on the Family* magazine, is a single mom who makes it a point to meet each of the young men taking out her daughter, Holly. At the close of her little *tête-à-tête* with each boy, she lets this thought sink in real deep:

"I know you two are just going out as friends, but I've lived long enough to know how quickly situations can change. So remember this: Treat Holly the way *you hope some other guy is treating your future wife tonight.*"

Zing!

From the Child's Side

We also talked to plenty of adult children who said their parents didn't want to face the teen dating issue head-on—

just like sex education or premarital sex. "Did my parents give me instructions on how to date growing up?" said Martin, a thirty-five-year-old man. "I would say no. I think they let me go with the flow."

This *laissez-faire* attitude was also found in the Laytons' home in Rhode Island. Bill Layton was *sure* his dad never taught him anything about dating. "Nor did I have that type of a relationship with my mom, a relationship where I could approach her with questions. Actually, anything I learned about dating was through the church."

Ah, the church. That can be fine, but parents, *they need to hear it from you first.* Anything the youth pastor says about dating should *augment* your guidelines, not be the first and last word.

When your son or daughter has discovered the opposite sex (Don't worry, you'll know when that is. They won't spend a half hour in front of the mirror to impress *you!*), start talking about the guy/girl issues you really believe in. Here's a short list of things to discuss:

For Guys

(1) *R-e-s-p-e-c-t.* Pull out your old Aretha Franklin record if you have to, but drill this point home. Between sitcoms, billboards, pornography, popular music, and friends, guys are learning one message: Girls are out there for your pleasure, so go for the gusto.

Dads, you can't sit idly by while their minds are warped by this philosophy. Sure, you want your sons to like girls and get to know them, but they need to see how a mature man treats them. Start early by setting the example at every opportunity. Open car doors for your wife. Don't turn your head (or your eyes) when you see a pretty woman in a low-cut blouse walking through the mall. Act as though your wife is your date every time you go out with the kids to a restaurant. Hold a chair out for her. Take the coat off her shoulders. Show boys the importance of treating girls like the unique and special creation they are.

(2) *The art of conversation.* One reason guys and girls start wrestling and "exploring" on dates is that they run out of things to talk about. Teach them how to ask questions and carry on a conversation—friendship skills that will last a lifetime. And it's not a bad idea to teach a guy how to use a phone, either. The idea is to encourage confidence in starting a friendship. Confidence builds security, security builds strong values, and strong values build morality.

(3) *Dating basics.* When I (Greg) was sixteen, my dad took me to a nice restaurant. After we were shown to our table, he wanted to introduce me to the waitress, whom he knew. "You should stand up when meeting a woman," my dad said. I'll never forget how grown-up I felt (and a little funny). Dad added that making eye contact was important. Afterward, he showed me the difference between shaking a man's hand and shaking a woman's, how to open car doors, and how to pay for the bill and add a tip. As best he could, he taught me how a man behaves while out in public. Do you think guys will learn how to treat girls right by watching "Beverly Hills 90210"? Nope, Dad, they need to hear from you.

While a father can tell his sons how to behave and show respect toward a woman, we know some moms who are taking the opportunity to be their sons' first date. Moms can often tell guys what the "other side" is thinking as they go through the basics. They can also relate funny stories of all the mistakes Dad made when they were courting! Besides explaining what girls like, moms can reinforce the idea that females need to be respected.

//

The Top Ten Worst Excuses for Missing Curfew

10. "My friends and I were discussing who had the best parents, and I, of course, had to stay and tell them how my mother and father are so patient and understanding." [This is commonly referred to as the "Eddie Haskell Defense."]
9. "The football game went into extra innings."
8. "What curfew? You never told me what time I had to be home by."
7. "All my friends get to stay out as late as they want."
6. "Uh . . . now I remember. We ran out of gas."
5. "Rats, my watch must have stopped."
4. "You wouldn't believe how slow the service was tonight at Taco Bell."
3. "It was dark. I couldn't read my watch."
2. "I was here by curfew, but then I went back outside."
1. "How was I to know that you'd still be awake?"

//

For Girls

(1) *Where a girl's worth comes from.* Nobody has to remind a grown woman about the unrealistic expectations that magazines and movies can give a girl. But you *do* need to point out to your daughters how devastating those ideas of what constitutes glamour can be—early *and* often. Yes, appearance is important, and it's a good idea to help them learn proper beauty or skin care. But there needs to be a balance between inner and outer beauty. Moms, that's your job.

Dads, don't be afraid of the emerging woman in your daughter. Learn what it takes to make her feel special. If she doesn't receive love from you, she'll go looking for love in all the wrong places.

(2) *The boyfriend trap.* Sad but true: Most adolescent relationships serve only to increase a teen's popularity. And if Sally Soshe is popular, she'll feel better about herself, right? Wrong! That's a false sense of security at best. Teach young girls to value themselves for the person God made them to be. Talk through the pressures of pairing up. Help them discover the real reason they want boyfriends. If their motives are to find guys they like to hang around with, great. But if they're looking to impress a pack of girlfriends or get more popular boyfriends, they're treading in dangerous waters.

Not only will some girls "throw" themselves at boys, but they'll also do whatever it takes to keep them. Build security into your daughters so they don't have to search for it in immature fellows.

(3) *Older boys.* Since girls have about a two-year head start up the puberty scale, they're sometimes not attracted to immature boys their own age. Some of the older guys smell this, and they aren't shy about pursuing younger girls. We hate to say, "Never trust an older guy," but in this case, we will.

(4) *Educate daughters on what "activates" a boy.* The way a young woman dresses and flirts—especially on a date—will send a subtle message to a guy looking for any signal of availability. Yes, even Christian guys! Moms and dads both need to teach their daughters what turns the crank.

We recommend that dear ol' Dad be his daughter's first date around age fourteen or fifteen. While you munch on mushroom burgers at Denny's, you can casually talk about what signals *not* to give if she wants a good, fun date.

//

What the Survey Said

We asked parents several questions about dating. Here are the results:

- At what age did your child start group dating? Between thirteen and fourteen.
- Were the kids chaperoned on dates? Not many answered this question, but those who did said they chaperoned their kids until they were fifteen or sixteen. You should know that chaperoned dating isn't very cool these days. It's all but extinct in the 1990s.
- When were the kids allowed to date on their own? Sweet Sixteen was the magic age—coinciding with the time they could get their driver's license. But a small percentage said they didn't start dating until college.

//

A Sore Point

Now, a *mega-huge* question: Should you allow your children to date non-Christians?

The fear, of course, is that they may end up unequally yoked with unbelievers (2 Corinthians 6:14). We interpret *yoked* to mean "joined" or "having close fellowship with."

Does one date qualify? Probably not. How about two or three? It's easy to see the dangers, isn't it? Dating means learning how to build a close friendship with the opposite sex. Close friendships can lead to romantic involvements. And we all know where that can lead.

Marriage to an unbelieving spouse usually does one of two things: (1) causes the believing spouse to put his faith on hold or drop it altogether, or (2) makes for a "challenging" marriage, where one spouse (usually the wife) winds up as the spiritual leader. Then you have a home out of order . . . and all sorts of problems.

That's why parents need to *discuss* their ground rules *before* dating begins. Most kids don't have the maturity to see that one date can capture a heart fairly quickly (especially if they're dating to become more popular).

We can hear it now: "It's just one date, Dad. Why do you have to be so old-fashioned?" Then your relationship becomes strained. It happens all the time in Christian homes. It could happen in yours.

In the year or two before they start dating, casually describe the value of a Christian marriage. And before that fellow knocks on the door or you hand over the keys to the family car, talk about how hard it would be if Dad or Mom didn't go to church. (Maybe that's already the case in your home.) Set the ideal, reinforce it constantly, and pray for wisdom. There may be times when you'll give in and let a son or daughter date a non-Christian instead of going to the mat over it. That's okay. Keep talking with your teens.

One more thought to ponder: Allowing your teens to date non-Christians could bring those young people to Christ. What an influence your youngsters could have during an impressionable period! We hesitate to recommend "missionary dating," however, even though that's how Greg became a Christian!

On Their Own

But there comes a time—especially after your teens turn eighteen—when you'll have to let go. We heard both sides regarding this question. Here's a comment from a New Jersey mom who pulled her hair out:

"Melody, our middle daughter, was dating a non-Christian

when she was nineteen. We were so opposed to the relationship that she spent most of her time at his house. It was hard for her to get to his house because she didn't have a car, but he would always drive her here and there. He gave her expensive gifts and took her to fancy restaurants. He had quite a hold over her.

"One time he got sick and was in a hospital. She had no way of visiting him because she had no car, and we weren't going to loan her ours. I wanted so badly to give her the car, but we couldn't condone what she was doing.

"Then my son wrote her a letter and said, 'You are breaking Mom's heart.' That made her feel guilty. But she took a taxi to go visit him anyway. That was probably our lowest moment. After several months, and I'm sure it's due to a lot of prayer, they eventually broke up.

"Then Melody went off to a Christian college in California, but she didn't like being that far away from home, so she returned. That's when her life started to turn around. She met a nice Christian guy from our church here, and they fell in love and married.

"Every now and then, we talk about what happened. She still believes we could have handled it differently. She felt we hated him, but we didn't hate him. It's just that we were so against the relationship. I know a family that has allowed their son to bring in a girl, and she lives with him in their house! I can't imagine not taking a strong stand. Yet despite all the hard feelings, Melody tells us she's very grateful she didn't marry that guy."

Remember Richard, the fellow who saw his daughter blow right past him at the beginning of this chapter? Let's hear what he had to say about how he handled the issue of dating non-Christians: "We did give dating guidelines. We said, 'No dating until you're sixteen,' but we didn't insist that they date only Christians. We talked to them about the importance of dating and what it leads to. We said that they needed to be selective from day one because people experience love in a growing type of process, and you may fall in love with the person you're dating.

"But we didn't make a hard line from that. We talked to them a lot about the importance of values and of two people agreeing on things. Unfortunately, my daughters sacrificed their values when they married non-Christians. Though they're good husbands and good providers, they're not believers.

"The tack we took with our girls was this: If we had said, 'Don't marry this person,' we knew we were going to drive a wedge between us. We would rather have a strong relationship and then let our example rub off on these guys and pray that they come to the Lord.

"When our son-in-law Ron met us, he told us we were the first people he had known who have been married for ten years. He was always real anti-Christian, but he likes us, so we are just praying God will do a work with his heart. But if we could have made a choice for the girls, we would have chosen differently. That's why I feel that if I could do it all over again, I would do it differently. I would have gone to a church where they had large youth groups so my teens could have had a lot of opportunities to meet other kids. I would have done that even if that meant we had to drive across town, even if it meant leaving the denomination."

SHAPING YOUR CHILD'S VALUES

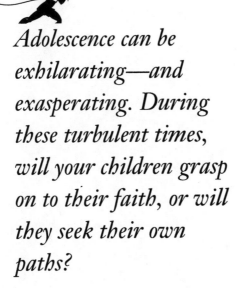

Adolescence can be exhilarating—and exasperating. During these turbulent times, will your children grasp on to their faith, or will they seek their own paths?

CHAPTER 16

REBEL WITH A PAUSE
Parents and Rebellion, Part 1

We're going to shift gears and tell you a story we heard from Alea Roberts, who grew up as a daughter of a Baptist minister in the New Jersey area. In our next chapter, we'll tell you what some of the parents and children we interviewed had to say about overcoming teen rebellion.

"When you're a preacher's kid," began Alea, "everyone in the church wants to be nice to you because they want to be close to the pastor. I never did like the attention."

Alea had it drummed into her that since her family was always being watched, they had to be examples to others. Part of being held to a higher standard meant that Alea lived in a home where movies were taboo and rock 'n' roll was outlawed.

Yet, when Pastor Roberts took the family on vacation, the first thing they did was find the local cinema. "One time," remembered Alea, "we went to see 'The Sound of Music' eight times during a two-week holiday. The whole family enjoyed it. You see, it was one of those forbidden things, something we couldn't do back home. The way Daddy explained this was, he was in a certain type of job, and that's the way things were. I mean, what would other people think if our family wasn't perfect?"

Alea, ten years old at the time, didn't grasp that line of reasoning. "I wasn't old enough to rebel against it," she stated. "But then my family started falling apart, and my parents started divorce proceedings. By the time I was in sixth grade, I was a tormented preacher's kid."

///// KEY THOUGHT

Alea was growing up under conflicting circumstances. This pastor's family always had to be "on" when they were in public. They had one set of behavior for the congregation and a "school's out" attitude when they left town.

The seeds of rebellion were being sown, however, as Alea discovered that her father's preaching really didn't match his faith. Coupled with a breakup of the marriage, Alea was an accident waiting to happen.

Kids need consistent discipline and house rules that don't change when the family leaves the city limits.

After the divorce, Alea's mother began taking her to another church—one where they weren't known and could fade into the background. Mrs. Roberts continued to instill a deep faith in her children by leading family devotions before school and doing her best to hook up Alea with Christian friends. "Not only did I enjoy being out of the limelight," she said, "but my mom made the Lord real to me."

In seventh grade, Alea met a special boy. One afternoon, they innocently held hands while they walked home from school together. Although this incident occurred in the mid-seventies, her mom made a *huge* deal about it. So Mrs. Roberts gave her daughter the silent treatment. This was her mother's way of dealing with behavior she didn't like. For *ten days* she didn't say a word to Alea. She finally relented after Alea got down on her knees and begged her forgiveness.

"Of course that was humiliating," said Alea. "After that episode, I gave up on trying to hold hands with boys. I didn't do that again until I was fifteen. Mom's reaction was that I should have nothing to do with the opposite sex. The only time she gave in was when she let me go to a Valentine's Day thing at the church when I was fourteen, but that was ultra-chaperoned."

At sixteen, however, Alea was allowed to start dating. There wasn't anyone in her youth group she wanted to go out with, however. Nor did her mother ever give her an explanation of *how* to date. "She just assumed that when I hit that magical age I would know what to do. But I *didn't* know, and I was very innocent and naive."

///// KEY THOUGHT

Alea's mom, who certainly had her own difficulties, nonetheless kept her head in the sand when it came to telling her daughter about the facts of life. Her style of noncommunication actually spoke volumes to Alea, who was left to figure out the opposite sex on her own.

After a while, children will stop coming to you with their questions about sex and dating if you fail to engage them when their hearts are open. Anticipate adolescent mistakes, and don't "punish" them to manipulate them into correct behavior. Remember, they're emerging sinful adults like the rest of us. Guide them to the truth. Then when they blow it, guide them back to the truth.

Testing the Waters of Rebellion

After Mrs. Roberts remarried, she continued working so she could pay for Alea's tuition at a Christian college. "Mom felt that if I was going to rebel, I would rebel the least at a Christian college," explained Alea. "Looking back, had I gone to a major state university, I probably would have been a much stronger Christian. It would have put me *in* the world, and it would have given me a chance to show my faith to other people. But being at a Christian college, we didn't have to witness. At my school, kids were huge hypocrites. It was hard to walk a straight line, so I joined the black sheep crowd. They all had hearts of gold and a solid faith, every one of them. They just liked to party a little. We were all in the same boat because our parents wanted us to be at this Christian college. I learned that there's something about breaking the rules that's a little fun, and it became exhilarating. We all knew we were gambling with our futures, because if we were ever caught, we would have been kicked out of school and lost all our tuition money."

Alea and the other black sheep participated in a lot of pranks, such as climbing up a nearby water tower, which was forbidden by school authorities. Sometimes they spray-painted graffiti about the college president on university property. Then they'd go off campus, way out in the woods, to drink and party. They usually made enough noise to attract the attention of the police. When the cops arrived, Alea ran deeper into the woods, her heart racing as she wondered if this would be the time she was caught. She never was.

Alea dipped her foot into the river of rebellion a bit farther. "Even when I had Christian boyfriends, I knew I wasn't going to stay a virgin until I got married. *I didn't want to.* Growing up, my mother never spoke about sex. She learned what sex was on her honeymoon night. I remember one time when she went to a Christmas party at the office where her second husband worked. Somebody grabbed her under the mistletoe and kissed her with his tongue. When my older brother heard about the story, he said, 'You mean he *frenched* you?' And Mom said, 'You mean there is a name for that type of thing?' Then my stepfather said he never heard of kissing with your tongue. That's how my parents were.

"In later years, at the height of my sexual escapades, I explained oral sex to her, and she was horrified. A part of me thought that was kind of neat about my mom—being so naive. But most of the time, her way was: 'Don't tell me, I don't want to know.' Total denial. Back then, she would call me on a Friday night, but I wouldn't be home since I was spending the night at my boyfriend's. I would call back on Saturday and say I just got home because I was at Gary's house all night. She *still* wouldn't confront me with the truth. For some reason, she felt it was better to ignore what I was doing."

All along, Alea wanted to be stopped in her tracks. "If she had ever sat me down and had an honest conversation about who I was and what I was doing, I know that would have changed my behavior. I needed some tough love back then. I didn't turn my back on the family. I spoke to her every Saturday, but Mom ignored *my* pain from the divorce and concentrated on *herself*. It was always *me* who had to make her feel better, to be the one to give her emotional support."

///// KEY THOUGHT

Like a professional wrestler who runs against the ropes and springs himself back into the ring, Alea was running faster and faster against the ropes, wondering where the breaking point was. Some of her actions were a demand for her mom's attention, but no matter how outlandish the behavior, her mother kept ignoring the evidence.

Rebellious children often *want* to be stopped in their tracks, if for no other reason than to have an excuse to stop their ungodly behavior. It's a courageous parent who loves his child enough to put a stop to destructive behavior.

The Die Is Cast

During the summer after her freshman year, Alea returned home and took a part-time job at her stepfather's office. She also continued to "see" her boyfriend—and then it happened. Alea walked into a Planned Parenthood clinic. She watched a nurse swirl her urine in a small test tube, but she wasn't paying much attention to the nurse's small talk. She felt her whole life hinged on the outcome of the test.

When the nurse stopped shaking the little tube, a crisp smile—almost a grin—creased her face. "You're pregnant," she announced. "What are you going to do about it?"

Alea coaxed her numbed brain to start thinking. She had thought of her options before she entered the clinic, but only one seemed feasible now. "I'm going to have an abortion," she heard herself tell the nurse.

"Why?"

"First of all, my mother would have a nervous breakdown if she ever found out. Second, I'm a Christian girl. I couldn't face my college classmates."

"Well, it sounds like you've thought this out. I wish you the best of luck."

Her boyfriend was waiting out in the car, and when he saw the tearstained cheeks, he didn't have to ask about the results. She sobbed and sobbed as the car turned into traffic.

Her boyfriend had it all figured out. "We have only one choice," he announced, "and you're going to have an abortion. I'll pay for it."

As Alea stared out the car window, she knew that's what she had to do. What other options did she have?

When she returned for a scheduling appointment at the Planned Parenthood clinic, the nurses explained to Alea that she "wasn't far enough along" and would have to wait another month before the doctor could perform a "complete procedure."

Even in the first trimester, she began to bloat. To her, the pregnancy was obvious. She confided to a couple of friends that she thought she was pregnant, but the test results were negative.

"I couldn't bring myself to tell anybody that I was going to have an abortion, so . . . I lied. My stepfather kept asking why I looked so pale. 'Would you please see a doctor?' he asked. I refused. My mother avoided my eyes. To this day, I was still waiting for her to confront me. I wanted her to be my scapegoat, to be the one who called me on it. Deep in my heart I wanted to keep that baby, I really did, but there was no one to help me."

She made arrangements to have the abortion the first week she went back to school. She never thought about marrying her boyfriend; the marriage would never last. But he did drive her to the clinic. When she reached the reception desk, she was handed a sheet of paper. Her eyes scanned the page; she remembers seeing the word "adoption" and a few addresses.

"What's this?" she asked the receptionist.

"It's your counseling," she replied.

"Oh."

When the nurses laid her on the table, she stared at the ceiling and kept telling herself it was just a blob of tissue, a blob of tissue.

Then the pain started. *Wait a minute,* she thought. *They never said this would hurt this much. Oh, God, this hurts! Just get me through this!*

"When I left that clinic, I was hardened. Hardened to the point where I would never allow myself to be put in a situation like that again. I was also hardened against God."

A Turnaround

For ten years, Alea kept the abortion bottled up, compartmentalized, off to the side. Life went on, and after graduation, she married a nice Christian man. She became pregnant, but at four months, complications set in. Her doctors suspected placenta previa (where the placenta starts to pull away from the uterine wall), so they ordered an ultrasound test.

When she saw her unborn baby on the monitor, it all came home for her. She turned to her husband, standing by her side. "My goodness, I was just weeks shy of this date when I had my abortion. And that's what I aborted!" she said. But that was the last time she allowed herself to discuss the past. After that, every time those memories of the abortion came back, she quickly shut them out.

It wasn't until she saw a Focus on the Family video, "Your Crisis Pregnancy," that she started to deal with what she had done ten years previously. She sat in a darkened room and listened to Dr. Dobson say on the TV screen, "I know I'm talking to a lot of women out there who have had abortions."

Her first instinct was to leave the room, but she remained in her seat.

Her ears continued to listen to Dr. Dobson. "I want you to know that the Lord has forgiven you. Your problem might be that you haven't forgiven yourself." *That's my problem, all right,* thought Alea. *How can I forgive myself for doing something so atrocious, so nasty? Nobody can be forgiven for that.*

Then she heard Dr. Dobson say that those who've had abortions should seek counseling, but she quickly dismissed that notion. Yet over the next few weeks, the flashbacks haunted her. She tried to keep all those little memories from surfacing, but they wouldn't go away. She felt deep, deep loneliness and a feeling that no one was there, not even God.

Then Alea heard about a Post-Abortion Counseling and Education class (PACE) at a nearby church. At the first meeting, she met other women who felt just the way she did. Over a period of several months at the PACE classes, she was able to turn her abortion over to the Lord and receive God's forgiveness so she could forgive herself.

Today, Alea is the mother of two, and as we write this book, a third is on the way. Her children are being raised in a Christian home, and though she regrets some of her past, that's history. Alea Roberts Price can't wait until tomorrow.

///// KEY THOUGHT

We've told this story as a reminder that rebellion can sometimes have lifetime consequences. Thankfully, Alea's story has a happy ending. But she would be the first to tell you that she walked through a long valley of pain before she reached the crest of a new life in Christ.

Keep the lines of communication open, and don't be afraid to gently probe and prod. Always give your children something to come back to.

CHAPTER 17

REBELLION 101
Parents and Rebellion, Part 2

Will any of your children follow Alea Roberts down the road of rebellion?

Some stretches, yes, but not the entire highway, according to the parents who filled out our survey. Here are a few thumbnail results:

- One-third said their children *did not* rebel.
- Thirty-seven percent said their children *definitely rebelled.*
- Thirty percent said their children went through *periods* of *minor rebellion.*

What type of rebellion are we talking about? Let's define *rebellion* as "the deliberate avoidance, neglect, or turning away from a faith they once held as their own."

What do our percentages mean? Two-thirds of parents can expect *some* stormy waters during the turbulent teen years. Typical was a comment from a Vermont mom: "All four of my children experienced some form of distancing—rebellion if you will," said Elizabeth Mailer. "Most of the children experimented with drugs and alcohol. But even Adam and Eve, in a perfect environment, rebelled and disobeyed. I like Billy Graham's advice: 'If you are going to err with your children, err on the side of love.'"

If love isn't the glue that keeps your children's hearts tender toward Christ, let it be the balm to salve their pride when they realize it's time to return. Every adult child we talked with who went through short- or long-term rebellion said it wasn't more *spiritual content* that brought them back; it wasn't an emphasis on their *behavior* (since the behavior was a symptom of their rebellion). Rather, it was the love of a parent, sibling, or other Christian adult that showed them the way home.

If you have a wayward child, be challenged by the apostle Paul's definition of love in 1 Corinthians 13: "*Love . . . keeps no record of wrongs. . . . It always protects, always trusts, always hopes, always perseveres. Love never fails.*"

//

The Importance of Chores

Before children get out of elementary school, they should be contributing to the maintenance of the household—both in chores and decisions affecting the family. Including your children in day-to-day tasks and decisions helps build responsibility. If they feel they're part of the family team, they won't ask the what-am-I-doing-here? type of questions as they get older.

Rebellion often occurs when kids don't have a well-defined family role. If family responsibilities are thrust upon them during the teen years, they won't always respond in the right way. Lack of responsibility breeds rebellion.

//

The parents said some interesting things about the rebellion they faced. (For a complete report, please turn to appendix 3.) But we're going to concentrate on two families whose stories impressed us. The first is from a father who works for a well-known, nationwide ministry that reaches out to teens. Even in the best of homes, conflicts can arise. All *four* of his children rebelled to some degree in their teens and twenties.

The Boston Nightmare

"When our oldest, Pete, was still at home, he probably did a few things with the football team that he shouldn't have," began Rich O'Neill. "A couple of times after he came home on a Saturday night, we could tell just by looking at him that he had been drinking. When he went away to college, he really got away from the Lord and did some heavy drinking. He probably even tried drugs a bit. I'm also fairly sure that he stopped going to church."

Karen, his oldest daughter, was a strong student who got into high school just as women's lib was starting to take hold in the mid-seventies. In her junior year, she was class treasurer, in line to be picked as a cheerleader, and heavily involved in drama. That's when Rich announced to the family that the ministry he was working for was going to move him from Boston to Baltimore.

"God may have called you to Baltimore, but he didn't call me," was Karen's reaction. Without telling anyone, Karen made arrangements to stay with a family in Boston.

"I, of course, didn't react well to that," said Rich. "I told her, 'I call the shots around here, and *you* are moving. It's cut and dried.' "

Karen moved with the family during the semester break that January, but she reacted poorly. Formerly an *A* and *B* student, she suddenly brought home a midterm report card filled with Ds. She began running with a rough crowd, and she did everything she could to rebel. "I refuse to live under this dictatorship," she screamed at her father.

Rich knew he had a *big* problem on his hands. He sat down with his pastor and laid out the story.

"How much do you love her?" asked the pastor.

The question startled Rich.

"A lot," he replied. Hadn't he been there in the delivery room? Hadn't he bonded with her in her first moments of life? Hadn't he helped raise her for seventeen years?

The pastor had a second question. "Do you think you love her enough to let her go back to Boston?"

"Why do you ask that?"

"Because I think you need to get the pressure off her. Let her finish her school year in Boston. It won't be the end of the world. This is not an indication that you are failing as a father."

After Rich discussed the situation with his wife, they called his former pastor in Boston and asked if Karen could live with them indefinitely. When he said yes, Rich told his daughter, "We know you are having a problem, so we've made arrangements for you to go back to your old school. There are no strings attached, and you can stay as long as you want."

Her parents' decision took Karen by surprise. When she returned to Boston, she found her "place" in school had already been filled. All her close friends had found other friends. On Father's Day, Rich received his first peace offering—a card from her. "I want to come back home," she wrote. "I'm willing to work at it if you are."

Back home, Karen was still a little distant and rebellious. After getting back into the routine, she lined her bedroom windowsill with empty wine bottles—probably to make a point. Rich knew his daughter was testing him, so one night after dinner he asked her about the wine bottles.

"Oh, I thought you'd get around to that."

"Look, you've only got one more year of high school," Rich said, "and once you're graduated and gone, we're not going to know what you're doing. You will be on your own. But you know what we stand for. If you want to develop a wine bottle collection, you can't do it in your window, because that says something to the community."

///// KEY THOUGHT

Though Rich could have offered different reasoning for why he wanted the wine bottles out of the window, his point is well-taken: Don't let a child flaunt values for which the home stands. Every household needs to stand on a foundation, and it's got to be a bedrock.

The Wind Changes

If you think Rich O'Neill was due a parental breather, he got it with his third child, David. Not that Dave didn't press his parents, but he did it with a smile on his face.

David was a high-energy, impetuous, never-a-dull-moment, fast-talking, merry-prankster type of guy. "He would tell us *everything,*" recalls Rich. "If he did something, he would come home and say, 'Man alive, I went to this party, and everyone was drinking beer, and I had some, too.' For him, life was an open book. Yet, he was very involved in his high school Christian club, although every once in a while he'd get caught with the wrong crowd."

Most of Dave's rebellion happened while he attended a Christian college. He told his parents that one of his collegiate "achievements" was rappeling off every building on campus. But things turned serious when Dave was caught out at three in the morning with a buddy and they each had a lit cigar. A "dorm daddy" ratted on them, and the two were hauled into school offices and told they might get kicked out of school—for smoking a cigar.

When Rich heard the story, he asked, "Didn't you sign something that said you wouldn't smoke or drink during school? You violated your commitment. They didn't force you to sign that."

The school authorities asked the boys to make a new commitment not to drink or smoke. Dave heard his father ask, "Are you going to live up to it? Don't sign it if you're not going to stay clean. If you have to go to a different school, that's what you'll have to do. But you have to live up to your word."

Dave signed on the dotted line.

"Of all our kids, Dave was the most sensitive to the Lord," said Rich. "It was never a sinful or vicious or anti-God type of thing. Rather, it was fun and pranks. When he did something he wasn't supposed to, he was always repentant. And when he signed that contract after getting caught with the cigar, he lost all his privileges. Yet he stayed in that school and lived up to his commitment. He redeemed himself."

And what about Rich's fourth child, Stephanie? "She was different, too," he mused. "She was witty but a little shy around people, but we never knew about her. In all my work with high school teens, I know that high school friendships pretty much dissipate. Still, to this day, Stephanie has close relationships with high school girlfriends. Though she probably did some pretty wild things, she never told us what happened. I'm sure the same thing was true in college. She was the one who was very slow to make a spiritual commitment."

While in college, Stephanie worked part-time in a hotel catering department in Baltimore. There she met a cute guy, a Mr. Hunk. One day he asked if she wanted to go with him to New York City for a frisbee-throwing contest. "We talked about that," said Rich. "I said to her, 'You've told me he's gone to bed with every waitress at work. Now, what does he want from you?' "

"Oh, I'm not interested in *that*," she said. "Besides, that's not why he's interested in me." She went to New York, but Rich never found out what happened because Stephanie never talked about Mr. Hunk again.

Rich said he really isn't sure what happened in his girls' lives after they left home. "I think part of it is that they would not want to hurt us. Stephanie was really concerned about that. She had seen our confrontation with Karen and how much we hurt each other. The boys were blunt enough to tell us things. Today, the boys are both in ministry, but the girls married non-Christians. I've read that boys relate to their mother and girls to their father, so I said to myself, 'Uh-oh, I screwed up.'"

But you didn't, Rich. You walked down the paths with your children until they reached adulthood. They have free will, and they chose the paths they were going to travel.

///// KEY THOUGHT

If the Prodigal Son's father had been an abusive, self-righteous man, the wayward son probably would never have even thought of returning home. But he knew something about his dad's character, and he eventually came to his senses. It was the same for Rich's children. None of them doubted his love and concern. They may have tested his values more than most, but the relationship was strong—and the door was always open.

If you close the door on your home or your relationship, you'll probably close the door on any desire of a rebellious child to return—to you *or* the Lord.

A Revisit

If you read our first book, *"Daddy's Home,"* you may remember that we started chapter 1 by telling the story of a Texas father,

Elliot, who spent the first ten years of his marriage devoted to the love of his life—and it wasn't his wife. It was his work.

One evening around midnight, lightning struck an electrical pole on Elliot's street, and the charge surged inside his home and started the TV set on fire. The flames quickly spread to nearby walls. Elliot, not quite asleep, smelled the smoke and hastily ushered the family outside.

As Elliot and his wife, Jerri, watched their house go up in flames, he heard a message from the Lord: *Quit working so much, and start spending more time with your family!* The next day, Elliot began making some drastic changes in his office schedule and home life.

We thought Elliot would be a good candidate to fill out a *Faithful Parents, Faithful Kids* survey. Not only had he been one of those rare birds to make major changes in his life, but both his children were in their twenties.

Then we received a letter from Jerri:

"The reason I didn't fill out the survey is it's just real hard right now for us. Although our children are in their twenties, we're not finished yet."

I (Mike) wanted to know more, so I called Jerri. After some small talk, I learned that her twenty-seven-year-old daughter, Linda Mae, was in full-blown rebellion and their twenty-three-year-old son, Jimmy, was in "rebellion lite."

"To be honest, it was a very painful thing to go through those questions you sent us," she said. "It's frustrating where we are now. I know we didn't do everything perfectly. We were God-fearing, Christian parents just trying to do the right thing. It's just real hard right now for us. My husband and I are hanging on to this verse: 'I know whom I have believed and am persuaded that he is able to keep that which I have committed unto him'" (2 Timothy 1:12, KJV).

By her account, the children were raised in a secure home. They took the children to Sunday school and church. Dad coached Jimmy in basketball, soccer, and baseball; Jerri was a Girl Scout leader. They pitched in at their children's schools, and they always helped with homework. The kids could always bring their friends over.

"We're not perfect people," said Jerri, "but good grief, when I look around today and see what's out there, it blows me away how solid our family was. Both sets of grandparents never divorced. Aunts and uncles had solid homes. I once joked, 'Our kids may have been deprived because they've had only one mom and one dad.' "

Linda Mae attended a Christian high school, and upon graduation, she wanted to go to a Christian college where Jerri was teaching part-time. Her parents, however, thought it would be better to send her to a small, private university where she could get in touch with the real world. Maybe this is where the parents should have stepped back and let their daughter make that choice—and live with the consequences.

But Elliot and Jerri didn't waver.

I asked Jerri when things started slipping off the track. "We have a classic strong-willed child in our daughter," she began. "From years back, she was always difficult to discipline. Though Linda Mae went through the motions of obeying, we could tell her will wasn't broken. In fact, it wasn't even bent.

"Our daughter was like a hothouse flower. She had been practically raised in the church, but when she got out in the world, she didn't know how to handle it. It's always been our feeling that we can't be salt and light if we are not *in* the world. We knew we couldn't protect them all their lives; that's hiding them. That's not living."

///// KEY THOUGHT

Should Elliot and Jerri have let Linda Mae learn about the real world sooner, when she was still malleable? Were they being *too* overprotective? Parents have to learn when to loosen their grip on their teens.

Things didn't improve as Linda Mae entered adolescence. "Linda Mae always considered herself an exception to the rule," said Jerri. "In high school, she was in trouble with her teachers a lot because she thought she could get away with things since Elliot was the school board chairman. That attitude carried over into real life. A couple of years ago, she got hold of a bunch of credit cards and really went wild with them. Now she's in a big mess—around five thousand dollars worth. Every credit card is maxed to the limit. Then she started writing hot checks. Her attitude is that *I really don't have to pay those bills.*

"Then she got speeding tickets left and right. Of course, she ignored them. Guess what? She was caught speeding again, and the state trooper ran her license plate through the computer. They had a warrant out for her arrest. 'I refuse to believe this!' she screamed at the officer. She thought it was *his* fault. "Naturally, she was thrown in jail because she didn't have the money to pay the $150 fine. Since this happened right before Christmas, we took the money we were going to spend on her presents and bailed her out. We also told her that if it happened again, she could stay in jail. Well, she got into another scrap, and when the police found more outstanding warrants, they escorted her into a jail cell. She made her one phone call to us, but when we reminded her that we weren't going to bail her out, she became very angry with us. She was resentful and bitter. She stayed in that jail from Friday night to Monday in order to pay her fine."

///// KEY THOUGHT
Elliot and Jerri employed some "tough love" tactics when their daughter landed in jail a second time. That was probably the *best* thing they could do. Although painful at the time, some children only learn when they suffer the consequences of their actions.

Meanwhile, Elliot and Jerri began praying, "Lord, how much more?" Because of Linda Mae's financial situation, she couldn't get an apartment, so she moved back in with her parents. They told her that she could stay there for a month. She did have a job. They wanted to encourage her, but she was twenty-seven years old, and the parents felt she had to learn responsibility and accountability sometime.

"Right now, you're talking to a mother whose heart is hurting. But God is faithful, and we know God is able to work a miracle," said Jerri.

///// KEY THOUGHT
You can do nearly everything right and still have kids who "just don't get it." Though Linda Mae received a lot growing up, some children will still choose to be irresponsible for as long as they can get away with it. For some, it's in their nature to shake a fist at God and believe he owes them a pothole-free existence. That's why some prodigals have to travel *all* the way down before they see how great they had it before. It doesn't do any good to tell them what life over the hill is like; they have to see for themselves.

He Never Graduated

Although their youngest, Jimmy, hasn't been introduced to the jail-cell life of "three hots and a cot," he's still struggling to find himself. College hasn't worked so far: Jimmy put in five years but didn't earn enough credits for a degree. He either flunked or dropped a lot of classes—about a third of his class schedule. Jimmy told a cousin, "Mom and Dad sent me to college, but I didn't take advantage of it."

During his last year, Jimmy saw a lot of his friends who had graduated fail to win decent jobs. That frightened him. He started drinking more and more as he struggled to keep up in his classes. To top it off, he had girlfriend problems. Everything caved in on the young man, and he returned home to Texas and checked into a Minirth-Meier clinic for three months of alcohol rehab.

"I don't know how much it helped," said his mother. "He doesn't think he had a real serious problem. Counseling is only good if you *want* to change."

After Jimmy left the clinic, Elliot and Jerri told him the gravy train wouldn't be carrying him any longer. If he wanted to graduate from college, he would have to pay the freight. So Jimmy took a job as a short-order chef at a Colorado ski resort to make a few bucks and figure out what his next move will be. He likes the work, and the scenery is nice.

Meanwhile, Elliot and Jerri are comforted with the knowledge that God is not finished with their children. Every morning, their alarm goes off at 5:30, and while Elliot is in the shower, Jerri has a quiet time with the Lord. When Elliot comes out, they will sit on the bed and read the Bible for fifteen minutes. Then they finish their devotional time praying over each other's day, their children, and other concerns.

"It feels good to start the day off together, asking the Lord to take care of our needs," said Jerri. "We aren't giving up. We are believing that God knows exactly where they are. Although it's been a hard year, Elliot and I have grown closer. And there is a real peace in us about the kids. During these painful and hurting times, we are trusting in the Lord.

"Another thing that keeps us going is that while we know we're held accountable for what we do, we also know we have done the best we could with our children. We are not going to be held accountable for *their* failures, just *our* mistakes and failures. The Lord set us free on that one. We had to swallow a lot of pride and a lot of expectations for our kids. There's certainly been a lot more peace in our hearts after we released them to the Lord."

///// KEY THOUGHT

Prayer shouldn't be the last resort in a hopeless situation; it should be the first thing we do every day for our kids. Though we don't believe in magic formulas, we do believe in God's miraculous power. He delights in hearing our requests, and he even suggests we wear him out by constantly lifting our requests to him. God wants us to bring everything his way so we can find comfort and help in time of need.

Perhaps the greatest investment we make in our children is the time we spend on our knees. We *need* supernatural help in raising faithful children. We can't do it with our own strength, knowledge, or wisdom; but we can with his.

CHAPTER 18

CONSTRUCTING GUARDRAILS
Parents Who Teach Discernment

During my (Mike's) first trip to Switzerland fifteen years ago, I was introduced to fast *Autobahns* and curvy mountain passes. The two-lane highways carved into the sides of the mighty Alps are narrow, exhilarating, and superbly engineered. Peering out from the passenger window, I could see old wooden barns and tidy, whitewashed villages below. For some stretches, a ribbon of steel guardrail was all that separated our car from the highway and the bottom of the valley thousands of feet below. But I felt safe. My father-in-law, Hans Schmied, had been driving in the Alps since World War II, and I knew the guardrails were designed to keep our car on the pavement.

Toward the end of my stay, Nicole (my wife) and I borrowed the family sedan for a two-day trip to Italy. We aimed the auto for the imposing Grand St. Bernard Pass—first crossed by Roman legions centuries ago. After an hour of switchbacks, hairpin turns, and seat-of-the-pants driving, we reached the summit of the Grand St. Bernard and a border stop. After a routine passport inspection, we began our descent into Italy. My mind quickly picked up three things about Italian roads: (1) They don't have any painted lines. (2) They do have potholes. (3) They don't have guardrails!

Well, not guardrails like we're used to. On the more treacherous curves, the Italians dotted the edge of the road with stone blocks, each about a foot square. About the only thing they'd do is rip off your oil pan cover if you went careening over the cliff.

Ever since that trip, I can see why parents want roads with solid *moral guardrails* for their children. The metaphor goes something like this: As kids grow up, parents choose the roads and paths their children will take. Parents select the safest roads, especially ones with good guardrails through the treacherous curves of life. As children turn into young adults, more and more responsibilities are transferred onto their shoulders. One day, they will leave home in their own cars and drive off into the sunset. Will they seek out roads with firm guardrails, or will they travel off the beaten track in search of more reckless times? Inside the home, parents also construct moral guardrails, ones engineered to keep the family's standards inside a protective railing. Betty Turner once wanted to see what was on the other side:

"I'd just graduated from high school, then went out of town all summer to pack fruit. I came back home in the fall, and my first week back I got invited to see 'Tootsie,' a movie in which Dustin Hoffman dresses like a woman in order to get parts on a TV soap opera.

"My dad, who is a pastor, said, 'No, you can't go. It's a bad movie. It's got things in it I don't want you to see.'

"I was furious! It was the last straw. I lost it that afternoon, and a good yelling match ensued between us. After we finally calmed down, he said, 'Maybe you have a point. You can make your own decision.'

"I went to the movie, and I had the worst time of my life. During the entire film, I noticed things in it that were unseemly. I came home and admitted to him that it wasn't a good idea to see 'Tootsie.' After that episode, I remember being a little more careful about what movies I went to. But at the same time, I definitely needed—and wanted—to break away from my dad's unreasonable demand of controlling everything I did."

For years, this father had thought that by constructing tight moral guardrails around what his daughter saw and heard, he could keep her from copying immoral behavior. That's not a bad goal. But he and his daughter had reached a point where it was time to see if *his* moral guardrails were *her* moral guardrails.

Getting Your Hands Dirty

How good are you at digging postholes and bolting on heavy-duty sheet metal?

Not the greatest? Well, too bad. Because at various times with your children, you'll have to dig, cement in, and bolt together *protective* guardrails for your kids. When your children hit the teenage years, you could be putting in a lot of overtime on the family road.

A day will come when your children will want to peer over the edge. For many, a quick glance will suffice. For a few others, that won't be enough; they will want to floor the accelerator and see how fast they can drive through the curves.

The story about Betty is a good illustration. The *protective* guardrails at their home had always consisted of Dad's making the choices about what movies the kids would see. Fair enough. If he's informed, Dad can protect his children from exposure to disturbing movies that could leave a scarring impression on young minds. That's his job. But the daughter was ready to make her own decisions (probably *past ready*). At eighteen, her request wasn't out of line.

In this instance, Dad could have *moved* the protective guardrails out a few feet—if he'd realized this was the time to do it. He could have said, "Betty, I've heard that 'Tootsie' isn't a very moral movie. You know I've always tried to protect your mind from inappropriate films. I'd really prefer you didn't go. But since you're an adult, I'll let you make the decision. I trust you. If you do decide to go, let's sit down and talk about the movie when you get home. I'd be real interested in hearing what you thought about 'Tootsie.' "

No yelling, no fights, no guilt-producing comments—and no hard feelings. He simply could have stated his beliefs, his motives, his trust, *and* his desire to use the situation to teach her discernment.

//

What Are You Teaching?

Our society worships the almighty dollar, so you figure that many homes are schools for teaching the pursuit of a buck. But a nationwide survey by the Shearson-Lehman Brothers investment firm said the American Dream is still rooted in traditional family values rather than wealth, power, or status. "It was a major surprise to us that people did not equate money with success and felt that success and happiness had to do with personal achievement and giving back to society," said marketing director Sara Lipson.[1]

You have to wonder about the parents who answered this survey. Were they merely telling the poll taker what they thought they should say, or were these deep-seated values?

//

Taking the First Steps

The nineties aren't the eighties. "Tootsie" is almost a Disney movie compared to the violent and depraved films that pass for Hollywood entertainment today. For me (Greg), it's tempting to make the protective guardrails one lane wide. That way I can be *sure* my kids aren't near the edge of the cliff. But, as mentioned before, I won't be able to protect them forever. In fact, I may not be doing them a favor by hemming them in between *my* guardrails when all they want to do is walk to the edge and peer into the abyss.

If you're raising teenagers today, you know that a one-lane guardrail means definite conflict as your teens constantly careen off each side. But what would you rather have as a parent: smashed-in guardrails (thus risking damage to your relationship with them) or sons or daughters who set their own guardrails—using you as a "construction consultant"?

Bob DeMoss, Focus on the Family's youth culture specialist, wrote a book called *Learn to Discern*. It's an excellent resource that should be read by every parent of teens. Bob states that it's the parents' responsibility to teach their children to think critically and "Christianly" about popular entertainment.

When TV shows, movies, music, magazines, and videos enter the home, they all need to be evaluated from God's perspective. That means we help our kids ask questions, from an early age, about the new Arnold Schwarzenegger movie, the latest Ice-T release, or Eddie Murphy's raunchy HBO special. We don't just give them the answers (*our* guardrails), but we take the time—and it will take more than a few hours—to help them discover where *their* guardrails should be.

As we mentioned earlier, if a child owns his moral guardrails, he'll try harder to stay inside them. If he's borrowed *yours*, he's more apt to make bad driving decisions—and bust through that guardrail.

That's what happened to Betty and her dad. Wisely, her dad decided to let her take a short trip on her own. When she scratched up the car, she realized her parents were right.

Hindsight Is 20-20

Talking to adult children *after* they left home gives us an excellent chance to pass along some "hindsight" advice. Here's what they said about learning discernment:

- "They talked us through TV shows and movies. When we were young, they turned or covered our eyes during bad previews."
- "Because they exposed me to a lot of good things, the bad things were self-evident."
- "They explained to us the consequences of following a certain life-style of an actor or musician we liked."
- "They often asked how it would benefit me to see a certain program or movie. That line of thought helped me to want the best."
- "When we were older, they saw some questionable movies *with* us. Then we'd discuss them."
- "They set a standard of morality and expected us to adhere to it."
- "They used Scripture to reinforce good moral character."
- "My father would use the phrase 'Would Jesus want to go with you?' "
- "They never agreed to let me see horror flicks. I'm grateful. I've seen only two to this day, and they still leave bad memories."
- "Mom and Dad talked a lot about the choices they had made in their lives; choices of standing up for what was right. I came to expect that of myself . . . to make godly choices."

Conscience, Discipline, and Compassion

We strategically placed this last comment at the end to highlight its significance.

Our society has raised a generation of baby boomers *without* well-developed consciences. Though all men are given a conscience at birth (Romans 1), a child's upbringing can either bury it or reinforce its value. Two of the most essential characteristics we can pass on to our children are a love for the work of their conscience, and the knowledge that the Holy Spirit lives within.

Building a sensitive conscience means we have to demonstrate *honesty*. We talked to several adult children who remembered their moms or dads giving back that extra change the sales clerk accidentally gave them. Kids don't forget the little stuff.

It also means we have to be *transparent*. We have two choices as our children grow: (1) We can wait until a situation comes up to explain the inner battle *we face* with right and wrong; or (2) we can seek out opportunities to explain that when we are tempted to do wrong, God helps us make the right choice.

One man said that when he was in junior high, his dad sat him down and walked him through the family's tax return.

"You see this column here?" the father said. "This is the place Uncle Sam trusts me. I could fudge a little bit, and they would likely never find out. But you know who would know? That's right. God would know, and I would, too. Three hundred extra dollars isn't worth not being able to sleep at night. Besides, if God thinks we can use three hundred dollars extra, I believe he could give it to me without cheating to do it."

The son learned two lessons that night: First, even though his dad was tempted to cheat—and knew he could get away with it—he chose not to defraud the IRS. Second, it's God who provides what we have, and he uses only honest means to give it to us.

Kids often put their parents on a moral pedestal. What children didn't see, of course, was the process we went through to make those right decisions. Since they didn't see us struggle with poor choices before they were born, we should tell the stories about our poor decisions. That's why transparency is so essential. When we come down off our pedestals, we can *talk* to our children at their level—not *pontificate* from on high.

Also let your children see you exercise some *self-discipline,* a value that's better *caught* than *taught.* When our children watch us use the TV flicker when one of those "jiggle" shows begins, or when they hear us discuss why we're not going to see the latest movie everyone is talking about, they will ask themselves *why* Dad and Mom did that. But children don't need a sermon from us, either. Seeing us calmly make the right choices and offer some commentary along the way will be enough. If you reinforce *why* that trashy TV show is not fit for family consumption, they'll catch your drift.

Take those beer-and-bikini commercials—please. When we flick to another channel to escape the latest antics of the Swedish bikini team, they'll ask what we're doing. That's the time to fight the self-righteous urge to say, "Because I don't think you need to see that stuff."

Instead, be honest. "Sorry if that bugs you, but I know those commercials don't help my mind at all." That's honesty!

Let's NOT Throw a Party

We should always show a little compassion for those caught in the downward spiral of poor choices. If we deflect attention away from our sinful nature by throwing a daily "congratulations party" every time we see people paying the consequences for their sin, our children will graduate with a master's degree in spiritual pride.

Finger-pointing, gloating over someone else's misfortune (AIDS victims, for instance), or taking the proverbial holier-than-thou attitude because we choose the "right" music, TV shows, and movies all speak volumes in support of the perception that Christians are "better" than non-Christians.

That's not the message of the New Testament. Whenever you point out a current example of sinful behavior—and the natural consequences those decisions wrought—it should be tempered with a statement like this:

- "It breaks God's heart to see his children going the wrong direction."
- "We need to pray for that baseball player who just got hit with a palimony suit."
- "I wonder what it would take to reach that rock star who is so far gone that all he can do is think about sex and drugs?"

After a few years of uttering those statements, you watch—your kids may someday make the same ones! Compassion for others will teach discernment faster than condemnation. If your compassion meter isn't registering very high, please ask God what you can do to get it higher. The world doesn't need another self-righteous, condemning Christian.

What are some other ways to teach discernment? We have some great advice from parents and some ideas of our own. Here's how you can handle the *major* entertainment battles:

//

Our Viewing Habits

- The average American household can now receive thirty-one channels; 68 percent can receive at least fifteen; 25 percent get seven to fourteen; and only 7 percent can choose from seven channels or less.
- In 1989, 92 million households owned TVs. Sixty-five percent of those have more than one set.
- More than two-thirds of TV households own VCRs.
- During the 1988-89 TV season, people had their sets on an average of seven hours and two minutes a day.
- The average child will have watched 5,000 hours of TV by the time he enters first grade and 19,000 hours by the end of high school—more hours than he will spend in class.

—Sources: *American Demographics* and *Time* magazines

//

Television

We're not going to take much time flogging this whipping boy. We'll get to the heart of the matter by asking you some questions:

- Is the TV always on as "background noise"?
- Could your family survive if you had one TV-free night a week?
- Do you turn the TV off when company arrives?
- Are different family members watching different shows in different rooms?
- Do you watch a lot of TV because you pay all that money for premium channels such as HBO, Cinemax, and Showtime?
- When you travel, do you always have to have the TV on in the hotel room?
- Do you ever wonder how your parents lived *without* TV?

Some tough questions there, we know. But the TV has become so ubiquitous, so all-encompassing, that many families can't imagine what life would be like if the dumb thing wasn't on from four-thirty to eleven every night.

But TV *can* be limited, and for some families, it means breaking long-ingrained habits. Here are a few ideas for accomplishing that daunting task:

- As tempting as it seems, try not to let the tube be a baby-sitter. Even if the "harmless" sitcoms appear clean, they are often antifamily. Again, set the example and keep a high standard.
- Use the chart system. Photocopy a weekly chart that has the agreed-upon number of hours your children can watch on weekdays. (Weekends could be different.) After each program, the kids color in their chart in thirty-minute segments. You could pay them a nickel a minute for every minute they don't use.
- Have a "matching" system. One family made the agreement that for every minute the kids read a book, they could watch one minute of TV. And every minute of reading the Bible "bought" three minutes of TV. The rule was relaxed a little on weekends, but not during weekdays when they had school.
- Watch and discuss together. On the average, children see twenty thousand commercials a year. As an experiment one week, whenever you watch TV together, write down on a sheet of paper what product a commercial is trying to sell. On the other side, write down their method. For example: Bud Light—young guys and gorgeous girls. Cadillac—older celebrity. Barbie—groups of girls having a party in

glamorous clothes. This teaches kids to recognize the real purpose behind TV, which is to reap advertising dollars.

- Develop a bedtime reading habit early. When the kids are young, always read to them before lights out. As they get older, let them keep the light on while they read themselves. This idea also fosters a love for books.
- Use the VCR. With your own VCR sitting on top of the TV, you get to be your own network. Don't like the latest offerings from NBC, CBS, or ABC? Fine. Tape some of the nature programs on the Discovery Channel. Looking for some sitcom laughs without being bombarded by double-entendre jokes? Then tape the old "I Love Lucy," "Mayberry, RFD," or "Leave It to Beaver" shows now in syndication.

You can also rent or buy prerecorded videos, especially those offering solid Christian entertainment. The McGee and Me! videos for kids (produced by Focus on the Family and Tyndale House) have been runaway successes. Both of our families have all twelve episodes. More and more Christian bookstores are renting videos suitable for the entire family. Check them out! If you get cable, you can also explore some excellent family programming on PBS, Arts & Entertainment, or the Discovery channels.

///

Sex on the Silver Screen

- "Childhood is no longer perceived as a time of innocence. Indeed, the steady diet of TV violence, sex and social problems insures that kids are not innocent any more. Children are now viewed as competent and sophisticated. This view can lead the parents of teenagers to feel that it is unnecessary for them to provide limits, guidelines and supervision."
  —Child psychologist David Elkind in *Psychology Today*

- "In 1991, the three networks displayed more than 10,000 sexual incidents during prime time; for every scene depicting sexual intercourse between married couples, the networks showed fourteen scenes of sex outside of marriage."
  —An American Family Association study
- In both 1979 and 1989 studies, every incident of implied or explicit sexual intercourse was between unmarried partners. Husbands and wives don't even talk about it on the screen. Sex was mentioned by married people only once, but singles talked about it ninety times.
  —*Psychology Today*

///

As we mentioned in *"Daddy's Home,"* fathers can also use the VCR to tape sporting events for later viewing. No reason to watch a three-hour NFL football game when it can easily be seen in one or two hours *after* the game.

Here are a couple of other comments parents offered about television:

- "We'd make comments while we watched TV together. Often we didn't have to even say anything. The kids would say it before we would."
- "We used biblical principles and evaluated our viewing decisions. ('I will set no worthless thing before my eyes.') We had lots of discussions about the choices we made."

Movies

Steve Fury was raised in a Christian home where movies weren't allowed. After he'd become a parent several times over in the sixties, he and his wife went to see "Bonnie and Clyde," the trend-setting Hollywood film about several Texas bank robbers during the depression years.

"The bad thing was that we found ourselves cheering for Bonnie and Clyde at the end," said Steve. "That shows how movies can twist and grab you and take you from your value system. We had to talk that out. We got duped as that movie went along." That's when Steve began to realize that movies are like books: There are good ones and bad ones, and it's up to the individual to steer away from the negative ones.

"I know movies are much more powerful, that they appeal to the senses," said Steve. So one of the things he tried to do with movies—and books—was to teach his kids there was good and bad in everything. He took them to the movies when they were young and watched TV with them, but he made the rule that they could not sit in front of the TV *ad infinitum.*

"Our dinner table was always our open forum time," said Steve. "We could always bring up anything, and we could agree to disagree. We would talk about the latest films and ask each what he or she had heard. I tried to point out that if the movie was based on a book with a bad moral to it, the film probably wasn't any good either."

What Parents Can Do

- Subscribe to a Christian movie review publication, such as *MovieGuide* ($40 a year for 26 issues. Write to the Christian Film and Television Commission, P.O. Box 190010, Atlanta, GA 31119) or *Preview Movie Morality Guide* ($30 a year for 26 issues. Write Preview, 1309 Seminole Dr., Richardson, TX 75080). The publications review the latest Hollywood films from a Christian perspective—including R-rated ones. Ted Baehr, publisher of *MovieGuide*, says his research shows him that Christians see R-rated movies in the same proportion as the general public. (Surprised?)

- Talk about new films in your Sunday school class. "Has anyone seen the latest Michael Douglas film?"
- Read movie reviews in newspapers and magazines. Even though the reviewers aren't writing to a Christian audience, you can certainly find out a lot about the film. The reviewers will often talk about how gory the movie is, how a certain sexual scene stayed in but the movie still earned an R or PG rating, or why this movie is "controversial."
- Realize that today's movies are tomorrow's videos. The time between theatrical release and the Blockbuster video outlet is shrinking; it's often less than six months. Exercise the same I-want-to-know-what's-in-this-movie mentality on anything being brought home.
- Remember that your strongest argument is, "Your mother and I don't watch those kinds of movies, and I don't think it's out of line to expect that you don't, either."

Here's what some parents said:

- "We taught them that Hollywood was a bad influence."
- "We didn't attend many movies, but my husband read newspaper reviews and would discuss with our daughter the 'message' beneath the surface."
- "We used the rating system as a guide and would always talk to a friend who'd seen that movie before making a decision. It meant a few more phone calls, but it kept us from making bad decisions more than once."
- "My husband and I were not Christians as teenagers, and we were very aware of how movies can mold your mind."

- "When they were fourteen and under, they were forbidden to see bad movies. After that, we verbalized our trust in them to make good choices."
- "We joked about movie values so they could see how shallow they were."

Music

I (Greg) know more about rock, pop, street rap, country, hip-hop, heavy metal, speed metal, death metal, and urban music than I care to know. Keeping track of that stuff is part of my job description, but hey, someone has to do it.

What I can tell you is this: If your parents hit the ceiling every time you wanted to buy a Beatles or Rolling Stones record, they'd hit the moon if you pushed "play" on the Red Hot Chili Peppers, Megadeth, or Madonna! You can't even go to a mall anymore without being constantly reminded of some degenerate rock group's world tour.

If your teens are in public school, they're probably aware of every group that's getting a steady rotation on MTV or the hit radio station. When I was in high school, I bought Jimi Hendrix records because my friends talked about them—and I hated the music! But there was a subtle pressure to keep up with the conversation and be one of the guys. That same type of pressure is probably on your kids.

Once that type of pressure hits, get ready for this question: "What's wrong with it?"

Because music is so personal, your response may determine the quality of your communication for the next six years.

If you want to see some fireworks, say something like this: "Look at those guys. They look like girls!" "I can't understand the words." "If they're on MTV, they must be evil." All you've done then is to reveal your prejudices and age. Such a statement may end the argument once, but because the logic is weak, you can expect more clashes in the future.

Now suppose instead you say: "So, you want to buy Madonna's new CD. Well, let's go down to the record store and listen to it. And we can check out the lyrics together. We can also discuss what her message is and see if it's something you really need to be pumping into your brain."

In that case, expect a brief tussle. Your children might think you don't trust them. But those comments show you're open-minded and fair.

If you should discover the music's garbage, calmly remind them of your responsibility to God to protect their spirits and their brains. Tell them that one day they'll be making their own choices about music, but that day hasn't arrived yet.

Should your kids listen to contemporary Christian music? We realize there are diverse opinions on this subject. Some parents don't believe that music can be Christian if it has a 4/4 beat. In other words, *it has to be old or slow if God likes it.*

We don't agree with that logic. If your children enjoy music, try what several families we spoke to are doing. "From an early age we introduced contemporary Christian music to our kids," said a Dallas father. "They're in college now, and *not once* have we had to fight with them about secular radio or album selections. They've all chosen the styles they like, and there are tons of quality Christian groups and singers in those genres. Fortunately for us, none of them liked heavy metal."

Here's what some other parents said:

- "We went with them to concerts, sitting a few rows away, of course, and discussed the music with them afterward."
- "Contemporary Christian music wasn't that prevalent

when our kids were young, but with the stuff our son got into, I sure wish it had been. He needed positive alternatives, and we just didn't have any to give him."

If your children are into music, encourage them to listen to the great Christian alternatives (in every style imaginable!). Dean Morrison said contemporary Christian music had always been a part of his home. The end result? "We've never had a fight about secular rock music. I simply wasn't interested in it because the Christian music I listened to was so good."

Teens may be captivated by metal, however. Perhaps they've already got quite a collection of Slayer, Def Leppard, and Guns 'n Roses. Bob DeMoss recommends parents discuss the lyrics of *all* their kids' music. If the music doesn't meet the family standard, offer to buy back their tapes at half price. Then go with them to the music store and pick out some good Christian alternatives.

The battle over the boom-box doesn't need to be divisive. It does, however, call for prayer, open discussion, and an early strategy to deal with this powerful medium.

Magazines

Teen magazines for girls—of which there are plenty—emphasize external beauty. In one issue of *Seventeen*, we counted 109 beautiful young women. No wonder impressionable girls don't feel good about themselves. As we mentioned, *Brio* does an excellent job of reinforcing biblical values without being hokey.

Boys' magazines are more specialized. Unless you have a son reading magazines about heavy metal music, skateboarding, or surfing (which are pretty raunchy), most are fairly tame. *Breakaway* has an eye-catching design, and features Christian sports personalities, music, and other general-interest topics that can really hold the short attention of boy readers.

Books

Without much effort, you can provide a steady stream of interesting books, many from a Christian perspective. Allowing a teenage daughter to read cheap romance novels when there is wonderful Christian fiction for girls—with appropriate amounts of romance—is totally unnecessary . . . and unhealthy for their minds!

Friends

Choosing the right friends is a skill, and parents should "direct" their little ones early on to play with "quality" kids. Then, as the teenage years hit, your children should keep right on rolling into friendships with teens who have been taught similar values. Although friend-making is a little hit or miss, you can do your part by explaining what it is to be a good friend. Mention why it's important to look for chums "just like you."

Adults in Their Lives

Whether it's teachers, neighbors, coaches, or employers, other adults can play a significant role in the values of your child. It's impossible to keep them away from every negative influence (you can't lock them up), so you need to be a student of the adults influencing your kids. Be a good observer, though. For instance, are any of the coaches yelling obscenities at players or referees? Is the shift manager dipping into the till? Does the next-door dad have "Playmate of the Month" posters all over the garage walls? Asking the right questions—but not making the right statements (especially to a teen)—teaches discernment, shows respect, and allows the children to value what you do.

CHAPTER 19

WHAT'S THE SUREFIRE FORMULA?

Parents Piecing the Puzzle Together

You would think that the scores of children who "made it" into their adult years with their faith intact could rattle off dozens of ways their parents pointed them to Christ. They did. They just didn't give us as many definitive patterns as we thought there would be.

Based on the responses we received (and they were all over the spiritual map), only *one* answer was common to every list. Read through the following statements. Can you guess which one it was?

- "Conversational prayer was often heard in our home."
- "I always saw Mom and Dad reading their Bibles."
- "My parents taught us how to spend daily time with God."
- "We had easy access to Christian books and magazines."
- "Sunday school attendance was a must."
- "We always had family devotions."
- "I made a profession of faith early in life."

- "What really helped was belonging to a great youth group during the teen years."
- "Every summer, I went to a Christian camp."
- "Other adults had a direct influence in pointing me toward Christ."

In case you're wondering, Christian schools or home schooling weren't popular when the adult children were growing up, so that's why you didn't see any remarks relating to them on the list.

Before we give you the answer, let's touch on each response and examine its importance. (Remember, no fair peeking!)

"Conversational prayer was often heard in our home."
In the early grade school years, about half the parents prayed consistently with their children. As their children moved into the junior high and high school years, we saw a *big* drop (to about 15 percent) in kids who said they prayed fairly often with their folks.

Why did that happen? As life got more hectic in the teen years, the sad fact was that most families didn't take the time to pray together—not even occasionally. Was it Dad's lack of leadership? Was it Mom's job? The kids' busy extracurricular schedule? It's hard to tell from our vantage point. But the impact prayer can have on a growing child isn't as tough to discern.

"Our life was surrounded by prayer," one Nebraska man told us. "We were farmers, so we were always worried about having enough money come in to pay the bills. We brought everything to God, including Bessy the cow if she wasn't milking. We learned as a family to praise God through trials. I learned the value of suffering. My father's prayers were simple, but he trusted the One whom he knew was in control. I learned a childlike trust from my dad."

Has your family slipped into the habit of saying *"mañana"* when it comes to praying? How do you feel about that? What is that teaching your children?

We asked a number of adult children how their parents' lack of consistent prayer affected their spiritual lives. After a few moments of reflection, most admitted their present-day prayer habits weren't that good.

Another side benefit of praying with your children is that you might actually receive what you ask for. Said a Houston father, "We saw that praying for our son's friends and his decisions really made the difference when Billy was growing up. I'd find myself being amazed and thinking, *Gee, God, my boy dumped those friends, and I didn't have to force him to do it!*"

"I always saw Mom and Dad reading their Bibles."

Here are the percentages of how often the adult children observed their parents reading God's Word:

- not at all (26 percent)
- once a month (12 percent)
- once a week (16 percent)
- several times a week (18 percent)
- daily (28 percent)

Did you notice any distinct patterns? We didn't either. But the chances of raising kids who love and obey God's Word will be greatly increased if they see *you* cracking open the Bible more often than every Christmas morning when you read Luke 2. While you never want to read your Bible just to impress your kids (they'll see right through that), spending time with God when your children "just happen" to be in the neighborhood is a nice example, too.

Building a hunger for the Bible in your kids starts with your own spiritual appetite. If you don't make much time for God's Word, chances are your children won't either.

"My parents taught us how to spend daily time with God."

Nope, it's not this one. In fact, parents were negligent in this area. Less than 10 percent of the kids we surveyed could ever remember their parents' showing them *how* to read their Bible and apply it to their lives. To us, this speaks volumes about the communication levels in those homes. And you can add a few appendixes about what their priorities were as well.

We did talk to one family that succeeded in this area. They used their nightly devotions to teach their children how to read the Bible. "A little after dinner, we'd meet for about fifteen minutes, never much more than that," said Laurie Calhoun. "We took turns reading and praying. My folks would answer our questions and help make the Bible interesting."

It doesn't always take a spiral-bound manual and a ten-week course to get a point across. For the Calhouns, the process of building an understanding and love for the Bible was as natural as waking up in the morning.

"We had easy access to Christian books and magazines."

Few respondents described their homes as places where Christian literature hung around their living rooms. We believe there were two reasons for this: First, it's only in the last five to ten years that so many Christian books and magazines for children and teens have hit the marketplace. Second, books and magazines (or tapes) are like meals. You probably can't remember what you ate last Thursday for lunch, but you'd sure remember if you hadn't eaten!

We know from experience that these resources are a wonderful way for kids to munch on spiritual values, not only during the early years, but during the all-important teenage years as well. And while reading Christian publications probably won't be one of the top three reasons your children stick with the faith, it's certainly an important part of the equation.

"Sunday school attendance was a must."
Many remembered these "formal" times of religious instruction, but they weren't the key. Besides, more than 50 percent said they quit going to Sunday school once they hit high school!

///

The Top Ten Reasons for Teens Not to Join a Youth Group or Go to Sunday School

10. It's better to avoid church and be thought unspiritual than to be asked a question about the Bible and remove all doubt.
9. Nine o'clock on Sunday mornings comes *way* too early.
8. Five days of school each week is already too much!
7. Because your parents want you to go.
6. You'll never hear those choruses on MTV.
5. You might be allergic to polyester suits.
4. If the kids at school found out, you'd never live it down.
3. You don't believe the Bible anymore because you think there's no way Moses could have gotten all those animals into the ark.
2. You might have to stop doing all those wild things that drive your parents nuts.
1. The youth pastor is a total dweeb.

///

"We always had family devotions."

Only 25 percent of the adult children said their parents led them through a formal time of Bible or devotional reading and prayer, which is how we define "family devotions." Several kids did comment about a father's feeble attempts at starting them, but Dad usually quit after a few times.

So, how did some parents persevere and keep family devotions fun and fresh?

"My father had a different family member lead them each time," one Wyoming man told us. "Every morning during breakfast, he would ask one of us to read from a small devotional book and take prayer requests. There were some days I wasn't into it, but many seeds were planted around the kitchen table. We continued that daily tradition until high school graduation. I don't even think my parents knew how much it would pay off later on."

///

Are Regular Family Devotions Possible?

Thousands of Christian parents struggle with how to live up to the Christian ideal of "family devotions."

I struggled when our children were growing up. Somewhere, Arlie and I picked up the idea that we *had* to have family devotions at a certain time each day (at the dinner table) and for a certain length of time.

But we found it wasn't always practical, or even wise, to live up to an ideal. There were nights when Little League practice, a school play, something at church, or a dozen other things crowded our family devotions and even crowded them out. We sensed that at times it actually would have been counterproductive to go ahead with our ideal. And we didn't want to risk turning the children off to the whole idea.

I believe our children love the Word of God today because we made our occasional visits into the Word times of delight. We tried lots of approaches. Sometimes they worked; sometimes they bombed. When they bombed, we admitted it and waited for a better time. Devotions at our house became "irregularly" regular times of delight rather than oppressively regular times of drudgery.

It may help you to know that all of our children are grown now, and the fruit is on the tree. They are all Christians, have married Christians, and are raising their children in Christian homes. My son and I have coauthored about twenty Christian books for children.

I've thought a lot about what worked and what didn't in this area of spiritual leadership in my home, and I've gleaned the following principles:

- Love for the Lord flows naturally from love for his Word.
- A consistent time for family devotions is great, as long as guilt and routine stay in the background.
- If you don't give up, you can find a format that works.
- If you ask him, God will give you abundant grace and wisdom to be good parents and spiritual leaders.

How do we apply these principles? With all my heart I believe that the first step in leading our children to Christ, and to a lifetime of walking with him, is not force-feeding Bible knowledge. Rather, it is helping them to *love* God's Word, to see it as a user-friendly reflection of the Living Word, our Lord Jesus. Jeremiah 15:16 says, "When your words came, I ate them; they were my joy and my heart's delight."

How can we help our children "consume" God's Word so that it becomes their "hearts' delight"? Here are some suggestions:

1. Speak with a positive attitude. Try not to say things like: "You will *not* get out of that chair until we are through"; "Be quiet and listen!"; or "One more giggle out of you and you'll go to your room!" Reinforce a positive attitude by saying things like: "Guess which wonderful person we're going to meet in the Bible tonight!"; "Let's have a contest to see who can . . ."; "I'm so excited about the Bible passage we're going to read."

2. Keep devotions on the bright side. Where did we ever get the idea that holiness is somber or gloomy?

Encourage a few giggles; don't squelch them. Let a child interrupt with something funny she heard that day. Make up a game to guess Bible facts. How about having cake and ice cream with devotions?

3. **Link learning about the Bible with building your child's self-esteem.** "Kathy! What a wonderful thought!" "Ron, you're a brave, young man like Joshua, you know." "Jan, you're my little helper, just like Dorcas."

4. **Use a Bible or Bible book geared to your child's age level.** When I couldn't find what I wanted, I wrote three age-graded Bibles for children: *The Toddler's Bible* (birth to age three, Victor Books); *The Early Readers Bible* (Questar); and *The Bible for Children* (elementary age to preteen, Tyndale House).

   Here are some of my favorite devotional books for children: Ken Taylor's *The Bible in Pictures for Little Eyes; Good News for Little People;* and *Wise Words for Little People;* Mack Thomas's *What Would Jesus Do?* and *The Bible Tells Me So;* and Stephen Barclift's *The Beginner's Devotional.* Mary Hollingsworth has written some books that should "delight": *The King's Numbers; The King's Alphabet;* and *Polka Dots, Stripes, Humps 'n Hatracks.*

5. **Ask yourself if you've delighted in the Word today.** If you haven't, read Psalm 119 and recapture some of your passion for God's Word. Most likely, your children's attitude will reflect your own.

   Above all, keep in mind the ultimate purpose of family devotions: to help your children know the Lord, love him, and walk in his ways. When your grown children make devotions with their own children a priority, you'll be glad for every moment you spent with them in the delights of his Word.

   —V. Gilbert Beers, president of Scripture Press

//

A Wheaton, Illinois, man told us the key to his family's devotions was the creativity of his parents. "My dad would do Bible quizzes, ones that he made up on his own. Or else he'd start out with some bizarre trivia question, like who was the tallest person in the Bible? When he told stories, he always added drama and excitement. He'd even scare us sometimes. During our teen years, he helped us be more literate with the Bible. Variety was the key. We never knew what would happen next."

Though family devotions are not the spiritual life insurance of the nineties, one thing is certain: God's Word will never return void. The tiny seeds of faith sown into a young mind will pay dividends later in life.

"I made a profession of faith early in life."
No doubt, when children dedicate their lives to Christ, everything else pales in significance! Most adult children told us they took that step early in life, followed by other professions of faith when they knew more of what they were doing—often in their late teens and twenties. Appendix 4 has an enlightening compilation of when and how the adult children we surveyed finally stuck with Christ. Many of us, however, know friends and acquaintances who made decisions for Christ early in childhood, only to drop by the wayside when they became adults. Something didn't click. Perhaps no one taught them how to grow spiritually.

While childhood—and even teenage—commitments to Christ don't always stick, we're still recommending that parents encourage those decisions. Whatever level children understand and commit to the gospel should be met with parental enthusiasm and support. But remember that their spiritual walk is just beginning with that small step.

"What really helped was belonging to a great youth group during the teen years."
Since many of the adult children grew up before the era of the

full-time youth pastor, belonging to a quality youth group was rare. These days, a pastor will hire a youth pastor before he'll hire a secretary; youth pastors are that much of a necessity. Why? Because teens need to be involved with other students in fellowship, teaching, and service. Several of the younger people we surveyed did say one key to their growth occurred when the family switched churches so they could be in a quality youth program.

We also talked to one father who regretted *not* getting his kids into a hot youth group. "If I could do it all over again, I would do it differently," said Richard Harris, the father from chapter 15. "I would have gone to a church where they had large youth groups so my teens could have had a lot of opportunities to meet other kids. I would have done that even if it meant we had to drive across town, even if it meant leaving the denomination."

Richard's two daughters ended up marrying non-Christians, and while he doesn't place 100 percent of the blame on a lousy youth group, he believes it was a factor. "I think the biggest problem with the girls was the whole dating thing. We went to a church with a small youth group. Neither were real glamorous girls. Both wondered: *How am I going to find a man? How choosy can I be?* I think they both opted not to be so choosy."

"Every summer, I went to a Christian camp."

Mountaintop experiences are important, but few adult children mentioned doing this. Granted, a summer camp or a foreign mission trip will stand out in a child's life as a high point—and rightly so. But a few weeks of those experiences can't compare to the day-in-and-day-out input a mother and father can have.

//

The Top Ten Worst Ways to Keep Your Children Following Christ

10. Adding ten more laws to the original Ten Commandments.
9. Forcing them to sit through church business meetings when the congregation is voting on amendments to the bylaws.
8. Making your son sing in the children's choir when he's going through puberty.
7. Committing your teens to helping out in the nursery.
6. Having the pastor over for dinner and asking him to reveal his deepest, darkest sins.
5. Dropping them off for church every Sunday morning, then going home to watch football.
4. When they're teenagers and asking about sex, replying, "God doesn't like to talk about that subject, so you shouldn't even be *thinking* about it."
3. Having them turn on the TV and watch a money appeal from a televangelist.
2. Giving them every stinking thing they ask for.
1. Saying no to every stinking thing they ask for.

//

"Other adults had a direct influence in pointing me toward Christ."

Finally, this is it! But you knew that, if only by process of elimination. More than *90 percent* of those we talked to could name significant adults who influenced them toward Christ: Sunday school teachers, Pioneer Girl leaders, aunts, uncles, brothers, sisters, grandparents, Scout leaders, schoolteachers, neighbors, youth leaders, baby-sitters, friends of the family—all were mentioned.

"The biggest problem I had," one pastor said about his kids, "was when they would secretly try to convince us they were in a right relationship with God and us. It was tough for my wife and me to figure out. What saved us was the people who were committed to our kids. Their youth leader could always pick up when our kids were straying off the track. He'd say—in a nice way, of course—something like this: 'I know what you're doing, and it's awful. You're developing into a dishonest person.' That would do it! Such incidents happened several times during their teenage years. That's the beauty of the body of Christ. God knows you can't do it on your own. The other people in our kids' lives serve as a safety net."

Another woman, Judy Davenport, told us about someone who took her under her wing during the turbulent teenage years. "She discipled me once a week when we did stuff together. She was a solid example because she'd admit her weaknesses. I remember her telling me she wasn't disciplined, that it was a struggle to read her Bible. She explained how applicable God is to real life, and she didn't mind challenging Christian traditions to help my faith come alive. I had so few peers who were seeking God and applying him to their lives that I soaked in all she said, even though she was fourteen years older than me."

At first, Judy's folks were excited about this relationship. But after a year, her mother became jealous of the amount of time Judy was spending with this other woman. Jealousy turned into anger. Finally, in her high school senior year, Judy's parents made her cut back on seeing the woman because Judy was developing a bad attitude.

Perhaps in that case, Judy's parents were in the right. Certainly, mothers and fathers do not want to abdicate their parental roles. But if another Christian adult is having a positive influence on your children, *work* with that person so you're all pulling on the same rope.

Throughout your kids' lives, expose and encourage them to seek out other Christian adults—people who will affirm what you believe. Your children need to hear truth and values from other voices. Yes, you need to monitor the relationship to make sure it's healthy, but don't prevent them from branching out to learn from other Christians.

Is Your Puzzle Missing a Few Pieces?

While we didn't come up with the sure-fire formula, one thing was obvious: Those who stuck with their faith—and are still going strong for the Lord—had a half-dozen "mentors" present during their growing-up years.

Adults who are presently in full-time ministry or active lay involvement said good relationships with their parents *and* Christian mentors were the two key influences in their lives. In addition, a balance was struck in the home between the ten elements discussed in this chapter.

If you want to raise faithful kids, try to find the right mix to put your children in the best possible position to grow. Within that twenty-year span when they're under your roof, you can't afford to leave many of those ten influences out. Not these days.

CONTEMPORARY ISSUES FACING TODAY'S FAMILIES

"Leave It to Beaver" families belong to another era. Today's families are facing issues that were unheard of a generation ago.

CHAPTER 20

MOM VS. MOM
Parents and Career Choices

Bailiff: All rise. The Honorable Harold Solomon presiding.

Attorney Amy Becker (representing mothers employed outside the home): Your Honor, may I approach the bench?

Judge: Yes, you may.

Attorney Becker: Your Honor, I represent millions of working mothers, many of whom have been unfairly maligned in recent years . . .

Attorney Carole Evert (representing stay-at-home moms): Your Honor, I object. *All* moms are working moms, especially those raising children in their homes. We don't sit around in curlers watching soaps and munching bonbons all day.

    Your Honor, do you know what it's like to be a stay-at-home mom on a school "snow day"? That's when your phone starts ringing at 7:15 a.m. All the working moms are frantically calling to ask if they can park their children with you for the day. One mom who lived across the street from an elementary school told me she received a call from the school nurse asking if she could watch a sick boy since his parents couldn't come and get him.

Attorney Becker: Your Honor, we're getting sidetracked here. A growing number of mothers either *must* work to bolster the family income or *want* to work to continue a career. I am here seeking an injunction against stay-at-home moms who continually make rude remarks about my clients. Just last week, one stay-at-home—who was watching the one-year-old son of a senior account executive—told my client that it was too bad she had to miss Brian's first steps. My client went home shattered by the experience. If we could have a little respect from stay-at-home mothers . . .

Attorney Evert: Respect? Your Honor, the only thing lower than stay-at-home moms on society's totem pole are toxic waste polluters. When's the last time you saw a TV Sunday night movie extolling the decision of a career mom to stay home and raise her children?

Attorney Becker: May I finish?

Attorney Evert: Sure. We stay-at-home moms always have plenty of time on our hands.

And so it goes. The issue of moms employed outside the home versus stay-at-home moms is guaranteed to shoot fireworks into the sky—any time of year. Whenever we run a story remotely touching this topic in *Focus on the Family* magazine, I (Mike) get an earful from both sides. This subject—along with schooling—generates the most mail to the editor.

Lest you think this "Mom versus Mom" stuff belongs only to the secular world, we have working Christian moms who tell us they feel the "gazing darts" from stay-at-home moms. "I wish Christian friends had been less judgmental," confided one mom. "I felt a lot of pressure that I was doing the wrong thing by working."

At the outset of this chapter, let us state our position. We believe, *if at all possible,* that children should be raised in a home where the *primary occupation* of the mother is to love, nurture, and raise the children. Our armchair perspective tells us that the chances of your kids coming out fine are greatly enhanced when Mom is doing the mothering. After all, when we pay someone else to look after our kids, we are asking that person to do for money what many of us will only do for love.

The Media Myth

In the May 1990 issue of *Focus on the Family* we published an excerpt from Dr. Dobson and Gary Bauer's book, *Children at Risk*. The article was drawn from Gary's chapter about how the media have promulgated the myth that "Ozzie and Harriet" families (i.e., families with a breadwinning father and stay-at-home mother) are finished, *finito*.

Perhaps you've seen the same stories in newsmagazines or your local newspaper. Usually, the writer begins his or her article with a look back—often derisive—at American families in the 1950s. We quickly learn that intact families with a breadwinning husband and stay-at-home wife are "dinosaurs" in the 1990s because "less than 10 percent of families fit the 'Ozzie and Harriet' model." Take that, you families with traditional ideas on raising kids!

It's easy to feel out of step with society when you read bunk like that. But it's not true! Bauer, who is president of the Family Research Council in Washington, D.C., says the "less than 10 percent" figure refers to a U.S. Census Bureau figure for a breadwinning father, stay-at-home mother, and *two*—count 'em, two—children.

I (Mike) am surprised that even 10 percent of American families can sit together under this tiny umbrella of a definition. Even though our family has two children, we don't qualify as a "traditional" family, either. That's because Nicole teaches a French class one afternoon a week for ninety minutes. My wife, according to the Census Bureau, is an employed mom.

Greg's wife, Elaine, has a part-time job, too: she occasionally sorts out contest entries from *Clubhouse* magazine readers. The modest stipend she receives disqualifies her from *pure* "stay-at-home" status, but she's still a traditional mom in anyone's book.

But what is a "traditional" mom? Ask that question of 150 moms, as we did, and you'll get 150 different answers. Although many moms had different stories to tell, here are some generalizations:

- Thirty-three percent said they were stay-at-home moms.
- Fifty percent said they worked part-time when their children were growing up.
- The remaining 17 percent said they worked full-time outside the home.

Of the stay-at-home moms we interviewed, many said that decision didn't come without sacrifices.

"I was fortunate I didn't have to work," said Susan Black, whose husband was in the air force. "I was always there after school for my three girls. We had Girl Scouts, and we had time to get involved in bowling leagues. Whenever the kids were in bowling tournaments, we'd spend the whole day together. I praise God for not having to work," she said.

"But I would sure not be critical of those who are working," she added, "because I know it does take two salaries for many families these days. We just didn't live high on the hog. We struggled financially, but that's not what a lot of people want to do these days. Yet I would do it again if that meant I could stay home with the kids."

More often than not, mothers said they came to a fork in the road and had to choose: career or kids. Carol Bentley's first child was born in 1960, and after leaving her son with a baby-sitter for a few months, she made a deliberate choice to stay home.

"My husband was in the navy, so the pay wasn't that great," she said. "I did things like child care in my home to make ends meet. We weren't starving, but it never did appeal to me to go out and work. I always felt sorry for anyone who had to wake up and drive their kids to the baby-sitter. That wasn't for me."

Moms Who Made It Work

Something noticed on the survey is the number of moms who worked jobs that allowed them to be there when the children arrived home from school. "I worked in the school system with the same hours as my children, so everything worked out well for me," said a South Carolina mom.

Said a Colorado mom: "I was a children's leader in a coop preschool program. I only worked while the kids were in school and was home before they arrived."

We also heard from career types who *wanted* to work but not sacrifice the family at the same time. "I enjoyed teaching," said Roxanne English, a mother of two. "My husband and I felt the children needed more adults than Mom to identify with. Being a schoolteacher gave me flexibility because my hours matched the time my children were in school."

Some moms backed off a bit on a full-time career. "I worked as a part-time teacher's aide for five years," said Melissa Kondon, "but that helped pay for my children's tuition. I enjoyed the work, but I was home when all the children were home. I was able to be part of my daughter's school environment, and she was even in one of the classes I helped. I performed all my home responsibilities and began some work on my own. I didn't experience empty nest as dramatically as some."

We also heard from some "tag-team" parents. Eva Tucker, a registered nurse, worked part-time nights when her son, Todd, was a baby. Her husband worked a normal eight-to-five and cared for Todd evenings. Eva didn't work at all for sixteen years until Todd was off to college and her two younger boys were in high school. "I started working nights again because I could be home when they left for school and be there when they arrived home. I had to work in order to put the boys through college, so I do not regret what I did. Now that the boys are all through school, I don't work outside the home."

Of course, for a certain number of moms—divorced, single, or widowed—working outside the home was not a choice. "Sure, I would have preferred being a full-time mom and wife," said one divorcée. "But I didn't have that opportunity. I had to be a breadwinner as well."

Said another single mom, "I was sole support of the family after the divorce. I think the ideal is for the mother to always be there when the children come home from school, though."

So, what should you do if you *have* to work? Here are some ideas:

- Work at a job that matches the hours your children are in school and their vacation periods.
- Work *in* the home. Do you have a skill that can be applied to a home-based business? Can you input computer data, make crafts, tutor, do bookkeeping, or watch other children?
- Job-share with another mom who wants to be there for her child. More and more companies are relaxing their rules about job-sharing in a bid to keep well-trained employees.

//

Something to Think About

Gary Bauer, president of the Family Research Council, points out that working moms usually bring in about 35 percent of the family income. In the last forty years, the tax burden on families has jumped from 2 percent to about 35 percent today. In other words, many moms are working in order to pay for the increased tax burden on families.

//

What's the Plan?

For couples contemplating marriage today, the question "Will Mom stay home with the kids?" needs to be part of any prenuptial counseling. Lorleen and her husband, Jay, didn't duck this one. "This was something Jay and I were firm about before we married," she said. "I grew up with my mother working full-time, and I really resented that. When I came home from school, I had no one to share my joys or problems with. We did not want this for our children, so I worked part-time. I wanted to keep my skills up in case I ever *had* to work full-time."

It's amazing how much it means to children for Mom to be there when they arrive home from school. When Nicole started teaching French on Tuesday afternoons, she couldn't be home when the kids arrived at 3:45. For a few weeks, Andrea and Patrick let themselves into the house and did homework and practiced the piano for an hour or so before Nicole got home. My children didn't like this arrangement one little bit, and they told us so.

So we made changes. I received permission from Focus to "flex" my Tuesday work schedule. I now work 6:30 a.m. to 3:30 p.m. Tuesdays, which means I have time to rush home and greet the kids. My kids think that's pretty special!

The last thing Nicole and I want is for Andrea and Patrick to be "latchkey kids." We've read too many articles about the dangers of being "home alone," and there's also the possibility they could get into all sorts of mischief. Latchkey teens, with their more-active minds, can use that free time to copy the bad behavior with the wrong crowd. "If I could have been home," lamented one Illinois mom, "my daughter might not have gotten involved with that rough group."

That's why some child-rearing experts, including Dr. Dobson, believe it's even *more* important for Mom to be home when the kids are teens. They can slip a borrowed X-rated video into the VCR, experiment with drugs, have a girlfriend (or boyfriend) in their bedroom—all while Mom is making a buck. The question to ask is: Is Mom's paycheck worth more than losing a child? Sadly, the choice of Mom working outside the home has already been made for hundreds of thousands of mothers. Through abandonment, divorce, or death of a spouse, they find themselves forced into the job market. Is it possible to raise faithful kids when you *can't* invest yourself full-time into the children? Of course, it is—with God's help. Our next chapter presents some practical ideas on how to accomplish it.

CHAPTER 21

FAMILIES FLYING SOLO
Single Parent Survival

When I (Greg) was twelve, Dad moved out for good and quickly married my mom's best friend. That set the neighborhood talking. It may have been a scene straight out of "As the World Turns," but it was being played out right in my own home. Any security I felt living in a normal family was shattered. My adolescent mind swirled with questions. *What do I do now? How am I supposed to behave?*

My mom was wondering the same things. After seventeen years of marriage and raising three kids, she had no marketable job skills— except for child-rearing. She couldn't cope. She'd either drink herself to sleep or spend endless hours on the phone (sometimes both). Then, after her mom died, she suffered a nervous breakdown.

Since we weren't a churchgoing family, Mom, my older brother and sister, and I were left to sort things out on our own. The soap opera got worse two years later, when Mom married a three-time loser and wife abuser. That union lasted three months, then we had to start all over . . . again. Finally, she found a wonderful man who treated her well, and since then she has been happily married.

I remember all too well, however, the struggles of my single-parent mom: loneliness, isolation from friends who didn't know how to help, feelings of insecurity, bitterness, and a broken heart. She needed us as much as we needed her—a common feeling in single-parent families. In the midst of this maelstrom, Mom's discipline disappeared. We used our freedom to experiment with drugs and alcohol during our high school years.

When I was eighteen, I became a Christian and totally changed the direction of my life—a life that was heading no-where fast. My brother and sister have yet to make that same change of direction. Though life hasn't been easy or fair for any of us, they have faced their share of disappointment from marriage. Both are now single parents.

The Facts Aren't Surprising

American Demographics reported recently that "if current trends continue, 61 percent of American children will spend some time in a single-parent household before their eighteenth birthday. In 1990, 16 million children lived with only one parent. That number has doubled since 1970. Forty-five percent of female-headed homes live in poverty. Thanks to Hollywood, the stigma of illegitimacy is gone as a motivating factor for marriage. As a result, one-quarter of all births in the U.S. are now out-of-wed-lock."[1]

If you're perceptive about your church's demographics, you may have noticed more and more single-parent families filling the pews. (That's actually *good* news, in a way. At least not all singles are leaving the church.) In fact, you could be reading this chapter because you're a single parent.

While one slim chapter can't address all the issues facing single parents these days, we know that you want to raise faithful kids just as much as the married couples—maybe even more so, if only to spare them the consequences and heartache of a busted marriage. While many of the principles and creative ideas we're discussing can easily apply to you, you're like a one-armed paperhanger. It's tough raising kids alone.

Dangers You Know So Well

We asked several pastors who are ministering to single parents how the ones successfully raising faithful children are pulling it off.

"The only single parents I see who are approaching success are those who don't fall into the tremendous trap of self-pity," one experienced pastor said. "These single moms are forced to go into the work force; they don't have a social life; and the kids demand a lot of time. It's not fair, and most singles recognize that parenting is a difficult, sometimes impossible task.

"The single moms and dads who become pessimistic and angry usually wallow in self-pity. You can't really blame them; those are just the facts. They have every reason to feel sorry for themselves because life has thrown them a major-league slider. I've seen several women, however, learn to live above their circumstances. They've decided they're going to walk with the Lord and be joyful, happy people. Their kids buy into their faith because they can see the miracle of a mom who has had it really tough over the years, but has maintained a good attitude."

The pastor quoted noted author Elisabeth Eliot, who has written extensively in this area. "She says, 'Your suffering can become the very place where Jesus shines. But American women expect life is going to get better, so they don't like to hear about shining during suffering. When you're a single parent, however, it often doesn't get better, it gets worse!

You've got to be able to live with this, and not succumb to anger, depression, and bitterness.'"

As soon as you do that, noted the pastor, you don't have anything else to give your kids other than those emotions. The key, then, is learning to make Jesus bigger than your circumstances. In other words, give *him* the problems. If the kids see the family succeeding, hope will reign. If not, they may feel he isn't a big enough God.

Hey, You Married Folks!

Please don't leave us. Reading this chapter will help you reach out to single-parent families in your church or on your block.

Advice from Single Moms

We interviewed several single parents and received some good advice, although space considerations won't allow us to cover this topic in greater detail. If you would like more information, please read one or more of the books recommended in appendix 10.

Don't Make Him Out to Be the Bad Guy

Divorces are rarely amicable. By the time the community property has been divvied up and the custody plans approved by the court, both sides have been shredded to bits. For some single moms, it's tempting to get back at a husband through the kids (and vice versa). The women we spoke with had been fighting that urge, even though some had been dumped on for years.

While you don't have to paint the absent parent as a giant-killing hero, don't color him bad to the bone, either. It's an old principle, but a good one: Let the children decide their father's character. The less bitterness or anger you show, the better example you'll be to your kids.

Sons Need a Man Around

Many of the single moms worried that their sons weren't learning how to be "masculine" since they were around females all the time. For some boys, the only male-to-male interaction came from a Sunday school teacher or Scout leader.

A young man who grew up in a broken home remembers what that was like. "After my dad and mom divorced, Mom went to the church and requested that some of the deacons spend time with me and my brother. They agreed. Though my brother and I saw through it, we went along with the scheme. We even became friends with some of them. Today, my brother's not active in his faith, but he still has those relationships to fall back on. That alone is important. Without a relational tie to the church, it's doubtful he'd ever come back."

Some churches start with good intentions for single parents, but fail to follow through.

"I went to a large church in southern California," a single mom of three children told us, "and one month they had this big thing about how the men were supposed to help single ladies with cars, fix screen doors, change the oil, things like that. It never happened. California families, I guess, value their weekends too much."

Another told us how hard it was to even *ask* for help.

"Being a single parent, and wanting to be able to do it all—and realizing you can't—was hard to come to grips with. I wanted someone to *offer* to be a buddy to my son. The last thing he needed was a one-time relationship. Fortunately, I knew a friend who was an ex-youth minister. His kids were all grown, and he agreed to take my son under his wing. It was great because I wanted my son to see that he could grow up and be a godly man—as opposed to his dad."

If your church is being negligent in this area, our advice is to holler loud and often until the leadership begins to respond. Though there might be some valid excuses for young dads wanting to concentrate on their own kids, the older fathers need to step forward.

Seek Family Counseling

Whether the children are young or old, the benefits of family counseling were often mentioned by the single parents we surveyed. Even if Mom has accepted the situation and the kids appear well-adjusted, there are still some deep waters flowing.

"Before I buried things underneath my hurt, Mom lined up counseling for us," said one young woman. "I learned the divorce wasn't my fault."

Added single mom Suzanne LeClair, "My son sees a counselor, and I'm fortunate that 80 percent of it is paid for by my insurance. He started when he was five because the school asked me to hold him back from kindergarten. The school counselor could see he wasn't adjusting well after the divorce."

"My son went to counseling for a year," another woman told us. "He was about seven, and even at that young age, he had a lot of anger. It took him a while before he was able to start talking. He soon improved, so I accompanied him to a few sessions. After the counselor showed me how to communicate better with my son, he told me something that made sense: 'Kids improve at the rate their parents do in emotionally handling the situation.' I've kept that thought as we go through this single-parent life together."

Not all single moms come out of divorce court. A widow relayed this story: "My kids were ten and eight when their father died after a long bout with cancer. We didn't see any counselors, but I wish we had. The kids were enrolled in a Christian school, and the teachers were saying the typical Christian stuff, like 'It must have been God's time.' My son withdrew and didn't talk. Though he eventually opened up, we had a very rough first few years."

Monitor What They're Hearing

"Sometimes my son will come back from visiting his dad and tell me about some weird spiritual things," one single mom said with concern. "My ex-husband is in A.A., and they leave it open as far as who God is. It's been hard because I have to counterbalance things my son's been hearing. Plus, my ex will take my son to attend movies I would never allow him to see. I have to constantly talk to him about what he saw and heard after he gets home from a visit."

Teaching proper values and spiritual lessons is a lot more difficult when one parent says one thing and another says something completely different. While such developments can lead to thoughtful talks—and the chance to point to the Bible as the ultimate source of truth—"deprogramming" may have to occur on a weekly basis. If communication is frosty between you and your ex, there's not much more you can do except pray and be prepared to do a lot of explaining.

Don't Forget the Discipline

"My husband was the fun one," one widow, Fran Billings, told us. "After he was gone, it seemed as if all the sparkle left the home. Since I was the one left with the disciplining of the kids,

I was always the bad guy. Then when the kids got older, they wanted more freedom and decision-making. But they still needed firm guidelines. That's probably been the toughest part of raising my kids alone."

The other difficulty, she said, was separating the tragedy of losing a father from the necessity of maintaining order in the home.

"Because my son had been through a lot, I'd give him plenty of leeway because I felt sorry for him," she said. "In addition, as I went through my grief, *I* needed him. I felt guilty about putting him in day care, and I compounded that guilt by purchasing more toys for him."

It *is* tough to say no when the kids have been torn apart by a death or divorce. But don't let grief or guilt keep you from sticking to your guardrails. The kids need you to *parent.* And if you're dealing with split custody or visitations, discuss your standards with your ex, if at all possible, so you can stay in sync on what's allowed and what's not.

Here again is strong support for the idea of teaching your kids discernment. Angela Elwell Hunt, in her book *Loving Someone Else's Child*, writes:

"When your child spends considerable time in a household with vastly different house rules, it is especially important to teach not just rules, but the *principles* behind the rules. Don't just tell your son not to go to R-rated movies; instead, explain that what we put into our minds and hearts stays in our subconscious. Show him Philippians 4:8, where we are told to think on things that are true, noble, pure, right, lovely, admirable, excellent, or praiseworthy.

"If you teach principles, your child will see the reasons behind the rules. He will learn to think and evaluate for himself."[2]

Establish Your Own Expectations

"When my son wanted to let his hair grow, I had to completely forget about pleasing others. I decided that this wasn't an issue to divide us, so I let him choose for himself. Guess what happened? I was judged for letting him have long hair."

Allowing church friends to determine which way your family ship will sail is a problem you're just going to have to get over. You'll be tossed and turned to do something, but don't let them get to you. Can you find one or two close friends who will talk honestly about how your kids are turning out? Discuss your struggles and parenting ideas with them.

Find Other Friends

As the children become older, it's tempting to subtly *change* the parent-child relationship to one of more equal footing.

"My daughter is twelve, and I have to make sure I'm not confiding in her," said a single mom. "She's at the point where we can chat about female things. I have to remember that I'm the mom and that she doesn't have to take care of me. That is really important. I need other buddies and confidants besides family members."

If you're a single mom it may be easy to begin depending on your kids for support—both emotionally and in doing more things around the house. While sharing the work at home is always appropriate, don't expect your young son or daughter to fill the role of your absent spouse. The older your kids are, the more you will struggle with keeping the parent-child roles intact. But children need you as a parent, not as a buddy.

One woman said it took her five years to find the friend she needed. "I prayed for that friend for quite a while," she said, "but I eventually found her."

Can Boys Talk?

When Lester Hayashi comes home after visiting his father for the weekend, it's usually Wednesday before he starts to open up to his mother again. Jean Hayashi says her fourteen-year-old son isn't a born talker and that she really has to pull it out of him.

The patient effort it takes to talk to boys—single parent or not—is difficult. But single moms must seek out those free-for-all discussions. The secret is finding out what hours of the day he talks best and plan them into your schedule. That's why you should always eat your meals together. The TV's off, his stomach is being warmed and filled, and he should be ripe to talk. Remember: Your son has many of the same feelings that girls have, but he's not mature enough to express them.

Put Yourself in the Children's Place

A single mom named Nancy Burke Smith wrote this after she started noticing looks of pity on the faces of friends and acquaintances:

"You think I have it tough? You think it's hard to juggle finances and work and caring and responsibility? Well, it is. But it's not nearly as hard as realizing, when you're a child of three or four years old, that your father doesn't want to see you. Being a single mom is not as hard as being a little boy and looking around and seeing only women and knowing that you're different somehow, but having no one 'like you' to talk about it with. It's not as hard as a mother who says, 'No, honey, not today. I can't buy you that toy or shirt or shoes or candy bar because the child support didn't come again.'

"It's not as hard as coming home one day and having Mom all excited, telling you that Dad's coming to take you fishing for the first time in all your six years of life, then watching Mom get angrier and sadder as the minutes tick off the clock. And it's not nearly as hard as pretending that you didn't really want to go and that you don't care and that you aren't going to cry when Mom puts you to bed that night.

"It's not as hard as letting Mom sleep in on Saturday mornings while you watch cartoons all by yourself. Or as hard as being sick and trying to pretend you're not because you know Mom gets worried about paying the doctor bills, and she doesn't have anyone to talk to about how to make you better."[3]

Find a Youth Program

Once the kids reach the teenage years, the importance of getting them involved with a lively, stimulating youth group can't be overestimated.

A mother of three told us, "The church I'm at now has a good youth pastor, and I'm going to stay there. I want my kids to make friends at church rather than school. If I had my choice I'd go to a church with a good singles' program, but if you lose them during junior high, it's over."

Emily Beach, a single mom, said, "I don't mind going to a church where I don't really get that much, as long as my son finds a good youth group. In the future, I'll want to find a place where my spiritual and social needs can be met—but that will have to wait until life gets more stable around here."

That's good advice. On top of that, you and your children need a web of relationships to enfold you. You may not find it in the first church you check out, or even the second or third, but don't give up. Give a church a respectable chance at ministering to your family—a month or more at least—but if you don't see the potential for healthy, supportive relationships by then, keep looking till you find the right place.

Make Church a Priority

Because single moms battle constant fatigue, Sundays are often the only "catch-up" day of the week. One single mom confessed that some Sunday mornings she doesn't want to get up, but she knows that worship and Sunday school are important. "I tell the kids, 'God is expecting us today.' And after church, I'll offer my youngest daughter a quarter if she can tell me five things she learned in Sunday school. That really helps her listen."

Continuing to build healthy attitudes about the church, the pastor, Sunday school, and the Bible in the midst of a divorce or the death of a spouse is *very* tough work. But even though fatigue and discouragement constantly nip at your heels, hang in there, Mom! With God's help, you can succeed.

CHAPTER 22

HEIGH-HO, HEIGH-HO, IT'S OFF TO SCHOOL THEY GO

Parents and Schooling Choices

On the cover of the April 1991 issue of *Focus on the Family* magazine, a cute, apple-cheeked boy of seven sat in a school desk, his left arm raised in the air.

"Where Will I Go to School?" the headline asked, and indeed, it's a question many Christian parents are asking themselves these days. In the ensuing article, we heard leaders in three branches of education—Christian, public, and home school— tell the Focus audience why they thought their avenue of learning was best.

You should have read the avalanche of mail that arrived on our doorstep! Parents in all three camps were quick to tell why their way was the only way.

Like the *Focus on the Family* magazine article, we will not take a position on public versus Christian versus home-school schooling. There are compelling arguments from all sides, and many of them make sense to us. As one *Focus* letter writer stated, our decision-making guide on this issue is not clearly spelled out in Scripture. He quoted Romans 14:5, which says, "One man esteemeth one day above another; another esteemeth every day alike. Let every man be fully persuaded in his own mind" (KJV).

Parents today are faced with a real dilemma about where to educate their children. For instance, the positives of a Christian school or home schooling are these: The peer group can be controlled; their education can often be accelerated; the teachers are Christians; and the curriculum isn't secularized as it is in public schools.

Perhaps you want to send your children to a Christian school, but the closest one is a hundred miles away. Or maybe the neighborhood Christian school is a three-room set-up in the back of a church that is heavy into legalism. Or perhaps—and this reason is more likely—you can't afford the tuition fees, which run anywhere from two thousand to five thousand dollars a year.

Public schools have their problems; there's no argument there. We're well aware of the shortcomings; we both send our children to public schools in Colorado Springs. We're also involved parents (Elaine and Nicole are classroom volunteers). But we believe there's a place for Christian parents in the public school system, and while we know religion is banned from the school-room, we aren't ready to throw in the towel—not yet.

Some of the reasons for staying in public schools are these:

- Christian school costs can be prohibitive. Home schooling your kids takes a patient and motivated mother (usually).
- Children can learn how to relate to non-Christians, hopefully without being negatively influenced themselves.
- If the parents are good models, the children have an incredible opportunity to reach out to non-Christians.
- Children are less likely to feel they are being force-fed

more "Christian information" than what most already receive at home, church, Sunday school, and youth group.

- Parents may need to take on this challenge in order to build communication and cement the relationship with their kids, rather than sending their children to a Christian school expecting *them* to teach *their* values.

Home schooling is for the truly committed. Quite frankly, we feel you have to be specially cut out for something as demanding as educating your own children. Only a decade or two ago this movement was on the fringes of education, but it has picked up steam in recent years because of the deteriorating public school system.

What Parents Said about Christian Schools

"Peer pressure is greatest in junior and senior high school, so a Christian school environment gave our children the opportunity to find believing friends. I would *not* have done things differently," said one mother.

We also heard from parents who felt the Christian school in their area was stronger academically than the public school. Several fathers and mothers added that they felt so strongly about Christian schools that they started such schools in their communities. That's a wonderful ministry to have if God calls you in that direction.

One mother told us she believed she "lost" her son, Caleb, in the seventh grade. "If we'd made the sacrifice then to put him in a Christian school, he would still be 'with us' today."

We did hear a downside. One parent with a seventh-grader in Christian schooling said her daughter had many classmates who were there because they had been problem kids in the public schools.

But generally, many parents wished they had sent their kids to Christian schools. Typical was this comment: "It would have been Christian schools all the way if we could have afforded it."

We also heard this from a mom who sent her children to public school: "We have strong convictions in favor of Christian schooling. Even though our kids chose to serve the Lord, they would have had a better education and a lot less hassles in the Christian environment. It seemed impossible for us to afford at the time, but I think we should have made more of an effort."

What Parents Said about Public Schools

We had many enthusiastic responses about public education— surprising, given all the abuse it has received over the years. Many parents expressed the view that their children need to be exposed to the secular world *while* they're still under the parents' influence. Some felt their experiences in public schools tested and strengthened their faith. Others who raised their children in the fifties and sixties argued that it's a different world in the 1990s, and they would rethink sending their children to public schools if they had to do it again.

Some parents, in deciding what was more important—Mom staying home or having her work so they could afford Christian school tuition—opted for the former. Those moms who did stay home said they volunteered to help in the classrooms and felt they were a positive influence on their children's teachers.

Here's an interesting story from a California mom: "Noah was in a government civics class at our public school, and they were supposed to simulate a legislature. The law they were working on was parental notification for abortion. Noah volunteered to work on the side *for* it. The rest of the class was against him, and they brought in a Planned Parenthood speaker to present their case. Noah asked me to come in and speak for parental notification.

"The woman from Planned Parenthood told the class that if this bill was passed, she would break the law and not notify the parents! And she would encourage her coworkers to do the same.

"The teacher allowed this whole conversation. But I was able to turn it around. Light will definitely shine brighter than darkness. I asked the teacher, 'How can you promote breaking the law?' He replied that you need to stimulate the children to think. But I hung in there, and I had an impact on those kids."

///

Need a Match?

If you've just moved to a new town or are unhappy with your children's school—or if you want to know how well your school stacks up to others in the area—a counseling service called School Match can help.

School Match has data on all U.S. public school systems and the nearly fifteen thousand private and parochial schools across the country. Parents fill out a detailed questionnaire or can call School Match's toll-free number (1-800-992-5323) and give their answers to a service representative. From that, they receive a printout of possible schools.

Cost of the service is $97.50, or $49 if you just want to know how well your school is doing. For more information, write School Match, 5027 Pine Creek Drive, Westerville, OH 43081.

///

What Parents Said about Home Schooling

Because home schooling was unheard of twenty and thirty years ago, only a few parents we interviewed kept their children out of formal education and taught them at home. Many felt home schooling is a good idea but believed it wouldn't have worked in their home because they didn't feel qualified to teach their kids, or they didn't have the temperament to handle the situation.

One mother who home-schooled said, "It's very important to keep *all* Christian children from public schools. We preferred home schooling because God holds the parent responsible for what the children learn."

Those in the home-schooling arena believe their children can receive a good education. Several years ago, the National Center for Home Education checked the academic progress of home-schooled students and learned that the average student scored above the 80th percentile on national achievement tests, such as the Stanford Achievement or Iowa Basic Skills. The average public school score, of course, is the 50th percentile.

Where Will They Attend College?

Christian college administrators often say it's even *more* important to send a child to a Christian college because when the high school graduate leaves home, parental influence ends, and peer pressure and the temptations of the world increase tenfold.

It's hard to argue with that statement. But again, every family is different. We had adult children tell us that they probably wouldn't have remained Christians if they had attended a state school; others, like Alea Roberts (in chapter 16), felt their Christian colleges made it easy to set their faith on the sidelines.

Either way, the choice of college is a crucial one—for many reasons. All parents want their children to receive a good college education without rejecting their faith. And from a worldly standpoint, it's getting more and more difficult to support a family *without* a college education.

One parent told us she believed the best gift she could give her children was a four-year degree. "When we're dead and gone, what good will their inheritance do then? We'd rather spend it now on a college education."

With the average cost of attending a private university, including tuition, room and board, and incidentals, heading past the ten-thousand-dollars-a-year mark, parents are looking for ways to trim costs. High school seniors can take advanced placement tests and receive college credit. I (Mike) took all those tests, and I entered the University of Oregon with two semesters of credit. Although I had to "load up" with classes for a couple of semesters, I graduated in three years and saved my parents a bundle.

Students can live at home the first year or two and attend a local college. Or they can pay in-state tuition and enroll in a public university before transferring to—and graduating from— a more prestigious school.

It's likely that you'll be footing the bill (or a large chunk of it). Either way, you should certainly take a role in planning *where* and *which kind* of college your kids will attend. One father, who said his children went to public high schools, told us with regret, "We left the choice of college up to them. We should have insisted on Christian colleges for the two children because they were spiritually immature."

Dan Masterson told us about his approach to picking a college for his teens. "I left the choice of college to my kids, but I told them that since I was paying the freight, they could attend a strong, biblically based Christian college or an inexpensive community college. That's because I didn't want to send them to a Christian college with non-Christian professors. They're too expensive and they don't always deliver when it comes to building a child's character."

If you do help out financially, you might do what John Wesson did. He told his kids that he would pay for college, but that once they stopped, they were on their own. None of this "taking a year off" stuff. Both kids finished in four years.

What the Adult Children Had to Say

About 85 percent said they attended public schools growing up. In college, however, more than half said they either enrolled in a Christian university or spent part of their collegiate years at one.

Here are a few sample comments on their schooling:

- "My mom never brought cupcakes or did playground duty. I would have liked that."
- "They showed no real interest. They were ultimately afraid that our education would take us away from God."
- "I really appreciated their financial commitment to our high education."
- "We moved a lot, especially in grade school. I wish we had been more settled so I could have kept the same group of friends and not had to keep starting over."
- "Paying for college myself really taught me responsibility." (We guess so! But these days, it's almost an impossibility.)
- "I think they could have encouraged participation in areas I was interested in: drama, track, and cheerleading. Church took so much time and priority that I couldn't make it to practices enough to be involved."
- "Their timing was perfect. In junior high, I switched to a Christian school because I was beginning to be influenced by the other kids' language and attitudes."
- "I had very little involvement with non-Christians, and I

was not encouraged to be involved in school activities. You see, they weren't important because they weren't Christian. Maybe I could have influenced more of my peers for the Lord if I had been more involved."

- "I went to Christian school from fifth to tenth grade, then public from eleventh to twelfth. My education was fabulous! The Christian school experience prepared me for my last two years of high school, where I was able to stand strong for Jesus."

Making Plans

Are you thoroughly confused? That's okay. Where you need to begin is with the Lord. Take your children's schooling options to him. Pray about them with your spouse. Talk to other parents. Ask your pastor for his view. Don't listen to anyone who says you *have* to send your kids to a certain Ivy League school or that particular Christian college.

Ask for God's wisdom, and then make your decision. But keep evaluating the direction you chose because your children only go through the education hoops once.

CHAPTER 23

McJOBS
Parents and Teen Employment

To work or not to work.

Not you, Mom. We're talking about your teenage kids, and like most things in the nineties, working as a young teen ain't what it used to be.

When our grandparents were growing up, teen employment was usually the domain of those destined to work blue-collar factory jobs, young folks who weren't going to—or weren't able to—further their education. As St. Louis Cardinal pitcher Dizzy Dean said during the Great Depression, "Those who won't say ain't, ain't working."

These days, the times are a-changing regarding adolescents in the work force. Teens are now twice as likely to work as they were in 1950, according to Simmons Market Research Bureau. The proliferation of McDonald's and Wendy's on every street corner has created an unprecedented demand for cheap labor—one that high-school-age students can easily fill. Teenage Research Unlimited, another market research firm, estimates that by their junior year, more than 40 percent of high school students will have jobs, and that the average teen has $60 a week in spending money from jobs and allowances. In addition, school-time jobs are predominantly held by middle-class students, the organization notes.

Psychologists Ellen Greenberger and Laurance Steinberg addressed this subject in *When Teenagers Work*, a book that demonstrates how teen jobs hurt academic performance and do not provide more family income. Instead, the authors note, the modest paychecks are tossed into a sinkhole of car payments, lavish dates, designer clothes, stereos, and TVs. Only 10 percent of high-school seniors said they are saving most of their earnings for college, and just 6 percent said they chipped in to help pay family living expenses.

In addition, high-school students in California and Wisconsin who worked more than twenty-one hours a week did much poorer in school (average grade point average: 2.66) than teens who worked ten or less hours a week (grade point average: 3.04). The students working long hours were so tired (many high schools start at 7:15 these days) that they struggled to keep their eyes open during class. Study hall was suddenly a coveted class period: a place where students could lay their heads on the table for fifty minutes of uninterrupted shut-eye.

Homework? Public schools have become less demanding since the 1960s because they can't enforce the higher standards. The average high school student has one hour of homework. That leaves enough time to put in a shift at Burger King, and if the students don't get around to what little homework they have, well, the teacher can't do anything about it anyway. So teens learn less.

"Everybody worries why Japanese and German and Swedish students are doing better than us," said Steinberg, a Temple University professor. "One reason is that they're not spending their afternoons wrapping tacos."[1]

///

The Top Ten Worst Excuses for Not Doing Homework

10. "The dog might eat it, and then I would have wasted all that effort."
 9. "But Mom, 'The Simpsons' *are* my homework!" [Don't laugh—this could actually be true!]
 8. "Only nerds do homework. If I did mine, none of my friends would like me."
 7. "I'll do it in the morning."
 6. "I need *you* to help me!"
 5. "Dad said I didn't have to do it."
 4. "Our teacher is crazy. Nobody can understand what he's talking about."
 3. "I forgot it in my locker at school."
 2. "Billy never does his homework, and the teacher never says anything."
 1. "But this is the season finale—I've *got* to watch this show!"

///

Some Questions

While we believe a moderate amount of working during the teen years can be beneficial, today's parents must ask themselves some hard questions: *Why* is my teen working? Is it to learn *how* to work? To learn responsibility? To pay for necessities I can't afford? To augment the child's college fund? Or is it to make monthly payments on that gleaming Z-28 sitting in the driveway?

Forty percent of teens seventeen and under have their own cars or trucks. Coincidentally, this matches the number of teens who have jobs by their junior year. If your teens say they *must* have cars because everyone else does, point out that 60 percent of their peers *don't* have their own cars. Tell them they can borrow yours, or do what this New Hampshire mom did:

"My husband and I know that a lot of kids work to have cars," said Patricia Witters. "It can be the most important thing in life to have wheels. We decided that if we provided a car, our kids could concentrate on other things, like their studies. So we bought used cars, usually old Suburbans because they're built like tanks. At one point, we had three kids in high school. Having one car taught them to share. They had to learn to work things out."

The Witters said their children learned to appreciate the well-used Suburbans. "These weren't fancy cars," said Patricia. "They were for getting from point A to point B. What we instilled in them was 'You can't have an accident.' Anyone who had an accident had to pay for it with his or her own money. One of the boys slid on some ice and busted up the light assembly. It cost a hundred dollars to fix. Even though that car was a junker, he had to learn to be responsible."

Before you think that the Witters had all sorts of extra money lying around, this is a family of six who operated a seasonal business—a bed-and-breakfast—in a depressed part of the country. Yes, her teens worked hard mowing lawns during the summer to earn money for school clothes, but the Witters didn't want them employed during the school year. "High school is a unique time," explained Patricia. "You can never go back to those carefree days, and there will always be work waiting for you in your adult life. So between September and June, we wanted them to put a lot of time into their studies and be active in after-school activities. We felt *that* was a full-time job."

Reasons Teens Should Not Work
High school is a stressful time for youngsters dealing with adolescence, peer pressure, dating, and learning to be independent.

Adding work to the equation can push some teens over the edge mentally. They won't have time to pursue outside interests, which means *sayonara* to football, track, drama, and the French club. No time for church activities—who has spare hours for the youth group? And finally, no time for family. Don't expect your working teens to be home for dinner when they're washing dishes during the evening "rush." This is the big reason we included this chapter in the book. Parents need to count *all* the costs before allowing their children to join the work force while their values are still forming.

Working teens are also likely to shy away from tough classes. In a public television documentary on U.S. education a few years ago, the filmmakers featured a student named Tony, who was a senior at American High School in Fremont, California, a San Francisco suburb. Tony said he wanted to become a computer technician; "That's where the money is," he added with a grin. "Well," asked the reporter, "are you taking calculus or any difficult math courses?" "It's my senior year," replied Tony. "I think I'm going to relax."

Will you allow your teens to skate through high school? We hope not. Instead, take an active role in planning their class schedules. Explain that no "senioritis" is allowed in your home. Then, walk through the reasons why (or why not) they're taking each class. Encourage *excellence*. Explain that tough classes mean more work at the front end (college being the back end), but that now's the time to get a head start on science, math, English, and foreign language.

Also point out that they will need good study habits in college, and that if they're used to cracking open the books in high school, studying will become as natural as breathing by their senior year of college.

If They Really Want to Work

If your sons or daughters really want to work, let them do so on Saturdays. However, this sacrifices youth group activities and time to "mess around" with friends and blow off some steam.

Another option is to let them work during the summers. "My mother always told us, 'When summer comes, you will be on the berry bus, and that will be your spending money,' " said Eddie Peek, who grew up in the Pacific Northwest. "So my brothers and I did farm work. We picked strawberries, cucumbers—whatever was in the field. Once, I got a job with a Christian potato farmer, and then I did a little cabbage cutting. Mom always said that if I wanted new clothes for school or a new bike, I had to go work because it was good for me."

If at all possible, let them work beside you. Talk about killing two birds with one stone! Seriously, this can be a great way to spend more time with your kids during those all-important teen years *and* impart some good work habits. I (Mike) manned a shovel and swung a hammer for my dad's small construction company during my high school summers. Dad specialized in remodeling homes (adding kitchens and bedrooms), and it was fun hauling lumber around and ripping down walls. I also learned how to show up to the job on time and a few things about construction (although I wish it were a lot more now). Working with my dad was a good reminder of how hard *he* had to work, and looking back, I can see how being "on the job" brought us closer.

Another father, who built apartment houses, told us his son always worked for him. "When Robbie was fourteen, I put him on construction clean-up, and then sometimes I gave him a job of running telephone wires through the new buildings. He made good money, more than he could have made at McDonald's. I mean, I would rather pay him than somebody else. He also learned something, too."

My dad paid me $3.00 an hour back in the early seventies. Imagine, I made $24.00 a day! My buddies were earning a lowly $1.65 working in fast-food kitchens, but here I was making nearly twice as much. Of course, you don't want to *overpay* your children, and I knew that older laborers were making five bucks an hour. I figured construction work paid more because we worked in the hot sun.

Finally, remember to hold the long view. The goal, in most homes anyway, is to raise happy, well-adjusted kids, and to do your best to get them through college. Like it or not, college graduates earn much more than high school graduates, and we can expect the gap to widen in the twenty-first century. In 1990, an average full-time male worker (twenty-five years old or younger) with four years of college earned 60 percent more than his high school graduate counterpart.

//

A Wonderful Surprise

My (Mike's) wife, Nicole, graduated from the *Kaufmaennische Berufsschule* in Baden, Switzerland, which is the equivalent of graduating from a four-year university here in the States. Because Swiss children go to school year-round and have longer school days than we do, Swiss teens are finished with university at age nineteen.

Following graduation, Nicole did office work for a manu-facturing company, but she still lived at home. Her father, Hans, began charging a hefty slice of her paycheck—three hundred Swiss francs a month (around $150)—for room and board. There was some grumbling on Nicole's part, but her father told her it was time she started paying her own way.

Several years later, Nicole and I married in Switzerland, and her father had a little wedding present for us. He handed her a bank book, and inside were several dozen three-hundred-franc deposits he had made over the years. Nicole burst into tears when she realized that her father had been putting all that money into savings for her, that it had never been for room and board. Said Hans, "You couldn't expect a father to be like that, could you?"

That bank book is now a nice little nest egg for Nicole, and it all happened because a father had the foresight—and courage—to initiate a savings program for his daughter.

///

What the Adult Children Told Us

The adult children we interviewed were uniformly positive about teen employment. Here are some excerpts:

- From a thirty-five-year-old Oregon woman: "We didn't have a lot of free money hanging around. I was nine when I first started picking beans and strawberries in the fields. Mom was the field boss. That bean money taught us its value. Then my parents bought a little resort business in the Cascade mountains. When I was twelve, we started working at the resort, helping out customers, watching over the marina. We did it all. And I think that's why we came out so well.

  "My parents would pay us a certain amount, and we had to buy our school clothes from that. We didn't buy real expensive brands because we had to make the money stretch. I didn't resent that, and I am sure no one else did, either."

- From a twenty-four-year-old Colorado woman: "In my junior and senior years, I worked at Long John Silver's, a fast-food place. I think everyone has worked fast food in their life sometime. Working there taught me how to manage what little money I earned. I bought Christmas

presents and anything I wanted personally, like a new
shirt. I didn't pay my parents rent until I was older and
out of high school.

"I'm glad for teen employment. I think by the time
teens are old enough to work, they should be working,
and it teaches a lot of responsibility. I hate to see kids
living at home and not doing anything. That's a little
problem I have these days. I'm a high school gymnastics
coach, and some of them do take advantage of their
parents. They say, 'Hey I need money,' and it's the
parents' fault because they give it to them."

- From a thirty-year-old San Diego man: "One year, Mom
'encouraged' me to sell the *Grit* newspaper. It was one of
those papers advertised in the back of comic magazines.
She didn't make me do this, but once I started, she
wouldn't let me quit. I couldn't stop until my younger
brother could take over the route. She was antiquitting.
'Even if this isn't going to lead to success, you don't stop
in the middle,' she said."

- From a forty-eight-year-old man: "I was in fourth grade,
and my dad was going to seminary. At any rate, Dad
worked the evening shift as a printer. It was a hard life. He
would come home late at night, study, get three or four
hours of sleep, wake up, go to school, and start it all over
the next day. He was under tremendous pressure. I, as the
only child, would stay up most of Friday night and sleep in
most of Saturday. I didn't want to do my chores.

"One day, he came home and sat me down. He
explained what the word *punk* meant. He said it was rotted
wood and did nothing. He explained that up to this point
in life, that is what I was—a punk. He told me I needed to
do something about that. So I went out and got a paper

route. It wasn't a monetary thing, but with my inactivity, that was a good start.

"Dad did a good job of explaining what work was, and I have worked ever since. After the paper route, I got into solid work in high school. I worked in the farm fields and the grocery store on weekends. In 1962, I worked from 7:30 in the morning until 7:30 in the evening for four dollars a day.

"I was at the grocery store before and after school, plus Saturdays, and I went all the way to box boy and checker. I worked my way through college selling insurance, fixing air conditioners, stuff like that. Then I went into the military, and after that, I went to work for Southwestern Bell. At the age of forty-seven, I took early retirement. Today, my wife and I run a 270-acre farm in Missouri. Now I can do what I want."

- From a thirty-five-year-old woman: "My first job was at Montgomery Wards, and I worked in the bookstore. It was after school and Saturdays that I worked. I know that I was only allowed to work so many hours. Basically, I could keep my job if I was doing my homework and my grades were up. I think I learned responsibility from that work. I was always happy if I just passed a class in high school. For me, a *C* was okay, but when I started to work, I learned I had to do my best. I remember learning that doing something fast, even though it was simple, wasn't the best way. If you're going to do it right, take your time and do the job right."

Other Suggestions
If your teens do work, here are some guidelines to consider:

- Keep the hours to under ten a week. Studies show that grades suffer when hours go past the ten-per-week mark.
- Let them work during vacation periods. Employers desperately need seasonal help during Thanksgiving, Christmas, and spring vacation times.
- No work after six o'clock. A full school day and three hours of work is enough for anybody, even for energetic teens. If your teens are not home for dinner, you're losing an important time to reconnect. Having them home by six or six-thirty also leaves them enough time to do homework and get adequate rest. Be on guard for burnout. Check with teachers to see if your kids are catching up on sleep during class.
- Remind them that a portion of their earnings should go back to the Lord. We hope they learned to give to God from their first days of receiving an allowance. The Lord delights in our offerings.
- Finally, force them to save. Have them put aside a portion of their paychecks into a savings account, one they need to get your permission to dip into. Yes, it is their own money, but explain that while this may sound harsh, it's for their own good. Tell them that money will come in handy for a car one day or to help pay for the expenses you won't cover during college.

BUILDING
A
LEGACY

*Like Old Man River,
some things about
families never change.
Keep your priorities
in order and your
kids will pass down a
lasting legacy greater
than any six-figure
retirement plan.*

//////////////////////////

CHAPTER 24

REMEMBER THE TIME WHEN . . .
Parents Making Memories

How does a family make a memory? The easy answer is doing something out of the ordinary. It can be as big as a long, cross-country drive to attend a family reunion or as simple as visiting the local cheese factory.

Sure, making memories can be a hassle. Who wants to drive through a Texas desert with a backseat full of hot, antsy kids? Who wants to endure "Dad, when are we going to be there?" for the fifteenth time since the morning bathroom stop? No one *wants* to battle traffic going to the ballpark. And strolling around museums with huge paintings of fat angels *can* be boring. But keep this in mind, young parents: With the passage of time, the bad memories will disappear, and all you'll recall is how much fun you had with your kids.

Years from now, will you complain about the forty-five minute wait in broiling heat for Disneyland's Matterhorn ride, or will you and your children remember the exciting bobsled ride down? Will you recall the three-hour flight delay at O'Hare, or seeing Gramps one last time before he died?

This chapter will not linger on the obvious. For many families, childhood memories are built around vacations, long weekend trips to see relatives, and attending sporting events. When we asked the adult children what their parents did to make memories, we could almost see their warm smiles across the phone lines.

Vacations and Special Trips

One father who stressed the importance of family drove his two children four hundred miles several times a year to see their cousins and their 102-year-old great-grandfather, who's still alive and kicking today. "My kids are past their teen years now, but I always made them go when they were growing up. They complained and dragged their feet, yet every time we went, they always said they liked the trip."

Family travels are also a good way for parents to step out of character, to let their children see another side of them. A thirty-five-year-old woman, Doris Summers, told us her soft-spoken dad rarely talked, but when they went hiking in Oregon's Cascade mountains, he would open up to her. She valued those times.

"I also remember we did a lot of things as a family," said Doris. "We went on hiking trips to California, and they really put the time into us. Nowadays, I can't believe some people go on vacation without the kids! We used to go to Idaho to see my grandparents every year. Other times, we went on Sunday afternoon drives. We've had family days, and then we would pick beans together."

One family told us they saved all year to take a train—the Empire Builder—from Portland to Minnesota to see relatives every summer. When I (Mike) was growing up in San Diego, my dad painted a Yuban coffee can white and a crude "Vacation

Fund" on the side. My parents put a few bucks away each week, and that paid for a mountain outing or a trip to Mexico.

//

The Top Ten Worst Places to Be on a Fourth of July

10. Any "abusement" park.
9. Standing on the interstate next to an overheated car.
8. The local water park.
7. In a strange town at eight o'clock in the evening without a room reservation.
6. The lost-luggage line at the airport.
5. Walking the state fair midway with bored teenagers.
4. The Safeway express line at five o'clock.
3. At the office.
2. Waiting in line at a safe-and-sane fireworks store.
1. Waiting in line at the hospital emergency room after those cheap fireworks blow up in your hand.

//

The richest memories seemed to come from those families who camped together. It must be the old family-that-sleeps-in-the-dirt-together-makes-memories-together routine.

Craig Udall, who grew up in the Northeast, said camping was an economical way for the family to see a lot of the country together. "My parents bought a tent-trailer when we were young," said Craig, "and we took camping trips to Nova Scotia and even the Grand Canyon. My parents also took us to places of historical interest, such as Gettysburg and all the monuments in Washington, D.C. They instilled a lot of history in us that continues to this day." In fact, Craig loves to watch Civil War reenactments in Maryland each summer.

When we talked to Craig's parents, recalling long-ago camping trips was a chance to revisit warm memories. Though it wasn't easy putting tents up and tearing them down, eating off a camp stove, and sleeping on the ground for a week or two, those memories have been long relegated to the back of the mind. As Marion Udall said, "I'm not sure the kids enjoyed it at the time, but they sure talk about it fondly now."

Marion added that her grown children often wish they had been thankful at the time. "Sure, they didn't want to leave friends, but now they realize how fortunate they were to see the country. We tried to build memories, and the way you do that is to go to New York City and Prince Edward Island and the Painted Desert. We have memories we wouldn't have had if we had stayed home," said Marion.

Other not-to-be-forgotten experiences can come from a long-distance move. Karl Hurst was born shortly after World War II, and in the 1950s, his family drove from Brownsville, Texas, to Berkeley, California, where Papa Hurst was to attend seminary while working a full-time job. The family was dirt poor; in fact, the Hurst parents always joked that the best insurance they ever had was well-fed children.

Karl continues the story: "Dad borrowed two hundred dollars from his stepfather and built a tandem trailer behind a local maintenance shop. We packed everything we owned in that little trailer and hitched it up to Dad's '50 Chevrolet. We drove all the way to California, which was quite a trip in those days. I remember him telling me that when he got his first paycheck, all he had left was one dime in his pocket."

Later, when the family returned to Texas, the Hursts bought a fold-out camper for their vacations, which often lasted for one to two weeks.

"The reason we took long vacations," said Karl's mother, Esther, "is that we couldn't take many weekends off since my husband was in the pulpit. So we really planned out those vacations, and that was just as fun as the actual vacation itself. But we've noticed that our kids take short vacations these days—three or four days—because both parents are working."

One caveat, parents. Don't be a nerd when the family is on holiday. Carol Minor, thirty-six, wishes her father had toned down the tourist act while she was growing up. "My dad was a big vacationer, and he always wanted to see all the sights," she said. "I never wanted to go. I was never into the sights, but he wanted to see everything in a fifty-mile radius. He told me, 'That's too bad, you're going anyway.' I don't know if that was the right response. I might have considered more what the kids wanted to do."

Making Memories at Home

As we said before, making memories can be as simple as playing catch in the backyard—which I (Mike) did every night after dinner during my Little League days.

Carol Ann, in her early thirties, grew up in a loving home, but one ruled by iron discipline from her Norwegian parents. "I can't remember doing simple things like kicking the ball with my parents," she began. "Sure, my parents would read us a story at bedtime, but they never really played with us. When my brother and I took tennis lessons, they never hit balls with us. Perhaps they were that way because they immigrated from Norway. But my mom worked on the family business at home, keeping track of the books. I know Mom's mind was on the books, especially during tax season. Luckily, that was for a short period.

"My mom often told me that she regretted there weren't books on parenting and 'making a memory' when she was raising us. She and Dad just didn't know much."

Her father did do some of the right things, though. When

Carol Ann was in junior high, he would drive her to school and stop along the way to buy donuts. "That was a very special time," said Carol Ann. "He did that for three years, not every morning, but several times a week. I haven't forgotten that."

Here are some more ideas to get you started on making memories at home:

- Install a basketball standard and rim, and shoot baskets with the kids.
- Buy a used pool table or Ping Pong table for the rec room.
- Bring in pizza once a month, and have the family watch home movies on video.
- Have a family "sleepover" in the living room.
- During the summer, pack a picnic and have dinner in a local park. Or better yet, if you belong to a club with a swimming pool, take the kids on a twilight swim.
- Make banana splits.
- Plan a "mystery trip." Have the family pack overnight bags, but don't tell anyone where they're going.
- Visit factories. The boys would love to see how automobiles are built!
- Take an airport tour, which can show you some of the behind-the-scenes areas, such as the baggage area.
- Make Saturday mornings a time for garage sales. Not only can you find great stuff at ridiculously low prices, but you can teach your children how to bargain!
- Have a "Back to the 1800s" weekend. Use nothing electric, camp out, and play games that pioneer families might have played.
- Go for a drive to visit several antique stores. The old furniture and knick-knacks provide great opportunities to talk about the past.

- Look at the "Calendar of Events" in the Friday newspaper.
- Plan an outdoor picnic on the longest day of the year—June 21.
- Go on a train ride. Many children grow up having never been on a train.
- Rent mountain bikes.
- Go fishing.
- Ride a ski lift to the top of the mountain—in winter or summer. Many ski resorts will sell you a one-time pass to the top.

//

In His Service

It's important for kids—especially teens—to get out of the what's-in-it-for-me orbit. One way to accomplish that is to encourage them to participate in service projects—with *you* helping out, of course! Some worthwhile projects include: volunteering at your local relief mission (and not just during the Thanksgiving and Christmas holidays); sponsoring a Third World child through an organization such as Compassion International or World Vision; traveling on a church missions' trip to Mexico; putting together a care package for a church-sponsored missionary; visiting elderly shut-ins at a local convalescent home; or building a house for needy families with Habitat for Humanity.

Don't wait until the kids are teenagers to tackle any of these projects. Anything that gets you and your family out of the consumer mentality and into a service attitude will encourage genuine faith in your youngsters, as well as build some great family memories.

//

- Get twenty neighborhood kids and go to a smorgasbord. Then sit back and watch them eat it out!

- Visit every waterfall within a fifty-mile radius of your home.
- Have each member of the family dress up like the "ultimate nerd." Then have a neighbor or friend take your picture. Hang it someplace where it will be sure to be the focus of conversation.
- Form your own "family band" by purchasing secondhand musical instruments—or use pots and pans!
- Visit anything you normally wouldn't go see; a deserted mining town, the annual rodeo, a planetarium, a lighthouse, hobby shows, dairy farms, Old West Days, dams, TV or radio stations, caves, cemeteries, battlefields, archeological digs, softball tournaments—anything you haven't done, try to do at least once.
- Rent a metal detector and go to a busy park and have your kids search for buried treasure. (P.S. Bring a small shovel.)
- Put together your family tree. Interview your parents, uncles, and aunts about the family's past on a tape recorder for posterity.

What's the Point?

There are certain general types of things your kids will always remember about you, but one way to hit the bull's-eye of building a strong relationship is to fill their memory banks with family activities—both big and small. Kodak moments just don't reach out and bite you on the leg. You've got to plan a lot of them. Your kids need to see how you respond when the tire goes flat on a long stretch of Kansas highway. Or watch how you keep your cool when the clerk at the Motel 6 says he doesn't show a record of your reservation . . . and they're full . . . and it's Saturday night at nine!

Activities, whether it's a cross-country trip or a hike in the hills, provide teachable moments you just can't create watching TV.

We've mentioned this before, but the importance of giving your kids something to come back to can't be discounted. Holiday memories are a start, but all the "Remember the time we . . . " stories you can pull out solidify the specialness of the relationship.

Probably the most joy we got out of receiving nearly two hundred essay surveys was reading the all too few who said this: "I loved my growing-up years. My parents always were doing stuff with us. We had a ton of great times together. I wouldn't have changed a thing."

You don't have to wonder if those children kept their parents' faith as their own, either. They did.

No matter what the age of your kids, you can start building a brain full of memories sure to stand the test of time. Start dreaming about things you can do the next three to five years to build memories that will cause your kids to smile twenty years after they're over.

By pursuing memories you'll want your children to store away, you'll not only give them a lifetime of smiles, but you'll enjoy their growing-up years immensely. Fun is the word we want our kids to recall when they talk about us to *their* kids. If that word isn't part of your kids' vocabulary, our next chapter will help you create a fun atmosphere.

CHAPTER 25

THE BEST YEARS OF OUR LIVES
Parents and Having Fun

As we come to a close, one of the last thoughts we want to leave with you is this: *Enjoy your kids.* Let the sound of laughter ring through your house. Roughhouse when they're little, play board games, linger around the dinner table, roll on the grass, and thumb through your photo albums. Will creating an atmosphere of fun help your children be faithful kids? Maybe, maybe not, but the odds are weighted in your favor when you're fun to be around.

Think about it. What's *really* important? Answer: that your children come to know Christ and receive eternal salvation. If that's what you want for your children, and we're sure it is, then start building those relationships long before they pack their bags for college.

One of the survey questions we asked parents was what they could have done to have more fun with their children.

That question sparked a lot of response, especially from some of the exemplary parents. Read several responses, and see if you can detect a pattern:

I would have had more fun with my children if I had . . .

- realized that other people were having more input in my children's lives than I was (from a mom who drove her kids from one activity to another)
- worked less and played with them more
- not lost my temper so often and spanked the children too much
- had more energy and been home more
- spent more time going places with them
- begun estrogen replacement therapy sooner
- not been so concerned about a perfectly kept house
- not been so busy working on unnecessary things
- not been so bent on routine, time schedules, and work
- listened to my children more
- been more relaxed and more understanding
- realized that everything has a way of working out
- forgotten about the house and my own things and spent more time playing with them
- not worked so hard at being a good parent and over-looked more—maybe
- learned to play tennis with my daughter, who started playing in fifth grade
- learned to swim, ski, and play tennis. Then I could be doing it with them now
- realized how soon they were to become adults
- realized how short the time we have with them really is
- laughed more and not been so solemn
- known they were going to turn out all right
- worked less overtime on the job
- left my kitchen floor unwaxed!

My (Mike's) wife, Nicole, is one of the best moms two children can have because she's always *doing* things with them. Andrea and Patrick are right around the ten-year mark, and it's scary to think that it's half-time. We want to finish the last two quarters with a flourish!

Remember those responses from the adults. Now compare them with those we received from the grown children.

I would have had more fun with my parents if they had . . .

- admitted that life is sometimes gray and not always black and white
- found out what I really wanted to do and done it with me
- turned off the TV, talked to me, and listened to me
- not gotten so angry about unimportant things
- let me have an opinion without always being wrong
- played and joked more with me! Life was always so serious!
- been more relaxed and easygoing on vacations
- told me they loved me and hugged more
- not always worried about what others would think
- played more sports with me
- spent time with me and helped me grow to what I wanted to be rather than what they wanted
- encouraged me to be honest about my feelings and thoughts even if it wasn't what they thought was "right"
- gotten excited about things kids get excited about
- developed a friend-to-friend relationship. We had a great parent-child one
- made the effort to solidify our relationship during the formative years
- done more activities together as a family, such as camping or skiing

- done more one-on-one stuff
- thought about someone besides themselves
- relaxed their standards only slightly. They were a bit too fundamental with their Christianity
- been more spontaneous
- been more secure financially so they could have spent more time with us
- not expected me to be perfect. I needed to feel I could have failed and still have been okay and loved
- played more sports with me. They would watch but not participate
- killed the TV and found something we could have all done together. Family camping trips were among the best times
- been there more and been willing to be vulnerable and share their own feelings
- hugged me and verbally encouraged me
- accepted that teenagers will always act like teenagers. They embarrassed me in front of my friends.
- understood us at all our various stages of growth. Let us be kids. Chosen their fights better. Not made such a big deal out of everything.

Wow! The grown children were pretty tough. Is that how you want to be remembered, as a pop more interested in NFL football than in your son's pee-wee football team? Or as a mom who was hooked by soaps and Harlequin romance novels and not your child's drama productions?

Sure, flipping the TV off and organizing a family outing on a Sunday afternoon isn't easy, but you can do it, Dad. *And you won't regret it.*

Homework

We know it's a pain when authors recommend stuff like this, but we haven't done much of it so far, so try not to complain.

Go grab paper and pen. Go ahead, we'll wait.

Write down ten things you want your kids to remember forever. It could be experiences you'll have, what good character qualities are, or what to look for in a mate. If you get on a roll, go for twenty.

See, that wasn't so bad!

Now, on another sheet of paper, write down ten things *you* want to remember about the child-rearing years. Again, it could be experiences or consistent positive attitudes you had.

After you've done that, pin both lists up in a place where you can constantly look at them. Or put them away in a safe place, but one you'll remember to come back to.

We have only eighteen or so years—years that will never go by faster—with those children under our roofs. Our influence often grinds to a halt when they leave home. Sure, we're going to have some input about their futures, but before they've flown the nest, we want to be able to look back and say, "I honestly did my best." While a simple plan like this helps, the key with children is hard work, a consistent effort, and the knowledge that you loved your children to the best of your ability.

One final thing to keep in mind: *Think like a child.* Do you remember the awe you felt seeing things for the first time? The fear you felt when the neighborhood bully was walking your way with his fists bunched up? The butterflies on your first date?

One of my (Mike's) daughter's friends, Jordan, asked her father, "What age will we be when we go to heaven, Dad? Will we be like kids or like parents?"

"Why do you want to know, sweetheart?" he responded.

"Because I want to be a kid when I go to heaven. Parents are so boring," she replied.

Maybe that's what Jesus had in mind when he gathered the children around him, but his disciples tried to send them away. Jesus said, "Let the little children come to me, and do not hinder them, for the kingdom of God belongs to such as these. I tell you the truth, anyone who will not receive the kingdom of God like a little child will never enter it" (Mark 10:14-15).

We are not going to pretend to know what age we'll be when we go to heaven, but my daughter's friend had a good point. Raising faithful children—ones who will be drawn to Christ—depends a great deal on parents who can lead them there. When they are young, you have to bend over and carry them. When they're toddlers, you have to reach out and take their hands. When they're in grammar school, you have to walk with them. When they're teens, you have to point out the right way. And when they leave home, you have to keep praying.

Be faithful to your children, and they'll be faithful to you—and to the Lord, as the following epilogue illustrates.

HE AIN'T HEAVY, HE'S MY BROTHER

One May evening in 1985, we (the Yorkey family) were visiting my Uncle Bob and Aunt Gay at their home in La Jolla, California. We were celebrating somebody's birthday when a last-minute visitor dropped in to help cut the cake. Who was it? My brother, Pry. He got his unusual nickname from his initials: Peter Richard Yorkey.

Pry was twenty-nine at the time, just sixteen months younger than me. We had always enjoyed a close—but competitive—relationship, and it had been a few months since I had seen him. Pry was a strapping six-foot, two-inch fellow with remarkably blue eyes and dirty blond hair that lightened with the summer sun. He was a California beach boy; we had grown up in La Jolla about one hundred yards from the pounding shorebreak of a beach called Sea Lane. From the end of school until Labor Day, we were in the Pacific every day, riding the waves on our belly boards and bodysurfing the shorebreak.

After high school, Pry drifted through a couple of colleges before learning the carpenter trade from my dad. The construction business had its ups and downs, and when the surf was up, Pry was down at the beach. He became a pretty good surfer and was living a nomadic life when he dropped by my aunt and uncle's that evening.

After enjoying dessert, Nicole and the kids and I left. Pry lingered for a second helping of ice cream. Out of the blue, his body began trembling involuntarily. His mind tried to comprehend, but his legs and arms shook and his eyes bulged as convulsions racked his frame.

Pry was in the midst of a grand-mal seizure. When paramedics arrived, they hustled him to nearby Scripps Hospital to stabilize him. Then the battery of tests began.

A CAT scan determined that a large tissue mass had formed on the right side of his brain. The decision was made to delicately lop the tumor off.

The operation was a success. When the neurosurgeon left the OR to greet my anxious parents, he had a smile on his face. "I think we got it all," he said. That was good news, because two weeks later, tests revealed the tumor was cancerous.

Meanwhile, Pry recovered quickly and resumed a normal life. He was one of the lucky ones. Every six months, he went in for a CAT scan, and he always walked out happy. "The doctor says I still have a hole in my head," he quipped.

Pry returned to the construction sites and his favorite surf spots, but in the spring of 1988, a seizure struck him again. He was rushed to the hospital for more tests, but this time the smile was gone from the neurosurgeon's face. The tumor had returned, bigger than ever.

Again Pry underwent brain surgery, but when the neurosurgeon talked to my parents afterward, he was shaking his head. "We'll have to wait until the tests come back" was all he would say.

I now understand why doctors do that—make you wait—when they already know. They want the patient to *get used* to the idea of dying. When Pry walked into the doctor's office that afternoon, he took the news like a man. "You have two to six months," the doctor said. "There's not much we can do."

Pry had a few questions. "What will it be like when I die?" he asked.

"Really, you'll feel nothing at all," replied the doctor. "In your last week, you'll be sleeping a lot, and one of those times you just won't wake up."

Naturally, I was devastated by the news. My thoughts turned heavenward. Pry knew *about* the Lord, but he had never accepted Christ into his heart—never had a *personal* relationship with him. He hadn't darkened a church door in ages.

We were living in the Los Angeles area then, and nearly every weekend we drove down to San Diego to spend time with him. During his "good" periods, we played a round of golf at Torrey Pines. During his "bad" periods, he sat on a couch and played an electronic backgammon game all day.

Nicole and I were looking for ways to present Christ to him. I brought him books that I thought he'd enjoy, like Pete Maravich's *Heir to a Dream*. I thought, *Maybe Pry could identify with Pistol Pete.*

Another time, I brought a Focus on the Family video with me—"Twice Pardoned," featuring youth speaker Harold Morris. When I popped it into the VCR that Saturday night, I counseled Pry to watch closely. My parents were impressed: "This ex-con can really speak," my dad said. But Pry didn't seem to be paying attention, especially when Harold delivered the gospel message at the end of the film. Although Pry was listening, he kept playing the hand-held backgammon game. I was watching *him* more than the video, and I wanted to reach over and slap the game out of his hand and say, "Pry, listen to what

Harold Morris is saying! You're facing eternity, guy, and you've got no time to lose."

But I didn't. I sensed the Lord telling me to wait, so I did.

All fall, Nicole and I tried to talk to Pry over the phone. One time I said I wanted to be sure I'd see him again in heaven.

"Oh, that's a ways off," said Pry—his way of not dealing with it.

Pry started weakening badly, and the cancer spread to his spine. He was checked into a convalescent home after Thanksgiving, but he was so weak he couldn't even decorate a foot-high Christmas tree that our mom had brought to his room.

Nicole and I knew the time was getting close. When we went to visit him that December weekend, all he could do was sit up in bed and talk to us. But after five minutes, we'd look over and he'd be snoring. Then we'd leave the room and come back in a couple of hours to repeat the scene all over again. After a few minutes, he'd fall asleep once more.

I prayed for an opportunity to talk to Pry directly, for one last shot. On Sunday afternoon, we were making our last visit of the weekend. We had to get on the road to return home.

Pry had just finished lunch and looked alert. We chatted for a few minutes, but then he fell asleep again! "Drats," I uttered under my breath. We gathered our things to go. Nicole said "Good-bye, Pry," out loud, and he opened his eyes. I rushed to his bedside and asked my parents to take our children for a walk.

Nicole went to the other side of his bed, and we each took a hand.

"Pry, would you mind if Nicole and I pray for you?" I asked.

"No, go ahead," he replied.

We lowered our heads and closed our eyes. I asked the Lord to be with Pry during his last few days on earth, to walk with him every step of the way, to comfort him and be there for him.

When we opened our eyes, Pry looked at me with a soft gaze. He didn't say a thing, but his blue eyes told me: *Go ahead, brother. You know what you are supposed to do.*

"Pry," I said, "would you like to ask Jesus Christ into your heart and repent of your sins?"

"Yes, I would."

"Then please close your eyes and repeat after me."

I led Pry through the sinner's prayer, and afterward, I felt as if a fifty-pound block of ice had been lifted off my shoulders. I also felt free to tell Pry things I had been bottling up for months.

"Pry, I'm really sorry you got sick like this. You are my only brother, and I love you. I'm sorry this has happened, but now I know that you will be waiting in heaven for me."

I hugged Pry's decaying body and wept. The warm tears were a welcome release. Pry didn't say much, but he looked happy.

After saying good-bye, Nicole and I walked outside and past his room. Through the miniblinds, he looked at us one more time. He raised his right arm and waved weakly, and I waved back. I knew it was good-bye until *next time.*

A few days later, Pry slipped into a coma. When I came down the following weekend, he was incoherent. Doctors were regularly injecting him with morphine, and I could smell death in the room. He died early on Sunday morning, one week after he had made peace with his Lord.

Although Pry waited until the eleventh hour and the fifty-ninth minute, he had something to come back to. My parents had raised him in God's faith. He had learned that Jesus Christ was his Savior, that he had come and died for *his* sins. When it came time to walk back to the Lord and make amends for his checkered past, Pry didn't have that far to go.

That's how you want it to be for your children. You can lead them to Christ, even introduce him to your kids, but only they can reach out and take his hand. Only they can take the final step to embrace him.

Your duty, parents, is to present Christ to your children. He will do the rest. Then, on that day, you'll hear our Lord say the best words a parent can ever hear: "Well done, my good and *faithful* servant."

APPENDIXES

*Quotes, notes, and
a few more stories from
parents we surveyed
and interviewed*

COMMUNICATING WITH YOUR CHILDREN

At what age did you and your children communicate best? Why? *(asked of parents)*

- "It has been good all along, even during the extra challenges of the teen years. After my divorce, I worked very hard at listening, and that has been the critical element."
- "We have always communicated very well. Supper was a great time for communication."
- "Probably starting in late junior high, and it got better through high school and really great in college. Now they are married, and they are our best friends."
- "Our daughter has always seemed to communicate well. During junior high and high school we had to prod our son to talk. Playing basketball or some game would help."
- "Grade school level were the best years. They were young and had open minds."
- "In college, when the kids started to feel they didn't have all the answers."
- "In their twenties. When they were little, we had no problems, either. It was just as easy to tell them rather than exchange ideas."
- "All of our children have different personalities—surprise! — so we tried to find a special way to communicate with

them based on what connected with them most, like games, sports, and answering questions."

- "We learned to communicate from the time of their birth until they left home on their own."
- "In college, they seemed more receptive to what I had to say. I tried to be a good listener when they were growing up, but I would often get 'preachy.'"
- "At age eleven, before he 'knew it all.' At age seventeen, when he realized he didn't know everything."
- "Up through junior high school was the best. In high school, the oldest and youngest were very much into their peer group, and they talked more to their friends."
- "I don't know exactly. Jeff never talked. We still don't communicate as I wish we could."
- "We worked very hard to keep talking. We tried to be shocked by nothing and accept their feelings as legitimate."
- "Grammar school and post high school. Probably because it was pre- and postadolescence."
- "We communicated well until they were age twelve or so. Our daughter had a rebellious streak in junior high."
- "Elementary age, because they acted as though we knew what we were talking about. As they became older, we became less aware of what the 'real issues' were."
- "I can't recall a time when communication was really closed with our kids. I believe they were both more open before and after high school."
- "At all ages. Our son enjoyed better communication with his father during the teen years. Now he shares personal issues with me and financial areas with his dad. The girls were born communicators."
- "During preschool and early elementary, they were so innocent and open. Also, communication improved— after a teen slump—when they were in their twenties."
- "We always had to pull answers from our son for anything."
- "In grade school and junior high, they were still willing to listen."

- "They were more to themselves in high school, but before grade school and now, after college, were good."
- "At age twenty-one, my daughter finally cut me a lot of slack and now understands things from an adult perspective."
- "In grade school, they were anxious to tell me everything."

At what age did you communicate best with your parents? Why? *(asked of adult children)*

- "At twenty-three, once I was established in my job, they seemed to think I could be listened to."
- "College to present. I was more mature and more appreciative of all they did for me."
- "Age eleven and under. I was very compliant."
- "When I was working on my homework around the kitchen table after school, my mom and I would talk about everything."
- "Until I got into college, Dad thought I was just a kid."
- "With Mom, it was junior high. She loved to be involved in all aspects of my dating life."
- "Post-high between the ages of eighteen and twenty. They began to treat me with more respect and trust my judgment. Until then, they just told me things and rarely asked my opinion."
- "At age twenty-four, when I was completely independent of them."
- "With my dad, in late elementary and early junior high. That's when he played sports with me."
- "In early elementary school with Mom. She read to us. It created great opportunities for conversation."
- "After college to present. My parents are now my friends and I feel that I want to be more open with them."
- "My senior year I learned to talk and listen."
- "From ages twenty-four to thirty-three, until my dad died."
- "After I came home from my first year of college, I realized how much I missed them and loved them."
- "I never communicated much with my dad. Mother was

more communicative on the philosophical level as I got older. It seemed like she was always exhausted when I was younger. I guess communicating with a child takes more creative energy. As I grew up, she was agreeably available."

- "The best communication occurred during my later college years. I always communicated best with my dad. My mom and I always seemed to have conflicts."

- "My mother was both Mom and best friend. She was always there when I got home from school, so we communicated almost daily. My dad is the quiet type. He listens well, but doesn't give a lot of feedback, so I talked with my mom more."

- "After high school, when I wasn't as smart as I thought as I was."

- "My interests and needs were always my parents' concerns. Even into high school they were willing to do research to answer my questions. They helped me to find alternate ways to view most situations, which caused confusion. For me, however, having my parents respond to my questions about sports, music, or peers wasn't the only kind of communication important to me. Even as a young child, I was aware when my parents, particularly my mother, were hurting. But when I asked what was bothering them or how I could make them feel better, I often got a denial of the emotional state they were in."

- "Mom and I communicated fine. I never really communicated with my dad very much at all."

- "I have always had great communication with my parents, because they were always willing to take time with me and listen."

- "With my dad we communicated best when I got into college. We were finally past the power struggle, and that's when we started sharing about values, struggles, and dreams."

- "Not until college and after marriage. My faith deepened, and I took the risk of self-exposure. After marriage, I finally cut some apron strings and became more of my own person."

- "From age nineteen and on. In our family, we tended to

discuss only the pleasant things. Unfortunately, Mom and Dad avoided confrontation like the plague. But my freshman year some special friends helped me come out of my shell and become a much more balanced communicator."

- "All my life my dad has been my confidant. At any age, he just seemed to know how to get through to me. Mom and I, on the other hand, just got on each others' nerves. As I have 'mellowed' with age, we get along beautifully. I think she just relates much better to adults than to children."

At what age did you and your children communicate worst? Why? *(asked of parents)*

- "We never did communicate badly. It was probably not the best in high school because they had other interests and friends."
- "From age eighteen to twenty-one. I don't really understand why, but they each wanted to make most of their decisions alone."
- "College age. I was never sure what was really going on in their lives. Being a single parent, I felt I lacked energy and time."
- "With our son it was worst during his teen years when I became most concerned with the secular rock music he listened to."
- "In junior high our kids wanted to be treated as adults, but they were not able to show that they were ready."
- "Probably high school." (We had a dozen or so responses like this one.)
- "In junior high we made the choice to let them become more independent. That hurt our communication for a time."
- "Probably ages twelve to fourteen—puberty hit!"
- "They were not willing to talk with us—we were 'too conservative' for their peer group."
- "There was never a wall, but during junior high and high school there was not a free exchange. We had trouble with our son—he sort of withdrew. He stayed straight, but he had emotional problems."
- "Our daughter got into bad company in sixth grade. Our

oldest son had his rebellious times in college. He felt we didn't care and that we showed favoritism."

- "When the divorce occurred, my daughter was sixteen and my son was eighteen. The grief and anger were there, but at least we talked. I never talked down their father, and now they trust me in that area. They can talk to me about their relationship with him."

At what age did you communicate worst with your parents? Why? *(asked of adult children)*

- "In high school, because of my attitude and their lack of acceptance."
- "In high school. I was independent and impatient."
- "Whenever I did something they didn't agree with."
- "Junior high through high school were the worst years. I was strong-willed, bossy, and selfish."
- "In high school, because I was tired of deferring to her needs. I felt little respect from her."
- "I never had a problem communicating with my parents, except on the issue of sex. Honestly, I never felt distant from them, probably because I always felt loved, accepted, and trusted."
- "There was never any conflict, but I wasn't as open in high school and college."
- "I was never allowed to be blatantly honest. A lot of denial went on. Any brush with hard truth clamped the communication lid down. That still is happening to some extent today, although there's some improvement."
- "High school was probably the worst. As the oldest child, I felt I was blazing new ground. I know my younger brother and sister had more freedoms. Our home was never a war zone—just a few battles here and there."
- "When I was a junior, I decided I didn't want to have anything to do with my parents, so I got really involved with activities at church. I decided not to share with them because of my anger toward my dad and his distant attitude."
- "At age eighteen, I thought I was old enough and smart

enough to make life-decisions; my parents didn't think so. They were correct."

- "Throughout my teenage years, it was a bit painful because Mom and Dad had a hard time listening—especially Mom. She talks, talks, and talks! I was never given the chance to express my heart because I was a natural listener. I bottled up a lot of things."

- "With my mother, it was in high school. We are both so similar in personality—stubborn, outspoken, and very emotional. It made for some very volatile and lively arguments."

PARENTAL INVOLVEMENT

What were the positive results of parental involvement in activities you did? *(asked of adult children)*

- "I think I respected my father more because of his involvement as my Sunday school teacher."
- "My dad was a scoutmaster who was always spinning yarns around the campfire. All the other boys looked up to *my* dad! He was my coach and always had an interest in my activities, helping me to improve and giving me encouragement."
- "I felt their commitment to us kids."
- "I enjoyed having both my parents around me. I was never embarrassed by them. I thought it was great they would spend time with me."
- "I learned more about them, that they did have something to offer."
- "It would have been more positive had they been involved at a younger age."
- "It was a lot of work for them, but it was very rewarding. I learned by my mom's example as a leader what it meant to love kids even if they were totally messing up their lives."
- "It helped form an early bond with Dad. Mom was just there, but Dad was always crafting us boys to be men."
- "They didn't coach or help, but they were always at my activities."
- "I was very proud of their involvement and felt that it

meant preferential treatment for me. My friends loved my parents."

- "Though I was proud of my folks when they were involved in my activities, I felt that it gave them way too close a view of my growing-up process and social interactions. I felt a little inhibited and restricted."
- "As my Sunday school teacher for a short time it was positive. It taught me to respect adults and showed me the frustration of teaching."
- "Their involvement gave me a feeling of security and belonging and helped boost my self-image. I was proud of my parents who loved me."
- "Always was secure at events or functions as we did them together. I was proud that my parents were servants and I wanted to be like them."
- "In elementary school, it gave me a great sense of security to have my mom one of the leaders. In high school, I felt embarrassment."
- "As long as they didn't try to parent me in front of other kids it was great. Other kids thought my parents were nice."
- "They modeled for me Christian service and involvement. I've actually determined I want to be more involved in my children's activities than my parents were in mine."
- "I wish my mom could have gotten involved, but I understood she had to work. It would have made me feel special to show her off."

What were some negative results of their involvement with you through the years? *(asked of adult children)*

- "Dad did not participate and I felt I was not so worthy—that I never pleased him enough for him to step outside his comfort zone to support me."
- "It was a further reduction in boundaries between myself and my mother. All negative."
- "We had seven kids. They were too busy to get that involved."

- "I felt I couldn't be myself."
- "I think perhaps my independence or 'responsible capabilities' outside my home could have developed earlier, if I was on my own earlier."
- "In junior high and under I loved it. Later, in high school, I kind of resented that my whole family came to all the teen activities at church."
- "When I was school-aged, I was usually embarrassed to be around them if they were involved because they did things that I thought were dumb."
- "I didn't feel like I had a life of my own."

If you were your child's Sunday school director, volunteer coach, Scout leader, etc., what were the positive or negative results of this involvement? *(asked of parents)*

- "It drew us closer together."
- "It was an opportunity to talk with other parents about the problems we were having and solutions we were finding."
- "I felt it was positive to see them with their peers. It was also good for them to see us as adults."
- "It was positive. The kids learned to love and trust an old geezer."
- "It gave us an area of commonality and discussion and gave us quality time together. No negatives."
- "I have never regretted being a youth leader for senior high youth group at church because we shared in many activities, ski trips, etc., as a family."
- "We would work together on the activity and children learned by observing and participating. We see ourselves being duplicated now as they are grown and doing some of the same programs."
- "The boys always seemed happy that we were involved in their activities."
- "I learned to better know my kids' likes and dislikes and could work to help them improve. As a Sunday school teacher, they felt that I was harder on them (they were right), yet the youngest, because of encouragement, won

a prize for memorization. I blew it though. She had to wait longer to get her prize than someone else's child would have."

- "They seemed to be proud of my involvement. They also seemed to be more comfortable having their friends at our home."
- "Sometimes as a coach it was hard for my son to determine if I was the parent or the coach."
- "I was a bit more informed as to what was going on. Being an aide in school allowed me to get to know the teacher better."
- "I gave my son an 'edge' by encouraging quality, especially in Scouts."
- "I really saw what the other kids in their class were like."
- "Being a scout leader for my son was the only way he would participate. My daughters loved my being room mother and working at the school. My sons did not. During junior high, no one liked me outside the house."
- "They knew I cared about their activities, friends, and them."
- "It was mostly positive. My eldest was very sensitive and seemed to be easily embarrassed with her peers, having a parent at a leadership position."
- "My children all loved my interest and participation."
- "They could see that what I believed was very important to me and that I was willing to put my feet, hands, and mouth to work for the Lord." (From a mom who worked in Christian Service Brigade, in youth group, and as a waterfront director where she worked as a counselor.)
- "It was very positive, but it required me to be sensitive to how they wanted me to be seen and known by other children. When they were older, I asked first before I volunteered."
- "When we moved to a new community, the kids were in sixth and eighth grade. I was a substitute at each of their schools early in the year, and it seemed to help them feel more at home."
- "Helping out helped me to understand some of their peer problems and pressure."

- "I knew what was going on so I could lend support or lobby for change. My kids knew that Sunday school, clubs, and school were valued by me, and my kids knew I cared about their personal experiences." (From a mom who was her child's Sunday school teacher, a classroom volunteer, and on school committees.)
- "They liked my involvement because most mothers weren't interested enough."
- "It showed our kids that parents could be involved outside the home while not neglecting them."
- "I think my involvement resulted in a positive relationship with our kids. We made sure we attended all their functions or sports, even if they weren't cooperating fully at home."

WHAT REBELS HAD TO SAY

Did any of your children experience teenage rebellion?
(asked of parents)

- "No rebellion at all, but there was some questioning of our values so they could establish their own."
- "Yes. They gave in to peer pressure with regard to disobedience and started using drugs."
- "Only a small amount of rebellion. We tried to keep the relationships open as they were growing up so that we would not have a lot of rebellion. We thank the Lord it worked. But it took a lot of time and effort."
- "We didn't have a lot of rebellion with the kids. If they didn't want to go to Sunday school, well, we said that was a rule of the house. They understood what that meant because they never pressed it on us too hard. We would sit and talk things out if it was a problem. Our kids had a lot of respect for us, and they could feel our respect for them. We kind of treated them like little adults. We had high expectations for them, of course. We asked a lot of them, at least compared to today's American family."
- "My son in junior high sometimes missed curfew. My daughter in high school started dating an older boy. She missed a lot of curfews."
- "Yes. She talked us into attending public school in tenth grade because she was interested in volleyball (she did get

a scholarship) and home economics. The Christian high school didn't have home economics."

- "Yes, but very mild. She smoked some. We never came down hard, but we did talk about the dangers."
- "Not to any great degree. We had our moments, but ultimately our kids liked living at home and enjoyed bringing their friends over. No drugs, no alcohol, just good relationships with the opposite sex, with one exception. Our youngest traveled with a non-Christian crowd, though."
- "Very slight with my son. He went through a year when he didn't get home on time a few times."
- "Dennis did, in a mild way, over the differences in our religious beliefs. He had difficulty with the hypocrisy of institutionalized religion. He is a very wise soul."
- "No. We praise the Lord that our girls were such a delight and our relationships were good. I [the mom] believe a great part of that was because of the positive affirmation and concern and love of their father. I believe this is why they were never 'boy crazy.'"
- "Our daughter got into bad company in sixth grade at the new school. Our oldest son had his rebellion twice in college. He felt we didn't care and that we showed favoritism."
- "Yes, when our daughter turned fifteen. She was quite involved with a young man who was into drugs and many other things. She didn't do drugs, as far as I could tell, but she also got involved with a girl at church who was involved with witchcraft. She also ran away twice. I believe she had an abortion, but she has never said so."
- "For our first daughter, typical mild adolescence, plus 'preacher kid' baggage."
- "Three out of five kids rebelled. The boys grew long hair and played hooky. One dropped out of high school and never finished. He did come home for curfew, though. One daughter wasn't too good either. She had fights at school, and I had to go see the principal."
- "Yes. All three of them tried alcohol and drugs, and two of them tried sex. Praise God, they did not become addicts."

- "Yes. Our oldest, who is nineteen, did rebel to the extent of a dysfunctional life-style of drinking and smoking and sneaking into nightclubs at the military base. She ended up marrying secretly, without our approval."
- "Our son drifted away at age eighteen. We continued to love him. He knew how we felt. It was a very hard time. We knew he was drinking some and not sure what else. It took lots of prayer, and we tried to follow Dr. Dobson's ideas."
- "Not to the extent of breaking communication with us. Naturally, they tried things."
- "Of course! Joanna had a struggle with our authority, faith, peer pressure, worldly values. Jonathan was very strong-willed, and there were strong confrontations. He moved out of the home for two months. Michael was compliant—made us think we were perfect parents!"
- "The area that our oldest rebelled in was choosing her friends. To her, her friends had the best things to say and do."
- "No serious rebellion, but we did have individual attitude problems. Peer influence had a major affect."
- "Three out of the four children did. They wanted the right to decide things for themselves before they were old enough to."
- "They wanted to do their own thing. Some made bad choices bringing heartaches to all, and some made good choices."
- "What child doesn't, to some degree? But I feel that our children were better than most, and I do not say that boastfully."
- "Our girl did a little with dating, but since she had already invited Jesus Christ into her life, we usually prayed about it. This helped us through difficult times."
- "They did the normal things: refusing to help out, excuses why they can't be kind to siblings, and doing a few things without permission."
- "Both girls wanted to stay out later than permitted, and they constantly tested my rules of behavior—who they

could date, where they could go, and they wanted to take charge of their lives."

- "Nothing extreme. Even during the divorce they accepted my limits on hours, activities, etc."
- "Our fifth child rebelled as a high school senior. He never went to college. He is still out of the Lord's will, but we have never cut him out of our family. We do not bug him about his life. We are on very good terms with him, and we are looking forward to the day when he will come back to the Lord."
- "Only after Mandi was out of her teens and into her mid-twenties were we able to get close again. We are super close now."
- "Our youngest, Jeff, is now twenty-three. He left home at seventeen upon finishing public school on his own choosing. He tried and was successful in getting kicked out of the Christian high. He rebelled against all of our values and is still not following the Lord."

Did you experience teenage rebellion? *(asked of adult children)*

- "Yes, I wasn't allowed to dress the way I wanted. I didn't feel as though I was treated as an adult."
- "Slightly, but mostly to find myself."
- "No. I wasn't kind, but I never rebelled."
- "No. I did stupid stuff, but never with a motive to hurt my parents."
- "I drank and spent as little time at home as possible."
- "Yes. Mom and Dad's rules were so black and white, while my world was gray. They wouldn't talk with me so I tried to discover it on my own in college."
- "Sort of. I did things behind my parents' backs."
- "No. I always felt my parents gave me enough freedom with limits."
- "Yes. I had an extended period where I didn't want to have anything to do with my parents. Home was only a place to eat and sleep."
- "No. No need to. I had lots of freedom."

WHAT REBELS HAD TO SAY

- "Yes. I felt my parents were too strict—definitely more than my friends' parents."
- "A little. I felt trapped in a small town and wanted to be different."
- "Yes. I wanted to test my boundaries. I wanted as much freedom as I could get."
- "I resented the continual lectures on being 'a nice girl.' I perceived God as someone impossible to please, because I could never be good enough to be acceptable. I did not understand grace, obviously, so I gave up. The world looked like a whole lot more fun."
- "Yes, mostly in the eighth grade. I wanted so desperately to 'belong' that I began to swear and act up in class to prove I wasn't a goody-goody. And there were real sparks with Dad at times."
- "No. Though at times I had a very rebellious heart because I didn't feel listened to. I was too loyal to my parents to give them pain."
- "Not really. I had a lot of common sense and was 'old' for my age. I could see that rebellious choices weren't wise, weren't what I wanted for my future. I knew my parents' way was best overall."
- "Yes. I felt bound-up and was not given enough freedom to express and choose—although now I'd rather have had that than have the opposite. I pushed hard, but came back in due time when I was a senior."

Was there ever a time when your children "walked away" from their faith for an extended period of time? How did you respond? *(asked of parents)*

- "No" (around half of the responses)
- "Each questioned their faith for about a year during college. We responded with prayer and encouraged them."
- "One of our five children has been away from the faith for about six years."
- "Our son left home because we required him to go to church if he stayed with us. He is still outside the fold. He still doesn't talk, but we go out of our way to let him know we love him dearly."

- "Our two sons are now, and our younger daughter often fence-rides. We have let them know we love them and are praying they get their lives in line."
- "All four stopped when they went to college. Not until the Lord dealt with them did they go back."
- "At one point when we sensed a lack of interest (in the teen years), we became involved in a home Bible study (which was outside our church body). This was a group of kids junior high through college age with a strong spiritual leader."
- "Only the fourth child stopped going to church in high school. It was her decision. We responded by letting her know of our concern for her. We wanted her to experience the very best in life and that, within Christ, all was possible."
- "Our son did. I expressed my concern but accepted his decision as part of his path toward 'wholeness.' He is quite spiritual and certainly moral. He is our idealistic, born philosopher."
- "My daughter said there was a bunch of hypocrites at church and she wasn't going to get involved in that. We told her that she had to go to church on Sundays but didn't have to be involved in the choir. She walked away from age fourteen to twenty (when she married). We prayed and prayed. Though she does read her Bible now, she hasn't found a church yet."
- "When my kids stopped going to church, I told them it was between them and the Lord. They always returned. They verbalized their struggles and questions freely."
- "I don't feel any of them walked away even when they didn't go to church while in college. We kept the lines of communication open."
- "Our daughter has not yet walked away completely, but it isn't a priority."

WHEN DID THEY GRASP THE FAITH?

At what age—and why—did you finally grasp the faith as your own? *(asked of adult children)*

- "At age five, then a thoughtful rededication at sixteen. The rededication happened while I was on a three-month missions trip in Haiti. It was eye-opening."

- "I accepted Jesus at five, but it really sunk in at fourteen. I'm not sure why, but I think the Holy Spirit came to reside and I began to read my Bible more."

- "At seven years old I received Jesus. At fourteen, I knew it was personal and not just a thing to do."

- "When I was eight I heard a preacher talk on the Rapture and those who would be left behind."

- "My initial commitment came in grade school. In college I finally turned the corner."

- "At age seven. I always *knew* about God because my mom told me about Jesus."

- "At twenty-five through independent thought."

- "At twenty when I was at Multnomah School of the Bible. I really had to decide whether I wanted to live off of my parents' faith or my own. I was a Christian before that, but I wasn't too committed. I think sending me off on a mission trip would have helped me form my own faith earlier. It sure worked for my brother, who went for two months one summer with Teen Missions. He was a junior in high school, and he really came back solid."

- "When I was ten, I had open-heart surgery and there wasn't much chance for survival."
- "At twenty, when I was away from home at Bible college."
- "When I was nineteen, I came to a point where I had to have answers to my questions."
- "My parents always made faith so real to me by what they said and how they lived. I know this sounds weird, but I used to pray *all* the time in junior high and high school. Other crucial growing times were my three summers at a Christian boys' camp."
- "As a sophomore in high school. I saw Christ as a strong part of the lives of one or two seniors."
- "I turned to the Lord 'full-speed' after moving out on my own. Funny how one decides he needs the Lord after his security base is gone."
- "I realized I'd be a Christian for the rest of my life at age five. I knew I was a sinner, and that I deserved death. But God had provided a way for me to miss that. Not out of judgment, but because he loved me. I gradually realized the implications of the gospel after that. In seminary, I was challenged with what kind of a Christian I wanted to be."
- "At eighteen, I realized how the Old Testament and the New Testament fit together. The faith was mine then."
- "When I was away at college, I discovered Christianity in a whole new way. I rededicated my life to him. I'm committed to serving him and thank my parents for their Christian example."
- "I'd been taken to church every Sunday forever, but it wasn't until I was an adult and had cancer surgery that God and I became close. It was like I woke up and realized I could have a faith of my own. Before that time, I had never looked at the world being lost with no hope. Until you really grasp the faith for yourself, you can't give it away."
- "When I got away from home I started to rely on God for things. I realized what my parents had taught me was

right. Plus, I got around others my age who were on fire a little bit more. They encouraged me to have a daily quiet time."

- "At sixteen, I went to a Young Life camp where I heard the gospel for the first time."
- "I finally realized when I was sixteen that I needed to make my own decision for Christ—not something based on my parents' decisions or on church attendance. I was at a Youth for Christ meeting."
- "At age twelve when my sister died. I had horrible feelings of loneliness and isolation. No one was talking to me, but God was!"
- "It was in stages: In grade school I accepted Christ. In junior high I learned about personal obedience. By high school I recognized the implications of the gospel. After that, I struggled with my faith because I went to a church that had different traditions."
- "When I got away from home and went to Wheaton grad school, I finally woke up. I had been raised in such a strict home where right behavior and propriety was everything that I didn't think you could be a Christian without being Baptist or Grace Brethren. At school, I made friends with people from all different denominations. They really challenged me about God's grace. I'd grown up with such a performance mentality that spiritually I was dead. I didn't want to go to church. I tested God to see if his grace could cover my neglect and lack of service. Back then, things were done out of duty; now it's like I want to do them."
- "It's sad but true. My faith wasn't totally mine until I went through years of rebellion. I was twenty-six when I finally started to get a grasp on God's grace. I didn't have to perform for God or my parents anymore."
- "At college. I matured and was surrounded by others who helped me find my own walk."
- "I gave my life to Christ at five, and then again in junior high. Although I believed and lived the best I could, I really realized it when I began to see him answer my own personal prayers—such as the summer of my wedding

when I couldn't find bridesmaids' dresses. I had been in every store in Wichita two times—except for Penny's. I had been there only once. We decided to change the whole color scheme when my sister suggested we go to Penny's one more time. There were the exact dresses I'd always wanted, on sale, and only in the exact sizes I needed. It was then that I realized God cared about what I cared about."

- "Sometime during my sophomore year of college. I turned the corner when I realized God was above human logic and he would exist whether I chose to believe or not."

- "It wasn't a onetime thing—but a process of a growing commitment and recommitment as I understood more and more."

- "In high school I heard a speaker at an outreach event with my youth group. It made me realize I needed to be sure Jesus was Lord, as well as Savior."

- "In college, I took a course in 'Christian Thought.' I realized my parents had given me the head knowledge, but I needed to believe in my heart as well as my head. It became a practical way of living then."

POINTING YOUR CHILD TO CHRIST

What were the top things your parents did to point you to Christ? *(asked of adult children)*

- "They never shoved their faith down my throat. They read the Bible to me and were living examples of being a Christian."
- "I saw their consistent relationship with God."
- "When my dad would pray with me at bedtime, he'd always ask God to help make him a better dad. That showed me he wasn't perfect and really wanted God's hand in his life."
- "We always had family devotions."
- "They read their Bibles in front of me."
- "They encouraged involvement in my youth group."
- "My parents *never* bad-mouthed the church in front of me."
- "They gave me a desire to seek God in all my activities and placed him in the front of my mind."
- "I could hear the sincerity of my dad's voice when he prayed."
- "Mom explained the gospel at an early age."
- "I remember specific times when they asked me for my forgiveness. Those were the times I was closest to them the most."
- "They encouraged us to have a daily quiet time."

- "They emphasized inward appearance, rather than the outward."
- "We memorized Scripture as a family."
- "I was encouraged to pursue Christian activities."
- "They allowed questions about the faith to be brought up any time we had them."
- "They instilled in us a love for Jesus, the church, and Christian music. They also taught us to have a love for the truth."
- "I'd often see Mom and Dad up early on their knees. This evoked a great amount of love from me for them. I knew they were praying for their children."
- "They never forced us to spend time with God, but often set aside time after breakfast and before school for a 're-treat to our rooms with God.'"
- "Mom bought me devotional books quite often."
- "As soon as I was old enough to understand, they showed me that their relationship with God was *not* enough for me to gain salvation."

TALKING ABOUT SEX

Did you receive a formal sex talk from your parents? If not, where did you hear about it? *(asked of adult children)*

- "My older sister told me. It was never really addressed by my parents."
- "No, the school did it. Mom was too embarrassed."
- "I had a formal talk around twelve. They basically answered our questions. Just prior to getting married they gave me a book and talked to me."
- "No, I suppose it was just assumed that I would learn it somewhere."
- "No. I was asked by Mother if I had questions when I was in high school sex education class." (from a male respondent)
- "No, I usually learned bits and pieces through peers."
- "At fourteen, we had an informal talk. Pretty skimpy."
- "No, it was not addressed."
- "No, I learned the hard way."
- "No formal talk—nothing, zip! Feminine hygiene pamphlets only."
- "At twelve or thirteen, my mother talked about the biological aspects."
- "We never had The Talk. I think my parents assumed that my sisters would tell me."
- "Never. The subject was avoided until a month before my wedding."

- "Yes, when I was young and didn't care. Mom was always open."
- "My sister asked the questions because she was older. I thought it was very disgusting and planned to never marry."
- "No. Dad asked what I knew when I was in seventh grade. Nobody ever told me about all of the different aspects of love and how it relates to sex."
- "At fourteen or fifteen, Mom gave the talk using Ann Landers' material. It was old news."
- "No. This is one of the few areas my parents could not bring themselves to discuss."
- "No. I was given a book when I was thirteen, but I already knew everything in the book!"
- "In sixth grade both Mom and Dad talked with me. Mom did most of the talking."
- "No, sex was not discussed. My mom tried to discuss feminine hygiene on my wedding day, but was too embarrassed. I did see a movie in Girl Scouts about puberty when I was ten. I learned what sex was from a girlfriend in seventh grade . . . I didn't believe her."
- "Not formal, but spontaneous. We had conversations as they came up."
- "No. In sixth grade I learned about sex at a slumber party, but I didn't believe my friends. So the next day I asked my mom if my grandma and stepgrandpa were married before my uncle was born. She said, 'Yes, that's the way it's supposed to be.' My sister laughed and that was the end of it. I knew my friends were telling the truth."
- "My parents purchased a set of books on sexuality for youth. I didn't have a formal sex talk."
- "In sixth grade. I just remember being very embarrassed."
- "My father attended a school presentation with me in sixth grade—I remember no discussion afterward."
- "No. I read the encyclopedia section in junior high study hall and extrapolated from there."
- "Not from my parents. The subject was covered in youth group at church . . . eventually."
- "No, I learned from my friends and my brother."

- "Not that I can remember. I read a lot, so I learned it all that way."
- "Yes, about age twelve or so—awkwardly done by my dad."

Did you give your child a formal talk on sex? How old was he or she? If not, how was the subject handled? *(asked of parents)*

- "We were very conversational, and it was handled as it came up."
- "I didn't feel like I did a very good job."
- "I talked to my daughters about menstruation and intercourse and gave them Christian books. I felt my husband should talk to our son. But I gave him books about fifth to seventh grade. They were ten or eleven years old."
- "No formal talk, just a short, casual talk at twelve to fourteen years."
- "In preschool, I took questions as they arose. In second and third grade, I gave them the Concordia book on sex. We had pretty free conversations."
- "We mostly talked about it at age thirteen or fourteen. I don't remember telling them any more when they got to high school. I probably didn't tell the youngest girl enough."
- "No, because they found out more from school and friends and didn't want to hear anything from parents."
- "We did try to discuss it some, but basically we gave her books to read. Also, we had a video by Josh McDowell."
- "We had books in the church library about sex. I talked about it with them."
- "My husband started teaching her about what to expect concerning sex when she entered first grade. I would talk to her along the way."
- "We tried to be open and answer questions from a very young age, so I don't ever recall having The Talk at one particular time."
- "Several times, beginning at age seven or nine."
- "All talks were formal and were held during the preteen and teen years. The issues were handled when they

spontaneously arose. Their schools had sex education, which we discussed with them."
- "Premarriage. That was it."
- "We talked some about sex, but we can't say we ever had a formal talk on the subject."
- "Having been raised by parents who found it hard to discuss it at all, it was a difficult subject around our house as well."
- "Our church library provided a Christian book series on sex education beginning at the first-grade level."
- "We went through the Dobson tapes when the kids were in junior high. I read a book on the subject geared to their ages."
- "I don't know if 'formal' is quite the word I would use. But yes, the subject was discussed from time to time."
- "It was mostly done in the early teens, but I believe it should have been done *sooner*."
- "Dad gave the boys a talk before dating."
- "No, I passed out booklets. They saw a film and I answered questions in upper grade school."
- "We talked about different subjects whenever the opportunity came up. To sit them down and launch into it was frightening to everyone."
- "We did not have a formal talk on sex. We were aware that they were reading the right books on the subject. In today's world, if we had young children, we would do it differently and talk about it."
- "We did not sit them down and have a talk. We did have books and tapes. We felt our public school did a good job in this area."
- "I bought a Christian book on sex, and I read it to them."
- "Their father explained the replenishment process to the son by observing farm animals. The school nurse explained sex and body development to the fifth-grade girls."
- "Sex was talked about in sacred terms. I don't believe we ever sat down and had a formal talk."
- "We always tried to use respectful speech and actions in regards to our bodies, relations, and sex. As young chil-

dren, we told them about sexual differences at their level of understanding. When our daughter was a preteen, my wife talked extensively with her. I had a weekend camping trip with our son and told him some basic things."

WHAT MOMS HAD TO SAY ABOUT WORKING OR STAYING HOME

Responses from stay-at-home moms:

- "I would not exchange the time I had with my children for money."
- "When our children were growing up, it was important for them to have a mother's influence and wisdom close by."
- "I don't function well or have the energy to keep up the home and work outside, too. More importantly, Jennifer had emotional conditions during the period of my employment. An ophthalmologist diagnosed severe problems with her sight, but the problem was completely solved within six months of my resignation. I was back home, where I belong."
- "I worked a Shaklee business from my home. It worked well for us. I was in the home when the children were home from school. We were able to be flexible."
- "I would not exchange all the material things in the world for our joy of my being home."
- "I rarely worked, and that meant we went without some of the 'extras.'"
- "I was glad the Lord gave me a husband who wanted me home with my children and also a job that provided

enough money for me to do that. I loved being a mother and wife. I liked housekeeping and nurturing children."

- "As a mother, I looked upon my family as the most important career I could have. My husband supported this conviction and was willing to work extra jobs so I could do this. We have never regretted this arrangement. We have passed this feeling to our daughters, who are also stay-at-home moms."

- "I know that psychologically I could not continue to be a good nurse and at the same time be a good helpmate and mother. I was fortunate enough to be a creative 'dollar stretcher.'"

Responses from moms employed outside the home:

- "I had a high energy level, a strong work ethic, a desire to share my husband's economic load, and a longing to influence children and society, so I worked part-time. I was involved professionally in my work to avoid becoming 'obsessively' absorbed in my first child, which may have given her the idea that the world revolved around her. My kids observe their friends' mothers who 'have no life' and are irrational and overcontrolling and are frustrating their college-age children."

- "My working worked out very well."

- "I enjoyed my work as an aide with learning-disabled children. I was also home when my own children were."

- "I taught for two years, full-time, and loved it. After my husband's brain surgery, I returned to full-time parenting and 'wifing.' Now my work is very flexible. I teach writing part-time, and I have created a wonderful balance in my life."

- "I worked full-time after both children were in school. It was very satisfactory. I taught school in the same elementary school they attended. Their father taught at the college they attended."

- "We, as a family, worked together as a team. Adequate instructions and arrangements were given beforehand, and the girls knew they were top priority. I was always there when they got home from school."

- "I would have preferred being home when my children were, at least through junior high. I was able to work because my hours weren't full-time and the children and I could communicate well."
- "I enjoyed getting out of the house and into the business world again. I was always home when the kids came home because I did temporary office work."
- "We were house parents to a boys' home where we had six foster boys in their teens. Our children were still in grade school. We did this for five years. Overall, it was very positive for our kids."
- "I wasn't away from home very often. Maybe four days a month. I limited it because I felt I needed to be home."
- "It would have been better, I think, if I had worked part-time consistently because I was home all the time when they were preschoolers. They didn't get to know their dad; he left it mostly to me. But full-time work when they were in grade school was too exhausting."
- "I worked for the school district. I left after the children went to school and got home before they did. Then I needed to help my husband full-time. I would have preferred to work part-time."
- "The kids were in junior high when I started working. They seemed to be proud that I returned to college at age thirty-eight to become a teacher. They learned how to wash, iron, cook, clean, and bake cookies."
- "I was worn out with my stressful job of twenty-four hours a day and therefore gave less to my children, energy-wise. I was less fun to live with, had less patience, etc. And they grew so quickly. I wished we could have managed another way."
- "My one-day-a-week sales job furnished our family with health insurance. My husband was self-employed, and he was home the days I worked. When we adopted Brittany, my stay-at-home 'mom' helped me!"
- "I worked out of my home, so I was always there. *But I worked too much.*"

BECOMING FRIENDS WITH YOUR CHILDREN

When did you start to become friends with your children and less of a parent? Why? *(asked of parents)*

- "We were friends and parents from scratch."
- "We were parents *and* friends with my kids early on, but we did less parenting after twelve years of age."
- "After high school. They were responsible adults then."
- "When they left home after high school."
- "After high school, I began to value them and their opinions. They are nice people."
- "As they grew older and we saw them maturing. They were taught to 'be on their own.'"
- "When they got into college, they were more willing to talk."
- "Around junior high, I started to treat them as a friend."
- "For me [the father], around junior high age. After a change in churches, I gained a better understanding of parenting, through teaching."
- "Our married daughter grew up on us, so we had no choice."
- "In the senior year of high school, we were more relaxed about what he could and couldn't do. He could tell we trusted him."
- "Our daughter, who was home-schooled, communicated

well, starting in ninth grade. For our college-age son, we're still working on it."

- "I think when they were married. I felt then a relief of pressure to parent."
- "After they attended college and were out on their own."
- "After they had children and realized *why* we did some of the things we did as they grew up."
- "During their college years, they were away from home, making their own decisions, and becoming leaders in their own environment. That's when we began sharing ideas, solutions, etc."
- "My nineteen-year-old still needs parenting sometimes!"
- "When they were in college, we felt they were old enough to make their own decisions. That's when they realized we are human, too!"
- "As they became teens. The rules we all lived by were instilled at an early age and we were consistent with enforcing them."
- "After college and when they married. I believe my children should 'leave and cleave' to their spouses. I *don't* want to be an interfering and controlling mother-in-law."
- "After high school. I felt we had done all the training we could, and they were old enough to make their own decisions. Discipline stopped and counseling continued."
- "Post–high school because of my letting go and their growing maturity."
- "Early twenties. I was widowed around then, and it drew us closer together. They became more concerned about my well-being."
- "We tried to develop a friendship since our children were small. We have tried to nurture them to mature so we could do less parenting. But we still do a little with our twenty-five-year-old son."
- "Letting go has been the hardest part of learning to be a parent."
- "When they left home after high school, we stopped authority parenting and became friends and parents."
- "After they left home and were *independent*."
- "Fifth grade for my daughter—she was very mature."

When did you become friends with your parents and less of a child? *(asked of adult children)*

- "After I was married. That's when they treated me as an adult."
- "When I married at age twenty."
- "When they saw me as an adult and could converse intelligently with me."
- "After high school. I guess I grew up."
- "In the last year or two. I made her understand I'm a separate individual."
- "When I could go along with my dad and contribute to family projects."
- "After college, when I moved out."
- "After high school, but especially after I left home to go to college."
- "After college, when I was grown up and self-sufficient."
- "It was in high school that my parents began treating me as an equal. I still see them as parents whom I love, respect, and spend time with, but not necessarily 'friends' in the same sense as friends we have at church."
- "After college, I could relate to them more."
- "After I moved out. I believe I was more perceived as an adult."
- "When I was eighteen or nineteen, I was able to make major decisions on my own and ask for advice when I wanted; they learned to let go."
- "At age twenty-four, when Dad was fifty-four. He initiated the man-to-man relationship. I am forever indebted to his respect for me and my directions."
- "They treated me differently once I went away to school. I guess they figured I was doing okay on my own away from home."
- "In high school, I started to treat them more as equals, not dependent on them for my learning."
- "In high school, maybe sooner. They treated us as adults and let us make decisions along with counseling us. Mom and Dad treated us as equals, and I loved them for that."
- "Around twenty-six, when I finally decided to be my own person."

- "After I graduated from high school. I had adult responsibilities, and they treated me more as an adult. I made decisions and suffered consequences."
- "During the college years. I felt I wasn't needing to view them as an authority anymore."
- "My dad was always very dominating until the last two years of his life when he was handicapped by a stroke. I was then able to approach him as a peer. I was thirty-eight at the time."
- "In the true meaning of friendship, we still haven't arrived. Friends accept you for who you are and love you in spite of failures. The world of 'legalism' doesn't promote that depth of friendship. All in all, a friendship was more a possibility when I married and had a family."
- "During college, I finally matured."
- "As I began to gain some freedom and independence in high school, they treated me less and less like a child. This took place on the basis of maturity and trustworthiness."

EDUCATION CHOICES

What convictions do you have regarding educational choices? Is there anything you would have done differently? *(asked of parents)*

On Christian Schooling

- "In today's atmosphere, Christian schooling seems to have the most advantages."
- "We have strong convictions in favor of Christian schooling. Even though our kids have chosen to serve the Lord, they would have had a better education and a lot less hassles in the Christian school environment. Even though it seemed impossible to afford at the time, I think we should have made more effort." (From a mom who sent her kids to public school.)
- "Our kids went to public schools. The choice of college was left to them. Since we were putting up the money, we should have insisted on Christian colleges for the two children who were spiritually immature."
- "I would never home-school, as I don't believe I have the gift to do that. I believe in Christian school education, but I also recognize the academic standards are too rigid for some young people."
- "I would have sent them to a Christian school if one had been available."
- "Our kids attended public schools growing up, but we always told them that we wanted them to go to a

Christian college for at least one year. They all did that except for child number five."

- "The junior high and senior high peer pressure is the greatest, so a Christian environment gave them the opportunity to find Christian friends. The somewhat smaller school gave them more opportunities. I would *not* have done things differently."
- "I felt that Christian education was much better than public, not only in the area of academics, but because of the principles taught. We felt so strongly that we helped start a Christian school in our area."
- "Christian education at the post–high school level is crucial. I would have sent my kids to Christian schools."

On Public Schools

- "I feel very strongly that the public school environment is the best to both learn about and apply biblical principles."
- "Grade school could be Christian, but a poor Christian teacher could have a far more devastating effect than would a poor secular schoolteacher. In junior and senior high, the child needs to be exposed to the secular world *while* he is still under the parents' influence. The semi-Christian college allows the mature child to see the non-perfect aspects of Christian people."
- "Most of their teachers were Christians. We tried to live in communities that had good teachers. Overall, we were pleased."
- "Public school showed our kids both sides of campus life."
- "Our daughters are in public colleges. You need to know what they're learning and be willing to talk to them. One of their best experiences was living abroad as part of a study program. I see negative effects of public junior and senior high, but the only Christian school was so legalistic. It may have had greater negative impact, plus we couldn't afford it since I was committed to staying home to parent."
- "I feel our boys had an excellent education in the public schools."

- "I couldn't afford anything else. But I think if I were raising my children in a big city, I would have done differently."
- "Although we would have liked to see as much Christian education as possible, public schools were good for both kids."
- "We helped lots in school. We parents were well thought of and their teachers responded to supportive parents. The kids knew we would stand with the teacher until convinced otherwise."
- "Christians belong in the public schools, to be salt and light."
- "We sent our kids to public school; now in the 1990s, it's a different society. We didn't urge them to be a lawyer, doctor, engineer, etc.; we left the choice to them. We might have been stronger in that sort of guidance."
- "Their experiences in secular schools tested and strengthened their faith."
- "My kids were bold in questioning some teachers. We did not have the choices in the fifties and sixties that are available today."

On Home Schooling

- "I would *not* have home-schooled, and I would have placed our child in public schools." (From a mom who used a mixture of home school, Christian high school, and public college.)
- "I didn't have enough confidence to help educate them until I went to work at an elementary school."
- "I would have home-schooled from preschool through high school." (From a mom who sent kids to public grade school, military junior high, and Christian high school.)
- "I would have home-schooled both kids through all grades. My son and daughter were in public schools until high school, when I home-schooled my daughter."

On Private Schooling

- "I felt that the private school took my son out of the mainstream of activity. I would not do that again."

- "There wasn't the option of much Christian education without being in a private school. It's a lot more open now."
- "I would have enrolled all my children in public or private *grade* schools instead of parochial."

SUGGESTED READING

For Young Families

Robert G. Barnes. *Raising Confident Kids.* Zondervan Publishing House.

Gary Bauer. *Our Journey Home: What Parents Are Doing to Preserve Family Values.* Word Books, 1992.

Tom Bissett. *Why Kids Leave the Faith.* Thomas Nelson.

Steve and Annie Chapman. *Gifts Your Kids Can't Break.* Bethany House Publishers, 1991.

James C. Dobson. *Dr. Dobson Answers Your Questions about Raising Children.* Tyndale House Publishers, 1986.

———. *The New Dare to Discipline.* Tyndale House Publishers, 1992.

Doug Fields. *Too Old Too Soon: Protecting Your Child from Instant Adulthood.* Harvest House, 1991.

Don and Katie Fortune. *Discover Your Children's Gifts.* Chosen Books, 1989.

Cheri Fuller. *Motivating Your Kids: From Crayons to Career.* Honor Books, 1990.

Marti Watson Garlett. *Kids with Character: Preparing Children for a Lifetime of Choices.* Multnomah Press, 1989.

Angela Elwell Hunt. *Loving Someone Else's Child.* Tyndale House Publishers, 1992.

Greg Johnson and Mike Yorkey. *"Daddy's Home."* Tyndale House Publishers, 1992.

Jay Kesler, Ron Beers, and LaVonne Neff, eds. *Parents and Children.* Victor Books, 1986.

Kay Kuzma. *Building Your Child's Character from the Inside Out.* Life Journey Books, 1988.

Ralph Mattson and Thom Black. *Discovering Your Child's Design.* David C. Cook, 1989.

Wanda B. Pelfrey. *Your Child's Teachable Moments: Making the Most Of.* Moody Press, 1988.

Bill Perkins and Rod Cooper. *Kids in Sports: Shaping a Child's Character from the Sidelines.* Multnomah Press, 1989.

Kathie Reimer. *1001 Ways to Introduce Your Child to God.* Tyndale House Publishers, 1992.

Gary Smalley. *The Key to Your Child's Heart.* Word Books, 1987.

Charles Stanley. *How to Keep Your Kids on Your Team.* Oliver Nelson Publishers, 1986.

Cliff Stunden. *How to Raise a Child You Can Live With: And What to Do If You Haven't.* Word Books, 1986.

Keith Wooden. *Teaching Your Children to Pray.* Zondervan Publishing House, 1992.

John and Susan Yates. *What Really Matters at Home.* Word Books, 1992.

Zig Ziglar. *Raising Positive Kids in a Negative World.* Ballantine/Epiphany, 1989.

For Building Family Memories

Rebecca Bertolini. *Mom's Big Activity Book for Building Little Children.* Victor Books, 1993.

Donna Erickson. *Prime Time Together . . . with Kids.* Augsburg Press, 1989.

Gloria Gaither and Shirley Dobson. *Let's Make a Memory.* Word Books, 1983.

Dean and Grace Merrill. *Together at Home: One Hundred Proven Activities to Nurture Your Children's Faith.* Focus on the Family, 1988.

Gwen Weising. *Finding Time for Family Fun.* Fleming H. Revell Co., 1991.

———. *Raising Kids on Purpose for the Fun of It.* Fleming H. Revell Co., 1989.

For Making Education Choices

H. Wayne House. *Schooling Choices.* Multnomah Press, 1988.

Raymond and Dorothy Moore. *Home-Grown Kids.* Word Books, 1984.

Bill Sanders. *School Daze: Helping Parents Cope with the Bewildering World of Public Schools.* Fleming H. Revell Co., 1992.

Dr. Cliff Schimmels. *How to Help Your Child Survive and Thrive in the Public School.* Fleming H. Revell Co.

———. *Parent's Most-Asked Questions about Kids and Schools.* Scripture Press, 1989.

David W. Smith. *Choosing Your Child's School.* Zondervan Publishing House, 1991.

John Whitehead and Alexis Irene Crow. *Home Education: Rights and Reasons.* Crossway Books.

For Parents with Teens

Stephen Arterburn and Jim Burns. *Drug-Proof Your Kids*. Focus on the Family, 1989.

——. *When Love Is Not Enough: Parenting through Tough Times*. Focus on the Family, 1992.

Jill Carlson. *What Are Your Kids Reading? The Alarming Trend in Today's Teen Literature*. Wolgemuth and Hyatt Publishers.

Jay Carty, *Counterattack: Taking Back Ground Lost to Sin*. Multnomah Press, 1988.

William L. Coleman. *Ten Things Your Teens Will Thank You For . . . Someday*. Bethany House Publishers, 1992.

James C. Dobson. *Preparing for Adolescence*. Tyndale House Publishers, 1992.

Richard and Renee Durfield. *Raising Them Chaste*. Bethany House Publishers, 1991.

Ellen Greenberger and Laurance Steinberg, *When Teenagers Work: The Psychological and Social Costs of Adolescent Employment*. Basic Books, 1988.

Pat Holt and Grace Ketterman. *Choices Are Not Child's Play: Helping Your Kids Make Wise Decisions*. Harold Shaw Publishers, 1990.

Kevin Huggins. *Parenting Adolescents*. Navpress, 1989.

Jay Kesler. *Energizing Your Teenager's Faith*. Group Publishing, 1990.

Jay Kesler and Ron Beers. *Parents and Teenagers*. Victor Books, 1984.

Dr. Kevin Leman. *Smart Kids, Stupid Choices*. Regal Books, 1987.

Margie M. Lewis. *The Hurting Parent*. Zondervan Publishing House, 1980.

Josh McDowell. *How to Help Your Child Say "No" to Sexual Pressure*. Word Books, 1987.

Al Menconi. *Today's Music: A Window to Your Child's Soul*. David C. Cook, 1990.

John L. Moore. *Loosening the Reins*. Zondervan Publishing House, 1992.

Dr. Cliff Schimmels. *What Parents Try to Forget about Adolescence*. David C. Cook, 1989.

H. Norman Wright. *An Answer to Parent-Teen Relationships*. Harvest House.

For Parents with Children Out of School

Shirley Cook. *Getting Along with Your Grown-Up Kids*. Accent Books.

Ruth Bell Graham. *Prodigals and Those Who Love Them*. Focus on the Family, 1991.

Carol Kuykendall. *Learning to Let Go*. Zondervan Publishing House, 1985.

Dr. Vern C. Lewis and Dr. Bruce Narramore. *Cutting the Cord*. Tyndale House Publishers, 1990.

Jerry and Mary White. *When Your Kids Aren't Kids Anymore.* NavPress, 1991.

General Christian Parenting

Sally Leman Chall. *Making God Real to Your Children.* Fleming H. Revell Co., 1991.

Robert DeMoss. *Learn to Discern.* Zondervan Publishing House, 1992.

John and Carol Dettoni. *Parenting Before and After Work.* Victor Books.

James C. Dobson. *Parenting Isn't for Cowards.* Word Books, 1987.

James C. Dobson and Gary L. Bauer, *Children at Risk: The Battle for the Hearts and Minds of Our Children.* Word Books, 1990.

Gloria Gaither. *What My Parents Did Right.* Star Song Publishing, 1991.

Wes Haystead. *The 3,000 Year-old Guide to Parenting.* Regal Books, 1992.

Jerry Jenkins. *Twelve Things I Want My Kids to Remember Forever.* Moody Press, 1991.

Jay Kesler. *Raising Responsible Kids.* Word Books, 1991.

Tim Kimmel. *Home-Grown Heroes.* Multnomah Press.

———. *Little House on the Freeway.* Multnomah Press, 1987.

Kevin Leman. *Getting the Best Out of Your Child (Before They Get the Best of You).* Harvest House.

Jean Lush and Pamela Vredevelt. *Mothers and Sons: Raising Boys to Be Men.* Fleming H. Revell Co., 1988.

Jim Marian. *Growing Up Christian.* Victor Books, 1992.

Anne Ortlund. *Disciplines of the Home.* Word Books, 1990.

H. Norman Wright. *The Power of a Parent's Words.* Regal Books, 1991.

Ed Young. *Against All Odds.* Thomas Nelson, 1993.

For Single-Parent Families

Sandra P. Aldrich. *Living Through the Loss of Someone You Love.* Regal Books, 1990.

———. *From One Single Mother to Another.* Regal Books, 1991.

Emil J. Authelet. *Parenting Solo: How to Enjoy Life and Raise Good Kids.* Here's Life Publishers, 1989.

Robert G. Barnes, Jr. *Single Parenting: A Wilderness Journey.* Tyndale House Publishers, 1984.

Andre Bustanoby. *Being a Single Parent.* Zondervan Publishing House, 1985.

Tom and Adrienne Frydenger. *The Blended Family.* Chosen Books, 1985.

Gary Richmond. *Successful Single Parenting.* Harvest House, 1989.

For Stay-at-Home Mothers

Debbie Barr. *Children of Divorce: Helping Kids When Their Parents Are Apart.* Zondervan Publishing House, 1992.

Brenda Hunter. *Home by Choice.* Multnomah Press, 1991.

Lindsey O'Connor. *Working at Home: A Dream That's Becoming a Trend.* Harvest House, 1990.

Donna Partow. *Homemade Business.* Focus on the Family, 1992.

Kathy Peel and Joy Mahaffey. *A Mother's Manual for Schoolday Survival.* Focus on the Family, 1990.

Carol Van Klompenburg and Joyce K. Ellis. *When the Kids Are Home from School.* Bethany House Publishers, 1991.

For Moms Employed Outside the Home

Karen Linamen and Linda Holland. *Working Women, Workable Lives.* Harold Shaw Publishers, 1993.

NOTES

////////////////////////////

Chapter 2
1. *USA Today*, November 1992.

Chapter 18
1. Interviewed on "Family News in Focus," week of July 2 to July 8, 1992.

Chapter 21
1. *American Demographics*, July 1992, p. 14.
2. Angela Elwell Hunt, *Loving Someone Else's Child* (Wheaton, Ill.: Tyndale House Publishers, 1992), p. 154.
3. *Grand Rapids Parents*, September 1990, p. 40.

Chapter 23
1. Quote from *Newsweek*, 16 November 1992, p. 80.

INDEX

/////////////////////////

Also from Greg Johnson and Mike Yorkey

"DADDY'S HOME"   0-8423-0584-X
The best ideas and most effective approaches to fathering, based on
interviews with hundreds of dads.

Timely Resources for Today's Parenting Issues!

THE NEW DARE TO DISCIPLINE
Dr. James Dobson   0-8423-0507-6
A classic for parents on maintaining order, developing responsibility, and
building character.

**50 PRACTICAL WAYS TO TAKE OUR KIDS BACK
FROM THE WORLD**
Michael J. McManus   0-8423-1242-0
Practical examples to help teens deal with the serious issues they face daily.

FROM DAD WITH LOVE
Chuck Aycock and Dave Veerman   0-8423-1333-8
Discover how to provide your children with gifts that money can't buy:
protection, identity, and confidence.

HELPING TEENS IN CRISIS
Miriam Neff   0-8423-6823-X
Exploring serious issues teens face, this counselor helps parents learn how
to prevent and work through problems.

**HOW TO HAVE KIDS WITH CHARACTER (EVEN IF YOUR
KIDS ARE CHARACTERS)**
Nadine M. Brown   0-8423-1607-8
Identifies specific character qualities and provides related Scripture and
activities for developing a child's character.

PARENTING TEENS
Dr. Bruce Narramore and Dr. Vern C. Lewis   0-8423-5012-8
Guide children through the dependent-interdependent struggles of growing
up and leaving home.

THE TEENAGE ZONE
John Souter   0-8423-1289-7
In understanding the changes of adolescence, parents can make a child's
transition into the teen years a little easier.

Fantastic!
That's what teens are saying about the *Life Application Bible for
Students.* Written and edited by the nation's leading youth experts, this
one-of-a-kind Bible addresses the issues teens face every day. Available in
The Living Bible version, hardcover or softcover.